Building a New Europe

Brookings Occasional Papers

Building a New Europe

The Challenge of System Transformation and Systemic Reform

WOLFGANG H. REINICKE

THE BROOKINGS INSTITUTION

Washington, D.C.

Brookings Occasional Papers

THE BROOKINGS INSTITUTION is a private nonprofit organization devoted to research, education, and publication on important issues of domestic and foreign policy. Its principal purpose is to bring knowledge to bear on the major policy problems facing the American people.

On occasion Brookings staff members produce research papers that warrant immediate circulation as contributions to the public debate on current issues of national importance. Because of the speed of their production, these Occasional Papers are not subjected to all of the formal review procedures established for the Institution's research publications, and they may be revised at a later date. As in all Brookings publications, the judgments, conclusions, and recommendations presented in the Papers are solely those of the authors and should not be attributed to the trustees, officers, or other staff members of the Institution.

CONTENTS

TABLES

FIGURES

APPENDIX TABLES

Acknowledgements

This paper was originally prepared in an abbreviated form for a chapter of a 1992 Brookings book, *The New Germany and the New Europe* (edited by Paul Stares), and was first presented at a conference held in Rottach-Egern, Germany, in September 1991. This longer version has benefited from the comments of Shlomo Avineri, Lilly Gardner-Feldmann, Ullrich Heilemann, and John D. Steinbruner, to whom the author is very grateful. I would also like to thank numerous officials from the European Community institutions and national government and non-government officials who shared their expertise. At the time the paper went for typesetting in late August, the French referendum had not been put to vote, nor had the subsequent crisis in the European exchange rate mechanism occurred. The author has added an epilogue that briefly discusses the implications of those events.

The author also wishes to express his appreciation to Lyle Goldstein, Robin Hodes, Andreas Luge, and, in particular, Daniel Turner for research assistance; to Venka Macintyre for editing the manuscript; to Caroline Lalire and Tricia Dewey for editing assistance; to Caroline Pecquet for preparing the manuscript for publication and collecting source material; and to Daniel Turner and Myles Nienstadt for typesetting the paper.

Brookings gratefully acknowledges financial support for this project by the John D. and Catherine T. MacArthur Foundation and the Fritz Thyssen Stiftung.

Wolfgang H. Reinicke is a research associate in the Brookings Foreign Policy Studies program.

1. Introduction

Referring to the sudden possibility of German unification, former chancellor Willy Brandt in November 1989 stated that "what belongs together will grow together." As recent years have made all too obvious, it is infinitely more difficult to merge two states and social systems that have followed fundamentally different political, economic, and social principles for the last forty years than it is to unify a nation with a common history, language, and cultural heritage. East and West Germany were the symbols of a Europe split into two opposing military and economic alliances. Now that the Cold War, and thus the formal division of Europe, has ended, Europeans stand at the beginning of a new political and economic era. For the first time since it was divided, Europe has the opportunity to unite on the basis of the rule of law, democratic political systems, and the principles of the market economy.[1]

This opportunity has arisen because the East-West conflict has unexpectedly dissolved at its core and new policies are needed for East-West interaction.[2] As long as the systemic conflict existed, economic and political cooperation between the two blocs was based on the concepts of peaceful coexistence and confidence building as they sought to make political relations more calculable, and military conflict less probable. Interaction was limited and change slow. Continuity and stability were the guiding policy principles.

This framework for mutual interaction is no longer valid. European policymakers (East and West) now have to cope with a radically altered political and economic environment created by both German unification and the transformation of the former Eastern bloc. But while the formal division of Europe has ended, the magnitude of their task to transform the economic and political systems of Central and Eastern Europe and the former Soviet Union, and to integrate them into the European and world political economies, is only beginning to emerge.[3] To ensure that the ideological and military division of Europe is not replaced by an economic and social one, policymakers must develop a strategy for the formation of the new European political economy.

In this paper I identify some of the central principles and policies that should inform such a strategy. I first examine the economic interdependence of

Eastern and Western Europe before the continent was divided by the Cold War and the place of Central and Eastern Europe in the minds of the architects of the European Community (EC). Although such historical extrapolations should be handled with care—particularly since the economic environment for all the European economies has changed drastically since the 1930s—policymakers concerned with developing a strategy for the new European political economy will find them instructive.

Next, I construct a framework for analyzing the challenges that the new Europe faces. I argue that the integration of the divided European political economy requires changes in both East and West. For the countries of Central and Eastern Europe this change is referred to as *system transformation*—the dismantling of much of the centrally planned economic system as it existed and the creation of the basic institutional infrastructure characteristic of any market economy. For Western Europe it requires a process of *systemic reform*—a considerable adjustment in the existing market structures to support the process of system transformation and to facilitate the East's integration into the West European political economy, in particular the European Community. This framework is used to develop a series of policy responses, East and West, that could provide the foundation of a new European political economy.

The experience with system transformation in Central and Eastern Europe so far suggests that it will be a long process, creating a period of political, economic, and social instability in the region. In addition to developing a strategy of system transformation, therefore, the essay proposes two short-term *policy initiatives* to stabilize the lengthy transition period and to shorten the process of system transformation itself.

The essay does not address the issue of system transformation in the successor states of the former Soviet Union. The developments since the dissolution of the Soviet Union, however, make the discussion of the system transformation of Central and Eastern Europe relevant to analysts of the former Soviet Union.

2. The Unification of Europe: Vision or Reality?

What role did Central and Eastern Europe play in the minds of the architects of the European Community? Is the Community primarily an alliance founded to overcome long-standing political and economic conflicts? Or did the Common Market and the idea of European integration emerge in response to the Cold War?

These are important questions to consider. If the Community is primarily a product of the Cold War, it is difficult to argue for the integration of Central and Eastern Europe on historical grounds. Instead, one might be tempted to conclude that the rapid military and economic dissolution of the Eastern bloc since the end of the Cold War will cause the Community to lose its rationale and disintegrate, and that Europe will return to the traditional state system of the prewar era.[4]

Perhaps the logical point at which to begin the discussion, then, is to see what kind of economic links existed before Europe was divided into opposing military alliances and whether they provide some clue to the future structure of the European political economy.

The first point to note is that the idea of a unified Europe as a way of overcoming the perennial state rivalries originated long before the beginning of the Cold War. The concept, said the former British prime minister Harold MacMillan, "is almost as old as Europe itself" and was certainly publicly recognized as far back as 1897, when Prime Minister Lord Salisbury referred to "the Federation of Europe" as "the only way we have."[5] By 1923 a pan-European movement was clearly under way, led by Count Coudenhove Kalergi of Austria, who called for the creation of a United States of Europe. In September 1929, in a now famous speech before the League of Nations Assembly in Geneva, Aristide Briand, the French foreign minister, with the backing of his German counterpart, Gustav Stresemann, proposed the creation of a European Union within the framework of the League of Nations. During World War II resistance movements against Nazi occupation in East and West developed ideas and concrete plans for a federal European order.[6] And in the aftermath of World War II, Winston Churchill, in his famous Zürich speech in

September of 1946, called for the creation of a United States of Europe, singling out Franco-German cooperation as the essential prerequisite.[7]

A united Europe would serve two principal purposes, both concerned with European problems of little immediate relevance to the Cold War. First, it would avoid renewed military conflict among the nations of Europe by creating the conditions for a lasting peace. Such a peace structure would be achieved not by imposing unilateral restrictions on Germany but by embedding Germany politically and economically into a grouping of European states. This underlying concern provided the basis for the treaties that established the European Communities.[8]

Of course, the emerging bipolar conflict also influenced the European integration process. Because of this conflict, the United States strongly supported the further integration of Western Europe into an economically and politically stable alliance, not least as a way to counter the Council for Mutual Economic Assistance (CMEA), founded in 1949. The record, however, is mixed. Whereas mounting East-West tension and the outbreak of the Korean War led Britain and France to propose a greater defense effort among Western European countries, including West Germany, in the context of the European Defense Community, the French National Assembly was unwilling to accept such far-reaching curbs on French sovereignty. At the same time, the Suez crisis and repression in Hungary forced Western Europe to close ranks and hastened the signing of the Treaty of Rome in 1958 establishing the European Economic Community and Euratom.[9] Thus, while the Cold War may have influenced the form and the speed of European integration, the principal purpose of the European Community was to address *European* problems.

Note, too, that the founding documents of the European Community do not make any reference to Europe's division. Rather, the architects of Europe considered the continent as a unit with a common heritage, culture, tradition, and geography. The Schuman declaration does not in any way mention the emerging division of Germany and Europe. The Treaty of Rome, although concluded in the midst of rising tensions among the two superpowers, was written in the same spirit. Emphasizing the unity and not the division of Europe, the signatories state that they are "determined to lay the foundations of an ever closer union among the peoples of Europe," and they call upon "the other peoples of Europe who share their ideal to join in their efforts."[10] These principles were embedded in Article 237 of the treaty, which states that "any European State may apply to become a member."[11] Walter Hallstein, the first president of the European Commission, made it clear that the founders of the

Community had all of Europe in mind: "We share one wish above all others, which is to overcome the division of Europe between East and West."[12]

Second, a united Europe would serve a purpose that attracted little attention at the time but is of considerable relevance today. By pooling the sovereignty of individual European nations, the founders of the European Community hoped to regain the influence that these nations had lost, but that none of them was capable of reestablishing alone. As a result of internal dissensions and wars, they argued, Europe was no longer at the center of the world stage. Its place was taken by the two new superpowers, the United States and the Soviet Union, each of which wielded far greater military, political, and economic power than Europe.

The architects of the Common Market recognized that if Europe failed to unify, it might have to return to complete military and political dependence on the United States. As one American observer of the European process wrote in the early 1960s,

> The unspoken assumptions underlying the Common Market are not anti-American, but they are opposed to American hegemony within the Western world: Western Europe is to become the master of its own fate, so far as that is possible. . . . In the measure that these nations . . . retain memories of this recent past, they are bound to view the US as a temporary overlord, whose sudden elevation to the rank of primus inter pares corresponds neither to innate virtues nor to the long-range interests of the Western world as a whole.[13]

Seen from this perspective, the European Community is indeed a product of the emerging superpower rivalry, but is not a part of one power's global political strategy. On the contrary, Europeans were eager to form an independent political and economic bloc that would represent a counterweight to other regional groupings emerging in the postwar international, political, and economic structure. However, the rapid emergence of the Cold War and the threatening superpower rivalry made such a strategy impossible to pursue in the immediate future.

Looking at the official reaction of the European Community to the revolutionary changes in Central and Eastern Europe, one notices a historical continuity. In April 1990 a special summit was held in Dublin to develop a response to the developments in Central and Eastern Europe. In the concluding statement, the European Council "applaud[ed] the continuing process of change in these countries with whose people we share a common heritage and culture. This process of change brings ever closer a Europe which, having overcome the unnatural divisions imposed by ideology and confrontation, stands united in its commitment to democracy, pluralism, the rule of law, full respects of human rights, and the principles of the market economy."[14]

To return to the question of economic relationships within Europe before its division, in 1928 West European countries sent 28.5 percent of their total exports (17.1 percent came from Germany) to Central and Eastern Europe. This represented 53.4 percent of all Central and East European imports (table A-1). West European exports rose to 31.3 percent during the next decade and increased to 59.4 percent of Central and East European imports as imports from other regions, especially Russia, declined (figure 1 and table A-1). For the countries of Central and Eastern Europe, the export markets of Western Europe were even more important. In 1928, 51.8 percent of all Central and East European exports went to the West: this represented 30.2 percent of all Western imports, with Germany's share at 13.4 percent (table A-1). By 1938 this share had risen to 60.7 percent, which amounted to 38.3 percent of West European imports (figure 1 and table A-1).[15] Eastern and Western Europe were also linked through the capital flows that financed this extensive trading network.

But although they were closely linked through trade and financial flows, the nature of these linkages reveal substantial structural differences between the economies of Eastern and Western Europe. In 1928 manufactured goods constituted an average of 67.3 percent of West European exports but only 24.5 percent of Central and East European exports. The Central and East European figure drops to 13.4 percent if the Czechoslovak share of manufactured exports (68.6 percent) is excluded (figure 2 and table A-2). Poland, Hungary, and Romania, known at the time as the "agricultural bloc," had agricultural export ratios of 59.2 percent, 54.4 percent, and 62 percent, respectively.[16]

On the financial side, all Central and East European countries were net debtors by 1931 and depended on a continuous inflow of mostly European foreign capital (table 1). By the end of 1929 Polish banks, for example, had taken up short-term foreign credits amounting to 676,000 million zlotys, 84.5 percent of which was provided by West European countries. The United Kingdom was the largest creditor (it contributed 20 percent), followed by Germany (17.2 percent), France (14.6 percent), and Austria (14.35).[17]

These differences between East and West were largely due to the fact that industrialization had occurred at different times and speeds in the various

Figure 1. Distribution of Europe's Trade,
Major Country Groups, 1938

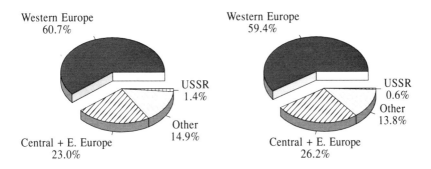

Exports: Central and Eastern Europe   Imports: Central and Eastern Europe

Source: See table A-1.

Figure 2. European Exports of Manufactured Goods, 1928
Average percent share by region

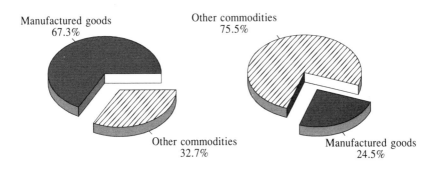

Western Europe   Central + E. Europe

Source: See table A-2.

Table 1. Central and Eastern European Foreign Debt, 1931[a]

Millions of U.S. dollars unless otherwise specified

Country	Indebtedness				Total	Per capita[b]	Annual debt service	1931 % exports needed for debt service	1990 % exports needed for debt service
	Long-term		Short-term						
	Public	Private	Public	Private					
Bulgaria	122	9	n.a.	7	139	23	7	16	16.7
Hungary	320	676	9	215	732	84	48	48	48.7
Poland	543	35	c	288	865	27	52	24	4.9
Romania	913	29	c	80	1,022	580	39	28	0.4
CSFR	283	45	c	68	395	27	20	5	10.4
Yugoslavia	578	n.a.	56	n.a.	634	46	24	29	13.7

Sources: Paul F. Douglass, *The Economic Independence of Poland* (Cincinnati: Ruter Press, 1931), p. 120. The exchange rate is from League of Nations, *Statistical Year-Book for 1930-31* (Geneva: League of Nations Economic Intelligence Service, 1931).
n.a. Not available.
a. Figures converted from Swiss francs to U.S. dollars using the 1931 exchange rate (1 franc = $ 0.194).
b. In U.S. dollars.
c. Included with the long-term debt.

European countries and that these countries had different amounts of natural resources. Thus, despite the close economic links between East and West before the division, structurally the economies of Central and Eastern Europe played a peripheral role in the overall European economy.[18]

Although the importance of this historical relationship should not be overstated, many of its patterns remain unchanged or are rapidly reemerging now that the formal division of Europe has come to an end. During the Cold War, trade between the two halves of Europe certainly declined sharply, but the European Community remained Central and Eastern Europe's most important trading partner in the West. In 1988—that is, even before the changes in Central and Eastern Europe began to unfold—11.4 percent of all CMEA exports went to the European Community, and only 2 percent went to the United States. In some cases the Community even took a greater share of trade than the Soviet Union, usually the East's major trading partner. In 1988, for example, the Community accounted for 24.4 percent of all Hungarian imports, in comparison with the Soviet Union's 24 percent, and it received 24.3 percent of Poland's total exports, which was 3.2 percent more than Poland sent to the Soviet Union.[19]

Within a year of the collapse of intra-CMEA trade, Germany reemerged as the most important trading partner of Central and Eastern Europe. As early as 1989, Poland and Hungary were importing more from Germany than from the Soviet Union, and their exports to Germany were approaching those to the Soviet Union.[20] In 1990 German exports to Central and Eastern Europe totaled $14.5 billion, or 30 percent of all exports from countries of the Organization for Economic Cooperation and Development (OECD) to Central and Eastern Europe.[21] Other historical patterns not only continued during the division of Europe but also expanded. For one thing, financial dependence on Western Europe increased, and most Central and East European countries accumulated large external debts.

Western Europe was also able to maintain a modern capital stock during a time of rapid technological development and experienced higher growth rates. Meanwhile, new investments in Central and East European countries declined sharply (between 1975 and 1988 the share of manufacturing plants less than five years old fell from 31 percent to 23 percent in the Czech and Slovak Federative Republic [CSFR], and from 34 percent to 19 percent in Poland). As a result, Central and Eastern Europe lost valuable export markets to other regions in southern Europe, Southeast Asia, and Latin America. Furthermore, the substantial differences in per capita income have grown

Figure 3.   European National Income Per Capita, 1937, 1988

Central and E. European income as a proportion of West European income

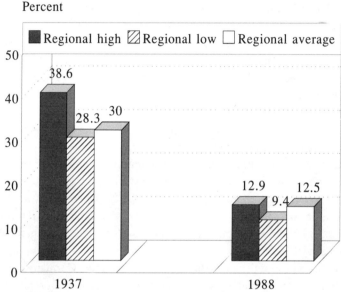

Percent

Regional high ▨Regional low ☐Regional average

1937 · 38.6 · 28.3 · 30

1988 · 12.9 · 9.4 · 12.5

Source: See table A-3.

larger. In 1937 Czechoslovakia ranked highest in income among the Central and East European countries, but its per capita GNP was still only about 39 percent of that of Britain, the most developed country in Western Europe at the time. By 1988 Czechoslovak per capita GNP had fallen to a mere 13 percent of that in Sweden, which by then ranked first in Western Europe. For the regional average, the ratios are about one-third and one-eighth, respectively (figure 3 and table A-3). Moreover, with the collapse of the Central and East European economies during the past two years, this gap is expected to widen until at least 1995.[22]

Today the greatest differences between East and West, however, exist because the division of Europe did not prevent Western Europe from moving ahead with economic and political integration in the context of the European Community. This integration has achieved many of the goals originally set by the EC founders. This state of affairs, however, will complicate the unification of Europe. As I explain later, unification is no longer simply a matter of renewing economic links among the individual countries as they existed between World War I and World War II. For European unification to succeed,

Central and Eastern Europe will have to be integrated into the institutional, legal and administrative, and political structures of the European Community.

When the treaty was signed establishing the European Coal and Steel Community, Jean Monnet remarked, "This isn't just coal and steel. It is the beginning of a process—a dynamic process to build a great market for all the people of Europe."[23] Monnet's vision of a single market, however, was interrupted by the Cold War. Today this vision has been given new life in a dramatic fashion as the Cold War has come to an unexpected end. However, unification will not come about without economic, political, and social change in both East and West. Indeed, it seems more difficult today, as both parts of the continent have grown even further apart during the last forty years. With the end of Soviet hegemony in Central and Eastern Europe, the national, ethnic, and partisan rivalries of 1920 and 1945 quickly resurfaced in Central and Eastern Europe and propelled the Community into a central position for which it was unprepared. Similarly, as Germany reunifies and moves to the center of the European political and economic stage, traditional rivalries among West European powers are reemerging. Thus, although the basic rationale for European unification has not changed, the challenge it poses is greater than ever.

3. Toward a New European Political Economy: Analytical Framework

As mentioned in the introduction, *both* parts of the divided continent will have to change if Central and Eastern Europe are to be reintegrated into the West European political economy. For the countries of Central and Eastern Europe this means dismantling the entire centrally planned economic system and creating the basic institutional infrastructure characteristic of any market economy—that is, system transformation. In Western Europe the change, or systemic reform, entails considerable adjustments in the existing market structures to support the system transformation and facilitate Central and Eastern Europe's integration into the larger European political economy, particularly the European Community.

As this section shows, however, system transformation is a highly complex process that is difficult to implement and will take many years to complete. The transition period has already brought such economic and social hardship to Central and Eastern Europe that it threatens to slow down or even reverse the transformation to a market-based system. Therefore the long-term strategy needs to be supplemented with short-term *policy initiatives* designed to stabilize as well as shorten the difficult transition period. (These initiatives may not necessarily be relevant to the establishment of a market economy.)

As many analysts have correctly argued, the primary goal of the adjustment process in Central and Eastern Europe must be to introduce an economic system that is based on private property and that relies primarily on the free exchange of goods, services, labor, and capital—a market economy. Though important, this free interaction of economic interests is only one of the elements of a market economy.

Much of the utilitarian tradition, including classical and neoclassical economics, envisions a market as an almost idealized state in which rational, self-interested economic actors interact free of constraint, whether it be legal, political, or of some other form, and are minimally affected by social relations, their history, traditions, ethnic allegiances, and other factors. In this atomized, undersocialized, and depoliticized conception of human action, the market is a separate, differentiated sphere of modern society, unrelated to the broader

13

political, social, and historical environment in which it is embedded.[24] Economic rationality prevails over political, social, or judicial rationality.

Such a concept does not fully capture the complexity of a market economy and thus would fail to suggest all the policy steps required to establish this kind of system. A market economy is more than a loosely structured agglomeration of individual economic actors that freely express their economic preferences, generating Pareto-superior or even optimal outcomes for themselves and the economy at large. Rather, a market economy is a complex organization based not only on the interaction of individual economic preferences but also on social relationships and patterns of behavior, legal norms and mechanisms, and political forces and institutions, all of which interact in a structured manner to produce relatively consistent behavior characteristic of any large institution.

A market economy is the principal form of social organization governing advanced industrial democracies. Any change in the economic circumstances under which individuals interact will thus also have a major impact on the political, legal, and social structures in which these economic activities are embedded. In other words, change in one area is inextricably linked to change in another and may often be its cause. The institutions of a market economy and the transactions they undertake also depend on the presence of collective goods such as trust, which cannot be provided by market processes themselves. The social organization of trust is thus an important constituent of a market economy, and it is one that economic theory has not been able to cope with.[25]

I have adopted this holistic concept of a market here for two reasons, one analytical, one methodological.[26] From an analytical perspective, only a holistic definition is likely to capture the complexity, scope, and uniqueness of the system transformation that Central and Eastern Europe will have to undergo. A number of scholars have adopted a similar approach in their studies of the transformation from feudalism to capitalism in Europe during the sixteenth and seventeenth centuries.[27] It takes into account the close interdependence of the legal, economic, social, and political aspects of system transformation. Indeed, from a holistic perspective, a market economy is an organic system that forms a social whole that functions through a network of its constituent parts.

The importance of individual systemic elements can be evaluated only in the context of the system as a whole. The institutions and actors that characterize modern market economies in the West are thus likely to come about through an endogenous process of societal change that places limits on the ability of exogenous forces to influence this process. Because of the organic nature of the various dimensions that define a market economy, the transformation of economic institutions and actors will affect political and social relations. Thus the conditions in which the economic transformation itself takes place will change. In other words, there will be a continuous process of change as the market economy develops.

From a methodological perspective, the concept of the market economy as the central focus of the analysis provides an appropriate framework of inquiry for the central question raised in this discussion: what policy responses can forge a new political economy of Europe? As already mentioned, the answer to this question lies not only in Central and Eastern Europe. The transformation there will have to be accompanied by changes in West European markets, especially in the European Community, before reintegration can occur.

Market mechanisms are firmly established in the European Community and are widely accepted as the dominant form of social organization. However, the structures, rules, and norms that define West European markets, and in particular the European Community market, will have to change considerably to cope with the transformation and integration of Central and Eastern Europe. Thus the size, shape, and structure of the political economy of the new Europe will be determined not only by the process of system transformation in Central and Eastern Europe but also by systemic reform in the Western half of the continent. Using the conceptual framework of the market—as defined in this essay—permits a theoretical integration of the required political, economic, and social changes in both Eastern and Western Europe. Ultimately, the degree to which East and West are willing and able to undergo such changes will determine how integrated the regions will eventually become.

For both sides, a holistic strategy of change would be based on two principles. The first principle is that the change should take place in at least three spheres of social organization: the legal and administrative, the economic, and the social and psychological. Economic interactions are the most visible characteristics of an economy and are most closely associated with the wealth-generating potential of a market exchange. However, all market interactions are firmly embedded in a set of administrative rules and regulations, which in turn are governed by the political forces structuring the market. In addition, every market economy operates on the basis of social and psychological norms and through the institutions that have internalized these norms. These norms and institutions are the wellspring of the individual behavioral patterns characteristic of and essential to the functioning of a market economy.

Most important, the three spheres of social organization are organically linked and depend on one another for their performance. Any strategy for

Table 2. A Holistic Strategy of System Transformation and Systemic Reform[a]

Level of social structure	Three market dimensions		
	Legal/ administrative	Economic	Social/psychological
Macro	Legislative structure Judicial system Bureaucracy	Efficient labor and capital markets Convertible exchange rates Free trade	Educational system Religion Mass media
Micro	Interest and pressure groups (unions, business associations)	Private/competitive enterprise system Free price system	The family Peer groups Schools Voluntary associations

a. The characteristics defining the various market domains are by no means exhaustive, and are for illustrative purposes only. Similarly, in reality the dividing lines between the various domains are more fluid, and one may want to introduce additional levels of the social structure.

creating or reforming a market, in view of new internal or external conditions, must deal with these spheres as a *whole*. This is not to imply that market economies cannot differ widely among themselves. In fact, many substantive differences in the institutional structure and the standards and norms of Western industrial democracies are now coming to light since the end of the overarching East-West ideological conflict. These differences are mirrored in the differing and often conflicting advice that Central and East Europeans receive from the West on how to transform their economies.

The second principle of a holistic strategy of change is that it must permeate *all* levels of society, from the major political and economic institutions, to mid-level organizations and associations, right down to the family and individual. If the strategy fails to reach the majority of citizens, the market economy that is to be created will lack a social base. Social support for the creation of a market economy or its reform is essential, both on the supply and demand side. On the supply side, the institutional structure will become fully functional only if it is adequately equipped with trained personnel who understand the dynamics of a market economy and who can espouse a professional ethic committed to its functioning. On the demand side, a large part of the population needs to be aware of the complexities and difficulties that system transformation or reform entail. The process needs to be supported by a sufficiently large share of the population and the organizations that represent them. If this social cohesion is lacking in times of difficulties, the transformation process is likely to stall.

When these two principles are combined, the multiple policy domains of a holistic strategy of change become obvious (table 2).

I. CENTRAL AND EASTERN EUROPE: THE CHALLENGE OF SYSTEM TRANSFORMATION

There is no doubt that the principal burden of change will fall on the countries of Central and Eastern Europe, which have engaged in an unprecedented experiment to transform their societies from a system that was primarily governed by a centrally planned economy and single party rule to a system that is based on the principles of a modern market economy and multiparty democracy. In section 4, I apply the holistic approach to the challenge of creating a market economy in the context of a democratic regime and develop a strategy of system transformation. To illustrate the need for a holistic approach in an applied context, section 5 briefly reviews developments in Central and East European financial markets during 1991.

Given the time period required to transform the social systems in Central and Eastern Europe and the problems that are likely to arise during the transition process, I propose in sections 6 and 7 two short-term policy initiatives—rebuilding regional economic cooperation in the former Eastern bloc and solving the debt crisis in Central and Eastern Europe—that would not only help to stabilize the transition period but also shorten the process of system transformation itself.

4. A Holistic Approach to Creating a Market Economy

For Western industrial democracies, the market economy has long been the dominant form of social organization. As a result, it is considered a "natural" part of everyday life, and observers tend to focus on its most obvious economic characteristics such as private property and a price system to allocate scarce resources. Many of its less visible, structural elements are taken for granted by its participants and policymakers alike. Once a market economy has been established, the primary task of policymakers is to manage it and, if necessary and politically feasible, to reform the management process.

Since none of the countries of Central and Eastern Europe has ever experienced a modern market economy for any sustained period, the challenge there is not to reform their respective economies by refining or reorienting macro- and microeconomic policies currently being practiced. The challenge is to *create* a market economy.[28] To do so, these societies will have to dismantle the political, economic, and social structures that have governed them for the past forty years. In the economic realm alone, many *vertical*-control hierarchies will have to be dismantled. These hierarchies enabled the state to use distribution as the primary mechanism to allocate both scarce resources and the economy's output. The hierarchy must be replaced with thousands of *horizontal* market links that will make information readily available and allow sellers and buyers to interact freely.[29]

Noneconomic Dimensions

The economic prerequisites of a successful market economy need not be discussed here. Many valuable reform proposals have been made concerning the various economic structures and elements that are in need of transformation. However, as the holistic approach makes clear, the economic dimension of the market cannot be detached from the larger sphere of which it is a part. It may thus be useful to look at the legal and administrative and the social and psychological dimensions more closely and to see what implications the close interconnectedness of all three dimensions has for a strategy of system transformation.

From a legal and administrative perspective a modern market economy depends not only on private property and free prices to facilitate exchange but also on a complex and differentiated network of organizations shaping that exchange. At the macrostructural level their function is often administrative. The network ensures the smooth and efficient interaction of participants in a particular market, and, if necessary, it employs legal means to obtain the required performance. For example, most labor markets in advanced industrialized countries operate through an extensive network of employment offices that not only provide unemployment benefits but also act as a support structure for the unemployed. They function as information exchanges and clearinghouses for job opportunities, and they provide career counseling and aptitude tests. In addition, most of these countries offer programs for vocational training and retraining, to smooth the transition in labor markets during times of industrial restructuring and adjustment.[30]

In conjunction with the transformation of the former East German economy, the German government has established a training and job creation fund. This fund was allocated an additional $6.9 billion for 1992 to help the five new Eastern *Länder* upgrade the qualifications of an additional 700,000 people. Between October 1990 (when job creation measures were started for the first time) and December 1991, 620,000 workers in East Germany were placed in jobs, 380,000 (or 62 percent) of them through job creation measures.[31] These measures are expected to help an additional 400,000 find employment under the Federal Labor Office's budget draft for 1992. Together, these numbers represent approximately 9.1 percent of the labor force in the five new *Länder*.

At the microstructural level, organizations often perform the function of interest aggregation and intermediation, providing policymakers with information and representing the interests of particular groups in the market. Chambers of commerce, unions, trade and business associations, and consumer groups are all vital elements of a modern market economy. In the example of the labor market, these organizations often facilitate adjustment by offering technical advice, expertise, physical space, and financial support for training programs. Their activities, both at the macro- and microstructural level, ensure that labor markets will allow demand and supply to clear at relatively low levels of unemployment and thus function smoothly and properly.[32]

Consider another example. Market economies rely extensively on multiorganizational networks of institutions representing individuals or groups of individuals. These multiple organizations indicate that a market economy promotes decisionmaking by individuals or groups of individuals, both as consumers and as producers. As a result, conflicts are a permanent feature of society at all levels and across many issues. To deal with these conflicts, market economies have established elaborate mechanisms to prevent or to resolve them, or both. These mechanisms operate in a legal framework ranging from commercial codes and antitrust legislation to arbitration procedures for industrial disputes, as well as consumer safety and protection standards.[33] To implement and enforce these laws, the system relies on a judicial apparatus consisting of both institutional and human capital. In contrast, the centrally planned economies of Central and Eastern Europe relied largely on mono-organizational structures. Conflicts among producers and consumers were rare, and rules and structures for conflict resolution were almost nonexistent. These rules and structures must now be created before a market economy can function effectively and efficiently in the region.

A strategy of system transformation must also ensure that the necessary social and psychological foundations are present. It must recognize, for example, that market decisions are often spontaneous and unpredictable and that the individual and society at large have limited influence on market processes, particularly in such central areas as production, investment, and distribution.[34] This is not to say that the command economies of Central and Eastern Europe could always predict results. Rather, unpredictability was considered a sign of confusion and was treated as an aberration—as something pathological and sick.[35] Thus an essential task during the creation of a market economy is to establish the social legitimacy of risk and spontaneity in everyday life. This legitimacy will not be accepted unless individuals shed their "learned helplessness," which is a reflection of the state's and party's monopoly not just over political life but also over economic, social, and cultural life. To do so, they will have to develop the skills necessary to deal with the insecurities and unpredictability that a market economy generates in everyday life. Entrepreneurship, innovativeness, creativity, independent decisionmaking, the acceptance of responsibility for one's own actions, self-confidence—all these characteristics make up the social and psychological foundation of a market economy.[36]

For a market economy to act as the principal mode of social organization, people have to understand how the market works, identify with it, and benefit from it. Only then will it have the integrating force it has in the industrialized economies of the West.[37] Not only will people have to develop the social and psychological preconditions of a market economy, but they will also have to come to terms with some of its consequences. The social acceptance of unemployment and the wide income differentials that will emerge in association with the rise of a middle class and a new managerial elite will lead to major adjustments in the social stratification of Central and East European societies.[38]

The mere recognition of these dimensions will not help create a market economy, however. Although it is important to adopt a commercial code and consumer protection laws, they will only have their desired effect if they are implemented effectively and their application can be monitored. Similarly, even if Central and East Europeans make the foregoing social and psychological adjustments, such changes need to take root in the larger society, not in just a narrow new elite. Unless these changes are actively promoted, it will take years for them to permeate the larger society.[39] Therefore, a successful strategy for establishing a market economy will include both an elaborate design for transforming the system and a *maintenance* scheme for managing and continuously adjusting the market economy in all three of its dimensions.

To recapitulate, the modern market economy comprises not just an exchange of goods and services and labor and capital, but also a legal and administrative framework in which these exchanges take place and a social and psychological foundation on which the exchanges are based. As mentioned, these aspects of a market usually receive little attention and are often taken for granted because they are not very visible, or because we have grown accustomed to them. Just because the most visible characteristic of a market economy—its output—is evaluated solely in economic terms does not imply that the input is equally unidimensional.

Linkage

Another important point for the policymaker to note is that these dimensions are organically linked. If progress in the economic realm depends on parallel progress in the legal and administrative and the social and psychological realms, then it is important to develop a *strategy of simultaneity* to ensure that transformation in one domain will be accompanied by equivalent or similar change in the other domains. That is to say, the *capacity* of a system to truly absorb economic transformations will depend on its ability to institute legal and administrative and social and psychological change as well as to sustain economic change.

This does not imply that economic transformation cannot be implemented rapidly, as has been often suggested. What it does mean is that even if the economic realm of a market is partly transformed, the potential for growth and for creating wealth will not be realized unless the forces in the other dimensions of a market economy also come into play. Economic transformation that takes place in a legal and administrative, and social and psychological, vacuum is likely to stall quickly. A reorientation will then be necessary to allow the lagging spheres to catch up with the level of transformation achieved in the economic sphere.

At the microstructural level, these feedback effects can already be seen in the slowdown in the Central and East European privatization programs.[40] In June 1991 the Polish government, in response to the slow privatization process, announced an ambitious program to privatize 400 state-owned factories, which account for 25 percent of the country's industrial sales.[41] Within a few months, however, the government was forced to scale back these ambitious plans and reduce the number of factories to be privatized to 230. One of the principal problems has been the absence of a legal framework for private sector investment both domestic and from abroad.

Continued difficulties with privatization forced the new government of Prime Minister Olszewski to once again adjust its privatization strategy. In February 1992 it announced a new program that would hand over about 200 companies to Western-managed investment funds, which would in turn sell shares to the population at a nominal charge.[42] This strategy, if it succeeds, is not considered optimal. Rather, in addition to lessening the debt overhang, it is a response designed to compensate for the lack of an adequate management cadre for the companies. According to an adviser to the minister of privatization, "It would be far better if Poland could import 400 first-class managers to run its ailing state enterprises."[43]

Czechoslovakia is also facing problems with its privatization effort. The so-called small privatization program (which involves state-run retail and trade shops, restaurants, and other small businesses) and the large privatization program (which involves state-run enterprises) both got off to a relatively good start. In both cases, however, irregularities occurred in the administration of the programs, and the program's execution was poorly supervised. In the case of the small program, straw men purchased enterprises for foreigners, even though this program was only open to Czechoslovak nationals. Moreover, an increasing number of shops were returned to the state enterprises after having been auctioned off because their owners could not survive the excessive maintenance costs.

The large privatization has taken place in a legislative vacuum and has also been disrupted by irregularities.[44] More than 300 largely unregulated private investment funds have sprung up across the country, offering to invest the vouchers of citizens.[45] Officials from the Ministry of Privatization consider the process to be very dangerous and have charged that these funds often mislead people with their advertisements. The lack of administrative capacity and supervision has led to the hoarding and even the disappearance of voucher books. In fact, the coupons were sold before the privatization projects had even been made public. As a consequence, officials want the program suspended.[46] Without an efficient stock market and the necessary accompanying legislation, the privatization program is likely to be paralyzed.[47] In addition, the breakup of Czechoslovakia threatens to undermine the entire privatization effort.

Feedback effects have also become evident at the macrostructural level. Poland, which initially followed the most rigorous stabilization program, has now altered its economic policy. The turnaround in the spring of 1992 under the government of former prime minister Olszewski, in response to increasing social discontent and unrest, demonstrated the limits of how far policymakers can move ahead in a single dimension of a market economy. Progress is also lagging far behind in the legal and administrative domain. Underpaid and overworked civil servants with no experience in Western-style bureaucratic administration are unable to collect all tax revenues or respond to all the requests to open new businesses. As a result, the budgetary crisis has worsened, further straining Poland's relations with the International Monetary Fund. The Polish bureaucracy is said to be less responsive to citizens than it was before the end of Communist rule. This has led to "a great disillusionment between the governors and the governed."[48]

To allow for more simultaneous progress in system transformation, authorities must distribute resources across all three market domains more evenly. *Systemic dysfunctionalities* are likely to occur if the organic links and the need for simultaneity are ignored. The transformation will suffer setbacks or collapse, the initial achievements will be obliterated, and the support for continued change will weaken.[49]

Holistic versus "Shock Therapy" Approach

Thus policymakers must also try to determine the appropriate speed at which system transformation can be implemented. This will depend in large part on the availability of the resources required for the transformation. A holistic strategy requires a broad range of resources. Economic stabilization programs that focus almost entirely on the economic dimensions of a market rely heavily on financial capital. A holistic strategy would also rely on vast amounts of human capital in the form of knowledge and experience to achieve progress in the legal and administrative and the social and psychological spheres. Unless these nonfinancial resources are being supplied in sufficient amounts to complement the financial ones, some of the capital originally allocated to the economic transformation will have to be reallocated to recruit more human capital. In view of the nature of the change that has to take place in the social and psychological sphere, much of the human capital is likely to accumulate as an endogenous process of social evolution specific to each country. Foreign capital, in whatever form, may be of only limited use.

This analysis suggests that a holistic strategy is likely to favor a gradual or piecemeal approach to system transformation. For this reason, the advocates of "shock therapy" believe the gradualist approach has certain built-in obstructive, or even destructive, tendencies. The critics argue that the more time that opponents of change have at their disposal, the greater the risk that the transformation process will slow down or even be reversed. Such criticism is appropriate if time is considered the central determinant of the success of system transformation. However, if simultaneity during system transformation is the central factor determining success—as it is in the holistic approach—a gradual approach will be more likely to succeed. In fact, it is shock therapy that is considered piecemeal and gradual from the holistic perspective because it concentrates its efforts on the economic dimension of a market economy alone.

The argument that increasing opposition to reform will undermine the transformation effort also carries little weight. For one thing, a strategy that relies on a surprise effect to overcome resistance to change by speculating on the lethargy and credulity of a democracy is equally if not more risky.[50] And although it is true that opposition often develops during system transformation, no conclusions should be drawn about the appropriateness of a certain policy before the source of the opposition is established. Is there genuine resistance to transforming a command economy into a market economy, which must be outmaneuvered by a shock therapy? Or is the resistance directed at the shock therapy itself, and therefore an indication that the strategy needs to be changed?

In discussing the merits of these two approaches, it is also important to keep the ultimate objective of system transformation in mind. This objective is not simply to privatize and stabilize the economy but to build the foundation for a market economy that can improve the living standards of Central and East European societies by generating long-term sustainable economic growth. Thus privatization and stabilization are necessary, but insufficient, conditions.[51] Large segments of society must also identify with the system transformation and have the incentive to participate in the process and support it. Human investment in the transformation process alone, however, will not suffice. Capital investment that can make use of the newly created market structures is equally important. Much of this investment will initially come from abroad, but it will flow only if both the legal and administrative and the social and psychological dimensions are firmly embedded in the overall market structure.

Given the more realistic assessment of the time and resources needed for system transformation, policymakers must be sure to target those components of a market economy that have high strategic value, both from a functional and a structural perspective. For example, the transformation of the telecommunications sector is likely to have great functional value. All industries and businesses, as well as individual households, are likely to benefit. Moreover, a modern telecommunications system may also become an important tool for facilitating the transformation in other areas, such as education, which plays a vital role in building the social and psychological foundation of the emerging market economy. Modern energy and transportation systems are two other central ingredients of a functioning market economy. The greater the "diffusion and demonstration effect" of transforming one specific sector of the economy, the higher its strategic value.

One sector of particularly high structural and functional value is the financial system. To illustrate the holistic approach to system transformation in an applied context I briefly review recent developments in Central and East European financial markets in section 5.

Yet another important consideration in devising a strategy of system transformation is the political context in which the transformation is to take place. The possible constraints must be identified at the outset. The extent to which system transformation can be undertaken at any particular point in time—whether by shock therapy or by taking a holistic approach—will depend on the *capacity* of the political system to design and carry out such a transformation.

This capacity is determined in large part by the degree of the government's legitimacy. Western politicians and bureaucrats are accustomed to advocating policies in the context of stable democracies, where the limits of feasible change are generally broad and the government's legitimacy is high. However, the legacy of the state and the party in Central and Eastern Europe has led to a low level of trust in public office and political institutions. There is also little sense of national identity. This lack of legitimacy and national consensus makes it difficult for Central and East European governments to enact system transformation swiftly, and it casts doubt on the political feasibility of using shock therapy. If transformation is enforced at a faster rate than the emerging democratic systems can absorb, it is likely to undermine and damage the fragile trust that has developed in favor of the new political elites. A political backlash is then likely to occur, and there may be a move toward authoritarian or even totalitarian forms of government or the country may split into different ethnic or national groups.[52]

A gradualist approach is more likely to prevent the emerging market economy from overloading the as yet fragile networks of the new democracy during the process of system transformation. The holistic strategy allows the market economy to evolve at a slower pace and thus leaves more time for the new political institutions to establish their legitimacy and thus to keep up with and implement the numerous changes required. By avoiding some of the economic and social hardships that are created by the shock therapy, the holistic approach itself is likely to help the government establish its legitimacy. That will strengthen political institutions and give the government the power it needs to proceed with the transformation process.

A holistic approach is also better able to cope with the complexity of system transformation. It generates a more realistic set of expectations regarding the necessary resources and the length of time it will take to establish even the most basic foundations of a market economy in Central and Eastern Europe. In many cases, attention has focused on the economic aspects of market formation, primarily at the macrostructural level, with the result that there is now a gap between what the majority of Central and East European citizens expect from the transformation and what can realistically be achieved in such a short time. These citizens have become disillusioned and frustrated, and many are beginning to withdraw their political support for systemic change.[53]

The Worsening Situation

The likelihood of a halt or even reversal of the system transformation in Central and Eastern Europe increased during 1991 and the first half of 1992.

In macropolitical terms, the countries of Central and Eastern Europe had, until recently, made considerable progress in establishing the basic institutions of democracy and the rule of law. However, the transition to a market economy is still at an early stage. Numerous complications are arising, and the record of the transformation process has so far been mixed at best.[54] Throughout the 1980s growth in industrial output had been stagnating in most Central and East European countries. Then, beginning in 1989, Hungary, Poland, and Romania experienced negative growth rates for the first time in their history. In 1990 and 1991 industrial output collapsed in all the Central and East European countries, declining at double-digit rates (figure 4 and table A-4). When the data are disaggregated on a quarterly basis, the drop in output during the last half of 1991 is even higher in most countries (figure 5 and table A-4).

As a result, unemployment is rising dramatically. Between December 1990 and December 1991, unemployment in Bulgaria rose from 1.7 to 10.7 percent, in Czechoslovakia from 1.0 to 6.6 percent, in Hungary from 1.7 to 8.3 percent, and in Poland from 6.1 to 11.5 percent (figure 6 and table A-5). Official government estimates project double-digit unemployment rates for most of the countries of Central and Eastern Europe by the end of 1992. Again, when the unemployment data are disaggregated on a monthly basis, there is no slow-down in the growth rates in most of the countries (figure 7 and table A-5).

Those people who were able to remain employed or find a new job saw their living standards erode dramatically. There was double-digit inflation across all countries even though some prices remained controlled or were deregulated at a slow pace (table 3 and table A-6). Finally, governments were limited in their ability to dampen the social consequences of these underlying macroeconomic conditions—either directly, through expanded aid programs, or indirectly, through fiscal expansion, as the budget deficits in most countries had reached the limits agreed upon under the stabilization program administered by the International Monetary Fund.

These economic statistics lie at the root of the deteriorating social and political climate across Central and Eastern Europe. They threaten to halt the transformation to a market-based system and to undermine the democratic achievements made so far. In a survey conducted by the European Community in the fall of 1991, more than 50 percent of the population in every Central and East European country indicated that the economic situation had grown worse in the preceding twelve months (figure 8, table A-7, and table A-10). In the case of Poland, the economic situation deteriorated with about one-third of the respondents in 1990 and two-thirds in 1991 indicating that the economy was

Figure 4. Industrial Output in Central and Eastern Europe, 1986–91

Percent change from previous year

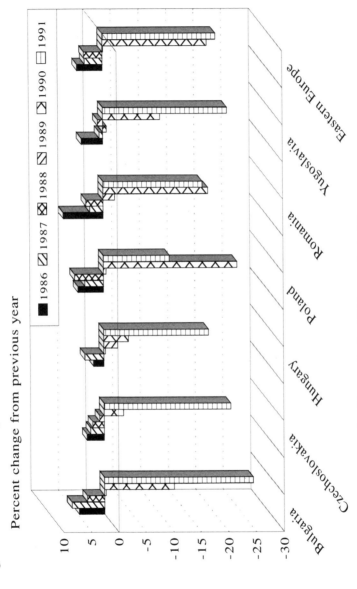

■ 1986　▨ 1987　⊠ 1988　▧ 1989　⊠ 1990　☐ 1991

Source: See table A-4. The figures for 1991 are national or ECE forecasts for the full year.

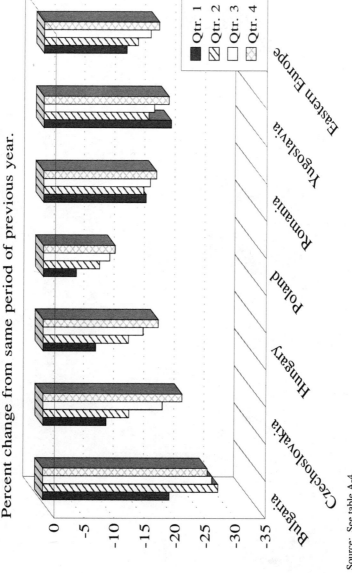

Figure 5. Industrial Output in Central and Eastern Europe, 1991 by Quarter
Percent change from same period of previous year.

Source: See table A-4.

32

Figure 6. Unemployment in Central and Eastern Europe, 1989–92

Percent of labor force at end of period

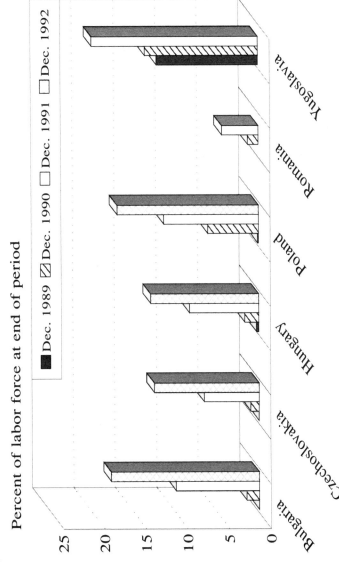

Source: See table A-5. The 1992 figures are estimates based on governmental and official sources.

Figure 7. Unemployment in Central and Eastern Europe, 1991 by Month

Percent of labor force

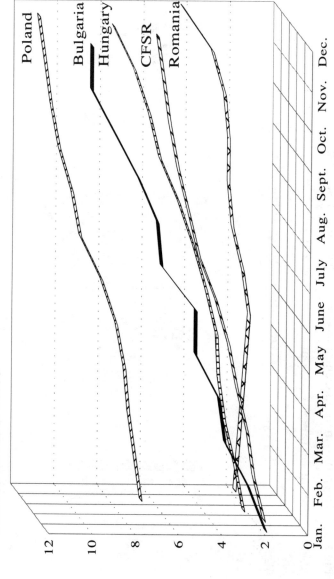

Source: See table A-5.

Table 3. Inflation in Central and Eastern Europe, 1989–92

Percent change over preceding year

Country	1989	1990	1991[a]	1992[a]
Bulgaria	6.2	20.0	249.8	n.a
CFSR	1.4	10.0	57.9	15-20
Hungary	17.0	28.9	35.0	35.0
Poland	244.1	584.7	70.3	45.0
Romania	n.a.	13.0	344.5	n.a.
USSR	n.a.	5.0	650-700	n.a

Sources: See table A-6.
n.a. Not available.
a. Forecasts by national or Economic Commission for Europe sources.

worse than in the previous year. For Czechoslovakia, the economic situation got slightly better, with about 10 percent more respondents in 1991 citing improvement than in 1990 (figure 9 and table A-10). The outcome of the poll at the microstructural level is even more troubling. Except in Romania, which has just started the process of system transformation, more than two-thirds of those surveyed said their household finances grew worse over the preceding twelve months (figure 10, table A-8, and table A-10). For the countries in which figures can be compared with those of a previous period, the situation has either stagnated, as in Czechoslovakia, or deteriorated, as in Poland (figure 11 and table A-10).

Confidence is declining not only in the economy but also in the political system, which is beginning to erode the legitimacy of the governing elite. According to the EC survey, in 1991 more than half the population in almost every Central and East European country was dissatisfied with democracy (figure 12, table A-9, and table A-10). Again, for those countries in which comparison with a previous period is possible, the survey indicates that satisfaction with democracy deteriorated, with the exception of Hungary,

Figure 8. Public Opinion on the Economic Situation over the Previous Twelve Months, 1991, in Central and Eastern Europe and Russia (European)

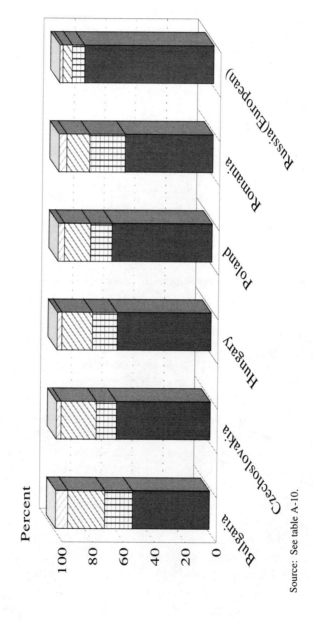

Source: See table A-10.

36

Figure 9. Public Opinion on the Economic Situation over the Previous Twelve Months in Czechoslovakia and Poland

Czechoslovakia

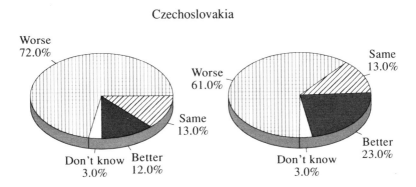

Poland

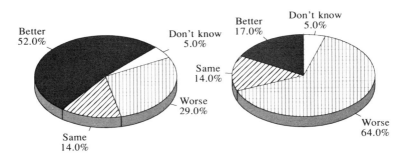

Source: See table A-10.

where 60 percent of the population remain unsatisfied (figure 13 and table A-9). In another poll conducted in Poland during the summer of 1991, 71 percent of the respondents agreed that "corruption in Poland today is a major problem," and more than half thought it was as bad now as under the Communist regime.[55]

Frustration with deteriorating economic conditions and the belief among Poles that the political system is unable to address these issues have manifested

Figure 10. Public Opinion on Household Finances over the Previous Twelve Months, 1991, in Central and Eastern Europe and Russia (European)

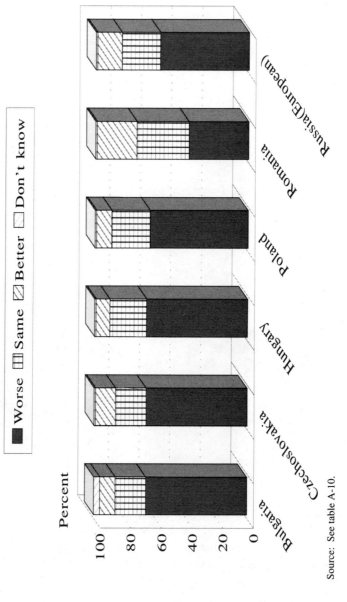

Source: See table A-10.

Figure 11. Public Opinion on Household Finances over the Previous Twelve Months in Czechoslovakia and Poland

1990   1991

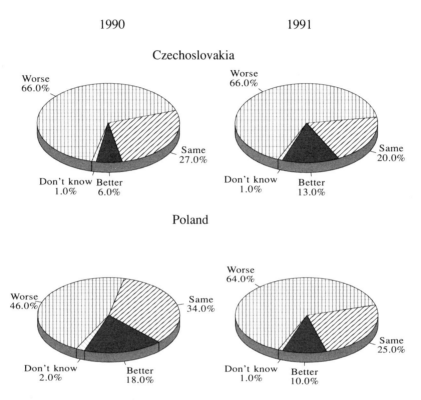

Czechoslovakia

Poland

Source: See table A-10.

themselves in active opposition and political apathy. This situation has begun to undermine the process of system transformation. In 1990 and 1991 the number of strikes increased sharply.[56] Solidarity has taken the lead in criticizing the government's economic program, calling it "reform through ruin."[57] The union warned that this policy "must lead to an increase in social conflicts, whereas the temptation to apply solutions involving the use of force generates even today a tendency to substitute authoritarianism for democracy."[58] Even more threatening to the political transformation process is the increasing political apathy in Poland. In April 1991, 50 percent of those surveyed did not intend to cast a ballot in the fall elections, but by July the

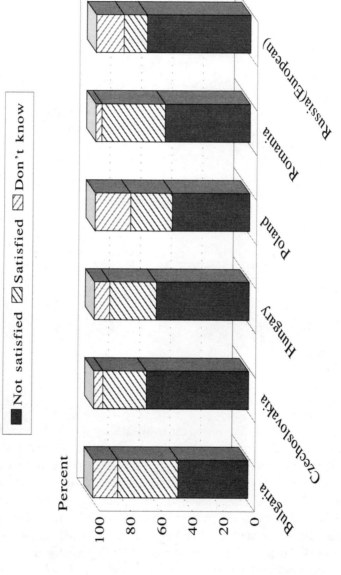

Figure 12. Public Opinion on Satisfaction with Democracy, 1991, in Central and Eastern Europe and Russia (European)

■ Not satisfied ▨ Satisfied ▧ Don't know

Percent

Source: See table A-10.

Figure 13. Public Opinion on Satisfaction with Democracy, 1990, 1991, in Czechoslovakia, Hungary, and Poland

1990   1991

Czechoslovakia

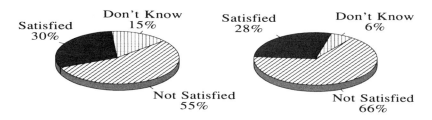

Hungary

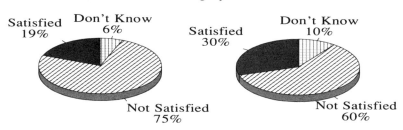

Poland

Source: See table A-9.

number had risen to 63 percent. These intentions were confirmed during the parliamentary elections in October 1991, when 56.8 percent of the population did not vote.[59] Since the elections, the government has been in a permanent state of crisis because of internal divisions and a failure to agree on an economic program that would satisfy both its domestic and international constituencies, in particular the IMF and the World Bank.[60] In democracies that have been in place for a longer period of time, voter apathy could also be interpreted as a general acceptance of a government's policies rather than alienation. However, given the fact that democracy and its institutions are only just beginning to emerge and considering the survey data just presented, there is little doubt that the apathy reflects the frustration and disillusionment among large segments of the population.

Other Central and East European countries are beginning to experience similar social and political strains as a result of the transformation to a market economy.[61] As in Poland, this discontent is reflected in voter apathy and declining government support. In Hungary local by-elections last August drew a turnout as low as 17 percent, and in mid-1991 a poll revealed that only 64 percent would go to the polls for a general election.[62] The current government has warned of the growing anti-democratic sentiment and of the population's increasing willingness to accept an authoritarian leader as the price for an economic miracle.

Differences over the strategy of system transformation have also erupted in other Central and East European countries.[63] In Czechoslovakia these differences continued to undermine the fragile federation throughout 1991.[64] Although the reasons for the impending disintegration of Czechoslovakia are numerous, there is little doubt that the economic adjustment program implemented by the federal government is one of the principal contributing factors. Unemployment in Slovakia has risen to 12 percent compared to 3 percent in the Czech lands, and Slovak industrial production has declined more sharply than that in the Czech lands. The policy of halting arms exports and arms production hit Slovakia more severely because most of the industry is located there.[65] The resultant greater deterioration in living standards and the resentment against the federal government's policies played into the hands of Vladimir Meciar and the electoral victory of his party, the Movement for a Democratic Slovakia, which initiated the breakup of the federation.

The inability to enlist and maintain public support and the deteriorating economic situation cast further doubt on the long-term viability of current transformation strategies. No strategy, however promising its eventual outcome, will succeed unless the transition period can be managed successfully and the outcome can be sustained. At the same time, a failure of the transformation process would not only have serious internal, social, economic, and political repercussions for each country, but would also jeopardize other countries' efforts to transform their social systems. Besides posing a threat to the stability of the entire region, such a failure would prevent the speedy reintegration of this region into the overall European political economy. This would weaken the European Community's role as the central external anchor of political and economic stability available to Central and East European countries. Although it is probably too late to reduce the "expectation gap" that has emerged in Central and Eastern Europe, a holistic approach could help to prevent it from becoming even wider. More important, by emphasizing both the multidimensional nature of a market economy and acknowledging the political constraints on system transformation, such an approach is more likely to provide a strong foundation for the emerging market economy (by reducing the risk of policy failure) and to ensure that the governing elite does not lose its political legitimacy.

5. A Holistic Approach to Financial Systems

One of the main causes of the collapse of the Central and East European economies is that they lacked an efficient mechanism for financial intermediation.[66] The history of economic development clearly shows that a working financial system is indispensable to the formation of a market economy.[67] Not only will a stable financial system facilitate and serve transformation processes in other areas of the economy, but it may well be a precondition for their success.[68]

Despite comparatively high personal savings rates and equally high rates of investment, the capital stock in Central and Eastern Europe in the mid-1980s was by and large outdated.[69] The allocative mechanisms of the available capital had failed, and it became increasingly clear that a market economy would be superior in allocating capital than the region's centrally controlled system of capital distribution.[70]

Besides channeling domestic savings from households and businesses to profitable investments, an indigenous banking system with positive real interest rates is likely to attract foreign investment capital that is much needed during the initial years of the transformation process.[71] Such a system will make the countries concerned less dependent on grants and loans and thus will slow down the accumulation of foreign debt, while allowing newly granted credits from banks and international financial organizations to be used efficiently.[72] A modern financial system is also essential for enabling policymakers to execute effective monetary policy.[73] Given that a considerable portion of the accumulated savings in Central and Eastern Europe is held in cash, monetary control may be difficult to achieve without the presence of a banking system that pools these savings. A market-based financial system will also benefit trade liberalization. Even viable Central and East European enterprises are likely to need credit to survive strong international competition. Since they no longer have access to money from the government, sufficient access to capital markets is essential.

The existence of a functioning financial system will also determine the success of the privatization effort. The absence of ready sources of financing serves as a barrier to entry and delays industrial restructuring and domestic competition.[74] Moreover, one important precondition for privatization is relative monetary stability. The high stock of savings in Eastern Europe and the lack of consumption, however, is likely to lead to a considerable monetary overhang.[75] One way to control this overhang without triggering inflation is to rely on a financial system that can offer households more attractive, but less liquid, financial instruments that reduce the excess cash in circulation.[76] The principal economic purpose of privatization is to create conditions for a more effective use of the factors of production. Unless a financial system is in place that can fairly and comprehensively distribute former state property to a broad base in the population, there is a risk that the structure of asset ownership will merely move from state monopoly to private monopoly.[77]

Basic reforms in the financial systems of Central and Eastern Europe have been implemented.[78] Historically, the banking system was nothing more than an extension of the state. As a result, the institutional structure of Central and East European financial systems was highly centralized, consisting of a state bank, which served as both central bank and the primary commercial bank as a lender to state enterprises. One or a few state savings banks collected deposits from the public and held most of the long-term housing loans at very low and fixed interest rates.[79] In addition, there were a few specialized banks, such as foreign trade banks, which financed and settled international transactions. As a first step, a two-tier banking system was created to separate the different functions of the state bank. One tier consisted of a small number of commercial banks, which took over the outstanding loans and now serve the private sector, leaving the responsibility for monetary and credit control with the state (now central) bank.[80] Although the most exposed aspects of the defunct banking systems in Central and Eastern Europe have been restructured, many inherited problems remain, and new problems are emerging that are in urgent need of consideration.[81]

For example, many (now private) commercial banks hold nonperforming loans to state enterprises. In Hungary, for example, at the end of 1989 nonperforming loans amounted to at least 28 percent, and as much as 44 percent, of domestic credits to enterprises, with a small number of insolvent enterprises accounting for almost 30 percent of those loans.[82] By the middle of 1991 the level of insolvency of Slovak enterprises had reached 20 billion korunas.[83] In Yugoslavia troubled loans accounted for 40 percent of the loan portfolio of the commercial banks, with potential losses totaling as much as 25 percent of loans ($7-9 billion), far in excess of the banks' capital.[84] In Poland in early 1992 between 20 percent and 40 percent of the assets of the commercial banking system were nonperforming.[85]

In some countries the state savings bank holds massive subsidized mortgage portfolios that yield about one-tenth of the current market rate. One Hungarian commercial bank estimates that the mortgage portfolio of around F300 billion of housing loans is probably only worth F30 billion. This leaves the banks and the government burdened with an additional loss of F270 billion. One study concludes that "most of the major banks of East Europe are effectively bankrupt if judged by Western standards."[86] Even though most of these loans were made under the old system, governments have so far refused to accept responsibility.

Moreover, several countries have been hit by banking scandals involving illegal loans or incidents of corruption. In Yugoslavia, for example, a commercial bank made an illegal loan of $1.3 billion to the Serbian government. Poland was also hit by several cases of fraud. One case led to the arrest of the president of the central bank, who was later forced to resign. The fraud cost the government $330 million and led to the detention of several other officials.[87] Another scandal involved the illegal purchase of Polish debts to private banks on the secondary markets by the head of the agency that manages Poland's foreign debt. It also led to the resignation of the deputy finance minister and the dismissal of Poland's chief foreign debt negotiator, damaging Poland's international reputation in international financial circles.[88]

These events not only are endangering the fragile financial system but are also weakening the credibility of public officials both at home and abroad, especially among the foreign banks and other investors whose help is urgently needed. The dismissal of Poland's central bank president and the subsequent nomination process of his successor turned into a power struggle between the Sejm and President Lech Walesa. The dispute lasted for more than seven months, during which time the Sejm repeatedly rejected Walesa's candidates. In March 1992 the Sejm approved a new candidate.[89] The controversial dismissal of the head of the central bank in Hungary has also caused some worries about the stability of the central bank there, which has just been given new and expanded independence.[90]

Clearly, the countries of Central and Eastern Europe need to establish a legal and administrative framework that will stabilize their banking systems during the precarious transition from a centrally controlled system to a market-based system, and they need to provide the financial system with the regulatory and supervisory standards characteristic of any market economy.[91] For the most part, such a framework is only beginning to emerge. Legislative activity is lagging behind market developments. Poland's Sejm approved the new banking law only late in 1991, and it took several months longer for it to be approved by the Senate.[92] According to the president of the National Bank of Poland, "the changes currently being implemented are the minimum for the National Bank and the banking system to function effectively," and much more work is needed "to create a banking system that will clearly define the working of the banking sector."[93] "Qualitatively," according to the head of the central bank, "the banking system shows considerable deficiencies and short-comings."[94]

A similar situation prevails in Polish capital markets. In 1991 Poland already had about 100,000 shareholders and trading was active, but legislation governing the stock market was passed only in March 1992.[95] Hungary introduced modern banking regulations for the first time in mid-November 1991, and set the legal foundation for the privatization of the banks.[96] The same goes for the CSFR, whose government in late 1991 approved a new banking law, which was approved after several months by the federal parliament.[97] In Bulgaria a banking bill was approved by the government in November 1991, and was passed by the legislature in February 1992. However, it falls short of a major reform, which may take another year or two.[98]

Only now are basic standards such as reserve requirements being established and executed. Few countries have succeeded in implementing up-to-date accounting rules, however, and few have introduced antitrust measures. As a result, the banking system is highly centralized, and many nonfinancial enterprises hold a large proportion of the banks' equity capital, thereby creating a high risk of insider lending. But problems would continue even with a comprehensive legislative framework in place because few trained personnel are available to supervise the banks. Even though minimum capital-to-asset ratios have been adopted in Bulgaria, Hungary, Poland, and the former Yugoslavia, many banks do not meet the standards. Capital-to-asset ratios in Czechoslovakia, for example, were only about 1.5 to 2 percent in mid-1991.[99] In Poland the bank supervision department at the central bank is seriously understaffed and the central bank has been criticized for being too lax in issuing licenses.[100] Since several countries have not yet implemented a system of deposit insurance, the consequences of a bank failure would be disastrous. This is true in political and social terms as well as in economic terms.

Similar problems prevail at the microstructural level. Few bankers in Central and Eastern Europe are familiar with, or have access to, the financial services necessary to support a modern market economy. Modern accounting rules need to be implemented, and loan officers need training in credit analysis and loan appraisal.[101] Many lack the experience or management expertise to process and appraise these loan applications efficiently according to market criteria. Ultimately, the success of the financial system will depend on its ability to attract domestic savings from the individual saver. A strategy to transform the Central and East European financial system must therefore concentrate on the social and psychological dimension as well.

For example, such a strategy must convince individuals that a bank can serve as a trustworthy depository and custodian of his or her savings.[102] Policymakers must communicate that personal saving is important for the investment potential it creates for the whole economy, not to mention its role in reducing the external debt burden. To gain the confidence of the community and the trust of each customer, the banking system must also ensure that its creditworthiness is unquestioned. Evidence of weak confidence in the current banking system was reflected in the run on one of the first private Polish banks, the First Commercial Bank of Lublin, after rumors began circulating that its founder was wanted in the United States for tax evasion.[103] It will take some time before confidence in the banking system is strong. Financial aid, however, is likely to play a limited role in establishing confidence in the emerging financial systems. Finally, banking reform is still not an official criterion for an adjustment program administered by the World Bank and the IMF. Both international organizations could ensure that adequate financial and human resources are allocated to the transformation of financial systems in Central and Eastern Europe if they included such a criterion in their official structural adjustment program.

This brief summary of the problems facing the countries of Central and Eastern Europe as they struggle to transform their financial system demonstrates that systemic change must take place in all spheres of society before a market economy can work there. In the legal and administrative domain, quick decisive action is needed to deal with both the old problems, such as outstanding debt, and with the new problems, particularly those related to the absence of a regulatory structure in the market-based system. At the microstructural level, individual banks need to address management and training problems. Confidence has to be restored in the banking system, and individual savers and investors must familiarize themselves with the basic roles of the financial system in a market economy.

Recent experience in Central and Eastern Europe suggests that three related steps can be taken to support the establishment of a safe and sound financial system, and to stabilize the transformation process—one domestic, the other two foreign or international. At the domestic level, the authorities need to deal with the nonperforming loans. Some moves have already been made in this direction. Several countries are now considering establishing a national banking agency that would take over the bad debt and sell it at a discount.[104] In the fall of 1991 Prague announced the creation of a recapitalization fund that will allow commercial banks to swap debt for equity in the companies being privatized.[105] Another way would be to swap government obligations for the outstanding claims that banks hold. To save the six largest banks, the Czech and Slovak government has decided to issue bonds worth approximately $1.6 billion.[106] More bonds may have to be issued in the future, because outstanding debts of state enterprises are currently estimated at about $16.6 billion. Such a socialization of the debt would help recapitalize the banks, but if the full value were to be swapped, it would represent a greater burden for the budget.[107] Still, unless the nascent banking system is unburdened of the nonperforming loans to the former state-owned industries, it will not attract new deposits—domestic or foreign. Similarly, at the microstructural level, authorities have to establish training programs and information campaigns in urban and in rural areas to familiarize employees and customers with Western banking systems.

Although the initiative for system transformation must come from national and local authorities, foreign actors—public and private—can play a decisive role in stabilizing and possibly shortening the period of difficult change. The European Bank for Reconstruction and Development, which plans to focus a substantial part of its activities on financial sector reform, could help by establishing banking agencies to handle the outstanding debt. Only a few bank failures could put the whole system of any Central and East European country at risk. Therefore, immediate attention should be given to establishing joint projects with Western central banks, addressing regulatory problems, and establishing a regulatory and supervisory framework for financial institutions.

At the same time, appropriate training programs and changes in the educational and vocational training systems are needed to ensure that banks in Central and Eastern Europe will not become too dependent on foreign advice. A modern market-based commercial banking system cannot be created in the short term unless human skills and know-how can be transferred quickly and on a significant scale. Foreign banks have so far remained somewhat reluctant to invest in Central and Eastern Europe and have instead concentrated by and large on trade finance business, which has not been conducive to the restructuring of the financial systems in Central and Eastern Europe. This reluctance has begun to cause some resentment among local bankers and public authorities, who for their part have become increasingly reluctant to grant more commercial banking licenses to foreigners.[108] The only fast and effective way to infuse human skills and experience and to transfer technology to Central and East European financial systems is to encourage joint operations by Western and Eastern banks. Those in the West can shorten the transition process, provide the necessary expertise, and equip the banks in the East with modern telecommunications systems that help the clearing process and other transactions.[109] The need for modern telecommunications equipment was underlined in one scandal in Poland in which billions of zlotys were deposited simultaneously in different banks around the country.

Some "twinning agreements" are already in place, the most prominent being an agreement between five European banks and five Polish banks to create a partnership to overhaul the banking system. The European banks will help with technical restructuring and teach commercial banking practices.[110] The Bank of England has established a training center that will teach people from Central and Eastern Europe about establishing regulations and supervisory practices. More recently, the U.S. Department of the Treasury awarded a $7.8 million contract to various private sector organizations to develop and implement training institutes of finance and banking throughout Central and Eastern Europe.[111] The Bundesbank, too, has established training seminars for Central and East European bankers. In the area of capital markets, the European Bank for Reconstruction and Development (EBRD) has established a program that will help Central and East European countries develop domestic bond markets. This would raise money in the local currency as well as guarantee and underwrite international bond issues by public and corporate borrowers.[112] In another case, the New York Mercantile Exchange (NYMEX) recently signed a cooperation agreement with the Budapest Commodity Exchange (BCE). NYMEX will provide technical and professional aid in exchange for information on mutual business opportunities.[113]

6. Rebuilding Regional Economic Cooperation

The first important policy initiative that would help to stabilize and shorten the system transformation would be to revive the regional economic and political cooperation among the countries of Central and Eastern Europe and the successor states of the Soviet Union. The close economic relationships among the economies of the Eastern bloc collapsed in the wake of the decision by the CMEA members to switch to dollar-based trading in January 1991 and the disintegration of the CMEA in June 1991. Trade in the CMEA had flowed in a radial pattern, with the Soviet Union, the largest trading partner of each Central and East European country, at the center.[114] As a result, bilateral trade with the Soviet Union began to decline in 1989 and continued to fall during 1990 (figures 14 and 15, and table A-11) and 1991. Trade literally collapsed after the Soviet Union banned all barter trade with foreign companies. By June 1991 Czechoslovak-Soviet trade had fallen to 55.4 percent of the level of mid-1990. Poland registered the greatest losses, with Polish-Soviet trade reportedly down as much as 80 percent. In the first quarter of 1991 Polish exports to the Soviet Union totaled only 30 percent of exports from the same quarter of the previous year. By the end of 1991 only 2 percent of all Polish exports went to the former Soviet Union, down from a share of 60 percent.[115]

Trade among Central and East European countries also declined sharply. In the first six months of 1991 Bulgaria's exports to Czechoslovakia plummeted by more than 70 percent from the same period of the previous year.[116] Even Hungary, which was able to increase its convertible currency exports by 29 percent in the first five months of 1991, suffered, because the increase in exports was more than offset by the estimated $1.5 billion Hungary lost through the collapse of CMEA trade.[117] The share of the former CMEA countries in Hungary's external trade had declined from 50 percent in 1988 to 16 percent at the end of 1991. Like Poland, Hungary experienced even greater losses in trade with the Soviet Union, which declined by 60 percent between 1990 and 1991.[118]

Countries incurred additional losses as a result of the CMEA's shift to hard currency trade in January 1991. The governments had to use public funds to

Figure 14. Intra-Group Imports among Central and Eastern Europe and the Soviet Union, 1988–90

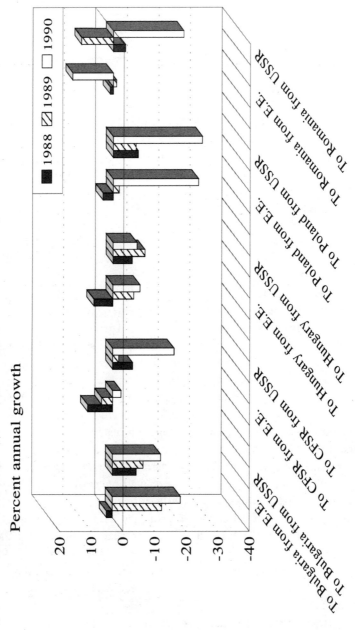

Percent annual growth

Source: See table A-11. Trade is measured in the value of transferable roubles.

Figure 15. Intra-Group Exports among Central and Eastern Europe and the Soviet Union, 1988–90

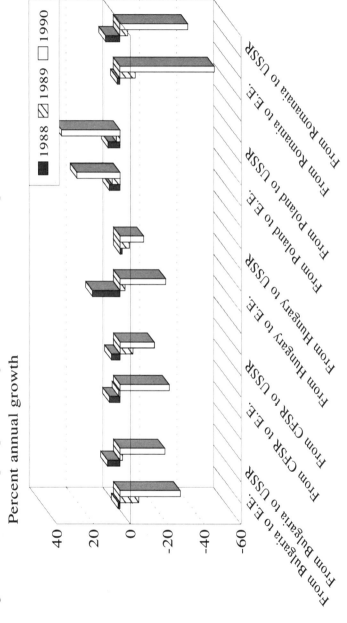

Percent annual growth

Source: See table A-11. Trade is measured in the value of transferable roubles.

buy up transferable rubles earned by private companies in trading with the former Soviet Union.[119] The collapse of regional trade has severely reduced output and employment for all Central and East European countries as well as for those of the former Soviet Union. The Czech and Slovak statistical office has estimated that by May 1991, 9 percent of the 12 percent decline in industrial production and 13 percent of the 36 percent inflation could be attributed to the collapse of the CMEA. The same trend was found in a similar study for Hungary.[120] In addition, all Central and East European members of the CMEA imported energy from the Soviet Union at prices below the world market rate, which amounted to a subsidy of about $5 billion. The subsidy ceased to exist in January 1991, when the Soviet Union switched to hard currency trade and began to sell its energy at world market prices.[121]

Measures to Rebuild Trading Links

To avoid the continued disintegration of their trading links, the countries of Central and Eastern Europe and the successor states of the former Soviet Union should make every effort to rebuild some of their former trading links and establish new forms of cooperation that could facilitate trade and payments among them. In principle, the renewal of economic cooperation would be beneficial to Central and Eastern Europe. As Czechoslovakia's former foreign minister Juri Dienstbier has pointed out, "Our modernization would be easier if we . . . could find new natural incentives for the true harmonization of our avenues, interests and goals with the countries of the former Soviet bloc."[122] Some members of the CMEA, in particular the former Soviet Union, had proposed such an organization, the Organization for International Economic Cooperation (OIEC), even before the CMEA was officially dissolved.[123] Poland, Hungary, and the CSFR refused to join. The three countries feared that any renewed economic cooperation with any of their old trading partners would limit their chances for speedy economic integration into Western Europe, particularly into the European Community, and that it would recreate the old system of Soviet-dominated trade.[124]

When the final communiqués to dissolve the CMEA were signed in Budapest at the end of June 1991, there was no longer any mention of creating a follow-up organization.[125] Some countries even took steps to promote further disintegration: in early 1991 Hungary raised tariffs for all imports from the CMEA countries an average of 15 percent; in mid-1991 the CSFR considered introducing protective tariffs on agricultural imports; and on January 1, 1992,

Poland began imposing higher customs duties on imports of certain goods. Although most of these duties will affect Western imports, they are also likely to affect Central and East European trade in some areas.[126]

After the middle of 1991, however, the resistance to renewed regional cooperation began weakening. It declined even further after the collapse of the Soviet Union. This change of heart was in part due to the fact that many countries were having difficulty negotiating association agreements with the European Community and in part due to the realization that only renewed trade among the former CMEA countries could bring immediate relief to domestic industry and employment. Thus the Central European countries engaged in negotiations over association agreements decided to coordinate their strategies to gain greater leverage; many countries also concluded barter agreements, primarily with the successor states to the Soviet Union, after a ban on barter agreements by the Soviet Union was lifted in the summer of 1991.[127] Until prices have been freed and convertibility has been established, such barter schemes could be an appropriate basis for cooperation. Table 4 presents a selection of barter agreements concluded during 1991 and 1992. In general, energy from the Soviet Union was exchanged for investment and consumption goods from the countries of Central and Eastern Europe.[128] Not surprisingly, some of these agreements have been difficult to maintain. The Russian-Polish agreements, in particular, were on several occasions in risk of being cancelled because Russia could not and would not fulfill its original commitments. Furthermore, some treaties had to be renegotiated as a result of the dissolution of the Soviet Union. In Hungary, a large outstanding trade surplus has for some time hampered the conclusion of any agreement.[129] Still, these agreements demonstrate that the desire for trade exists and is considered beneficial by both parties.

New proposals have also been made to revive regional cooperation in trade and other matters among the former CMEA members, the emerging Baltic states, and the former Soviet Union. One proposal has suggested creating a European consultative economic forum, which would be structured as an intergovernmental organization composed of the former European members of the CMEA. It would in no way limit the sovereign rights of the member states to conclude agreements among themselves or with third countries.[130] The most serious efforts have been made by Hungary, Czechoslovakia, and Poland. As early as February 1991, at the Visegrad summit, Hungary proposed that the three countries establish a free-trade zone. A month later Hungary officially proposed to start formal talks, with the goal of establishing such a

Table 4. Selective Barter Agreements, 1991, 1992

Agreement date	Country	Trade	Value
Autumn 1991[a]	Czechoslovakia Siberia	Food and consumer goods Oil (200,000 tons)	n.a.
May 28, 1991	Czechoslovakia Russian Soviet Federated Republic	Food Crude oil and raw materials	$260 million
July 13, 1991	Czechoslovakia Russian Federation	"Trade Agreement" of mutual payments in mixture of hard currency, national currency, and barter	n.a.
August 2, 1991	Czechoslovakia	Polygraph and medical equipment, pharmaceuticals, and spare parts for Czech machines	n.a.
January 1992	Estonia Czechoslovakia Russian Republic	Furniture, construction materials, electric motors, and fish products Debt retirement ($163 million) and other items Oil (7.5 million tons), natural gas, fuel elements for nuclear power plants, and nonferrous metals	$1.7 billion
November 1991[a]	Bulgaria Sverdlovsk province, Russia	Mechanical, engineering, and chemical industry products, mineral fertilizers, and electrical appliances Fuel oil (10,000 tons)	n.a.
November 7, 1991	Bulgaria	Handling machines, spare parts, electric truck storage batteries, and medicine	n.a.
November 15, 1991	Lithuania Bulgaria Ukraine	Fertilizers, consumer electronics, and fish Mechanical engineering products, medicine, and natural gas Electricity (850–900 million kilowatt hours)	n.a.
February 1992	Bulgaria Russian Republic	Calcinated soda, machines, tobacco, medicine, meat, and baby food Crude oil (5 million tons), diesel fuel, fuel oil, natural gas, and raw materials	n.a.

Date	Country	Goods	Value
November 1991[a]	Lithuania	Electrical equipment, washing machines, light industrial products, and fish	n.a.
	Azerbaijan	Fruits, tires, and oil	
November 1991[a]	Lithuania	n.a.	50 million rubles
	Kyrgyzstan	Wool and light industrial products	
November 1991[a]	Lithuania	Paper and consumer products	n.a.
	Tajikistan	Metals, cotton, and agricultural machinery	
June 14, 1991	Hungary	Buses, grain, meat, butter, pharmaceuticals, and light industrial goods	$670 million
	Russian Republic	Coal, oil derivatives, wood products, tractors, construction materials, and artificial fertilizers	
June 20, 1991	Hungary	Yamburg gas pipeline construction	758 million rubles
	USSR	Natural gas	
September 9, 1991	Hungary	Grain	$110 million
	Ukraine	Electricity and coal	
November 17, 1991	Hungary	n.a.	$20 million
	Ukraine	Agricultural and light industrial products	
March 3, 1992	Hungary		n.a.
	Uzbekistan	Cotton and chemical products	
March 26, 1991	Poland	Cement	$16 million
	Ukraine	Coal	
July 23, 1991	Poland	Medicine	$325 million
	USSR	Oil (7 million tons) and natural gas	
September 21, 1991	Poland	Medicine and electrical engineering products	$200 million
	USSR	Iron ore, natural gas, and cellulose	
September 21, 1991	Poland	Food (620,000 tons)	n.a.
	USSR	Gas (1.5 billion cubic meters)	
January 1992	Poland	Coal, coke, sulphur, pharmaceuticals, and food	n.a.
	Russian Federation	Oil (5 million tons) and natural gas (6.6 billion cubic meters)	
January 1992	Romania	Caustic soda and soda ash, medicine, consumer goods, and machine tools	$520 million
	Russian Republic	Coal (2.4 million tons), lumber (120,000 cubic meters), asbestos (40,000 tons), pulp (30,000 tons), and synthetic rubber (8,000 tons)	

Sources: Various issues of Foreign Broadcasting Information Service, *Daily Report: East Europe*; Radio Free Europe/Radio Liberty, *Daily Report*; *Financial Times*; and *Washington Post*.
n.a. Not available.   a. Approximate date.

zone by the end of the year. Exploratory talks opened at the end of July, and they continued throughout the fall. At the Cracow summit of the "Visegrad Three" in October, the three leaders reconfirmed their commitment to such cooperation, once the association agreements with the European Community were concluded. In early December they signed a document expressing their will to sign, by July 1992, an agreement gradually removing trade barriers.[131] The agreement is modeled on the European Free Trade Association (EFTA), and the liberalization of trade will be spread out over a period of five to ten years. It will proceed in parallel with the association agreements to be ratified by the same countries and the members of the European Community before the end of 1992.[132] Similar arrangements are currently being discussed by the three Baltic states.[133]

If successfully implemented, this agreement could be the basis for expanding cooperation into other areas. Indeed, close cooperation in rebuilding and modernizing the transportation systems of Central and Eastern Europe to accommodate new trade flows is a natural complement to a free-trade zone. Countries should also cooperate in modernizing their telecommunications systems, preventing environmental pollution, and producing and transmitting energy.[134] In all these cases, a regional approach represents the only real and comprehensive policy solution and avoids unnecessary barriers to the free flow of economic resources. It also avoids waste that would result from a lack of information or from a duplication of efforts during the process of system transformation. Cooperation could also be extended into other areas, such as foreign and military policy, visa-free travel, and cultural and educational exchanges.[135] Cooperation should be evaluated for both its political and economic benefits.[136] Given the multinational and multiethnic character of the Central and East European societies, and the rising tide of nationalism among ethnic groupings in all of Central and Eastern Europe, regional cooperation over a wide variety of issues could help to ease the tension among various nationalities and ethnic minorities. Closer cooperation could possibly help prevent the outbreak of military conflicts similar to those occurring in Yugoslavia.

It is of the utmost importance, however, to ensure that this policy option remains open to *all* countries in Central and Eastern Europe and the successor states of the Soviet Union. The rejection of Romania by the Visegrad countries as a participant in the summit may be understandable as a short-term response, but it cannot be accepted on a long-term basis.[137] A Central and East European free-trade and economic cooperative area must not become an exclusive club of the wealthier countries that have had moderate success with system transformation. This would recreate a new division in Europe farther to the east that would encourage political instability, economic decline, and ethnic unrest. Entry into the regional cooperative zone should be based on the same political conditions applied in the association agreements with the European Community, and stepwise integration should be open to all countries.

Role of the European Community

Furthermore, the European Community should encourage the countries of Central and Eastern Europe to engage in greater regional cooperation. First, it should encourage national parliaments to ratify the European agreements as soon as possible. Once these agreements are firmly in place, Central and Eastern Europe are less likely to interpret the Community's encouragement and support as an effort to institutionalize their continued exclusion from Western markets, particularly those of the European Community. Indeed, the European Community should publicly reassure those countries that increased regional economic and political cooperation would not in any way jeopardize their prospects for eventual membership in the Community. Second, the Community could make continued Western support in some areas conditional upon increased regional cooperation. Third, it should allocate a larger share of its current aid, within the PHARE program, to regional projects and should convert some of the projects that are currently national into regional ones.[138] Finally, the Community should offer its patronage to such an undertaking.[139]

The Community and the European Free Trade Association (EFTA: Austria, Finland, Iceland, Liechtenstein, Norway, Sweden, and Switzerland) could encourage economic cooperation by providing technical and financial assistance as well as the expertise needed to establish a free-trade zone. In one case the Community has begun to support the renewal of trade between Central and Eastern Europe and the Soviet Union.[140] Through so-called triangular trade arrangements, the European Commission has begun to help pay for Central and East European farm exports to the former Soviet Union.[141] In September 1991, and after the temporary collapse of the negotiations over the association agreements between the Community and Central and Eastern European countries, Jacques Delors proposed that the West spend at least $2 billion for food to be sent from Central and Eastern Europe to the Soviet Union.[142] This approach is favored by France, in particular, which sees it as a way of relieving the pressure among Central and East Europeans wanting to increase their agricultural exports to the Community. Subsequently the European Commission approved about one-quarter of the ECU (European currency unit) 500 million credit to the Commonwealth of Independent States (CIS) that could be used for this assistance scheme; another larger aid package amounting to ECU 1.25 billion was blocked by disagreements over counterpart guarantees from Russia.[143]

Although the idea of diverting farm exports to the Soviet Union away from the Community's agricultural market is particularly appealing to Community members, they should consider widening the range of exports that could be financed under the triangular scheme. The Hungarian minister for international economic relations suggested to the European Parliament's Foreign Trade Committee that the EC subsidize the export of Hungarian pharmaceutical exports to the USSR.[144] According to officials from the Hungarian pharmaceutical industry, an agreement was reached to ship products worth $200 million to Russia in early 1992. Negotiations for a shipment worth $50 million to $100 million to the Ukraine are under way. Total demand from the former Soviet Union is estimated at $350 million to $400 million.[145] A similar agreement has been concluded between the Community and the CSFR.[146] Other products include shoes, garments, textiles, and transport vehicles. The prospect for increased triangular trade has improved recently. During the conference on humanitarian aid to the CIS, which was held in Washington, D.C., in January 1992, Czechoslovakia, Hungary, and Poland presented a joint document outlining a much expanded plan for triangular trade that would also include technical assistance. Although the Community has indicated its support for such a program, there appears to be resistance from Western industries that would prefer to export their own goods to the CIS.[147]

As previously mentioned, numerous other loose cooperative arrangements exist or are being planned, many of which involve one or several Western countries. The best known is the former Hexagonale, which brought together Poland, the CSFR, Hungary, Austria, Yugoslavia, and Italy to cooperate on economic, technological, and cultural matters.[148] Other cooperative plans envisage the formation of a Black Sea Common Market, closer cooperation among the six Balkan states, a free-trade zone in the Italian city of Trieste, the formation of a cooperation committee between the Nordic Council and the three Baltic states, the revival of the Hanse trading region, and negotiations between EFTA and all Central and East European countries over closer cooperation and possible membership.[149] In March 1992 foreign ministers from all ten countries bordering the Baltic Sea agreed to revive their historic trading and cultural links and to create a community having its own specific identity but having close links with existing European organizations. Foreign Minister Uffe Ellemann-Jensen of Denmark has argued that this Council of the Baltic Sea States should become a region within the European Community.[150]

Although such efforts are laudable and promising—since they involve Western partners and thus automatically involve the transfer of technology, know-how, and expertise—too many different arrangements are more than likely to complicate matters. They may encourage different trading blocs to emerge that not only reflect Central and East European interests but also compete with West European commercial interests. To avoid such bloc thinking, the Community should give its full support to the recently concluded triangular free-trade zone, while ensuring that it is open to all interested countries in Central and Eastern Europe.

Central and East European countries should establish a payments union to support the formation of such a free-trade zone. Such a union would help revive trade between individual countries, since transactions would not involve hard currency payments.[151] Exporters would accept payments in the importer's currency and then deposit the funds for clearance at regular time intervals. Only the aggregate difference between each republic's total imports and exports would have to be settled in hard currency.

Such a clearing system could work only if all participants were fully committed to it. Moreover, it would require Western expertise as well as financial support to finance the payments union during the initial years of system transformation and until prices adjusted to international levels. Such a system was proposed in December 1991. Three West European banks, with the support of the EC Commission, and Central and East European central and private banks proposed to finance such a system using the European currency unit as a common financial unit.[152] Its implementation would be relatively smooth and quick, because it could rely on computers and payments procedures of the existing West European ECU payments system. A system that was established in 1986 involves forty-five banks and handles payments of up to about ECU 30 billion ($37.5 billion) a day. Initially, the Central and East European system might only handle a small number of transactions involving a dozen banks in Central and Eastern Europe. As the volume of trade increased, participation could be increased, and the scheme could be extended to finance East-West trade as well.

A more recent proposal suggests the formation of an ECU zone. Under this plan, Central and East European economies would pool their currency reserves to create a stabilization fund, and the Community would provide standby credits. Central and East European exchange rates would be pegged to the ECU, however, subject to adjustments, given the different stages of economic development the Central and East European economies are likely to enter over the next decade. According to its authors, such a plan not only is more comprehensive but is also a more flexible approach than a payments union.[153] Although not in a position to act as creditors, the EBRD and other international organizations, in conjunction with official export credit agencies and private banks, could act as guarantors and thus also help to revitalize increased regional trade as well as support the triangular trade arrangements.[154]

There is little that the countries of Central and Eastern Europe can do at present apart from trying to revive some of the regional economic cooperation that existed in the context of CMEA and to foster new programs for economic, political, and sociocultural integration. They simply lack the necessary financial resources to implement policies that would help to stabilize and shorten the transition period and thus ensure the successful completion of system transformation. As a consequence, the majority of support for the transition period will have to come from the West. Numerous efforts are currently under way. One program the Western countries could implement to stabilize the transition period that has not been given much attention would be to alleviate at least temporarily the external indebtedness of the Central and East European economies.

7. Solving the Debt Crisis

The second policy initiative that would contribute to a more stable transition period is a solution to the debt crisis. External indebtedness is a major hurdle on the road to Central and Eastern Europe's transformation. External indebtedness has continued to increase over the past two years and there is little sign of improvement (figure 16 and table 5). Between 1989 and the end of 1990, Central and Eastern Europe's total gross debt rose by $13.1 billion, jumping from $77.1 billion to $90.2 billion.[155]

Debt in the Individual Countries

Bulgaria was second only to the former Soviet Union in being the least creditworthy country in this period. Although not very large in absolute amounts, its ratio of net exports to outstanding debt increased by almost 100 percent within one year, rising to 327 percent. In 1991 Bulgaria ruled out debt forgiveness to improve its international standing but was forced to ask the Paris Club to reschedule its $1.8 billion debt with official creditors. It had hoped this action would pave the way for a complete rescheduling of its $8.5 billion debt to the London Club. But early in 1992 the government announced that it would seek a reduction of the debt with the London Club and deferment of the part owed to the Paris Club.[156] Preliminary talks opened in April 1992. Given the recent export performance and the fact that the transformation process is still at an early stage and on an unknown path, the debt situation remains precarious. Poland succeeded in reducing its official debt of $33 billion by 50 percent shortly before the end of the one-year moratorium extended by the Paris Club in March 1990, and after agreeing with the IMF on a restructuring program.[157] It remains to be seen to what degree this will decrease the pressure to incur new external indebtedness in the short term.

Before its disintegration Yugoslavia's debt was estimated at about $20.6 billion, and in 1991 the country asked the Paris Club to reschedule 60 percent of its principal ($1.3 billion).[158] This request follows a sharp fall of foreign currency reserves from $10 billion in 1990 to $4.7 billion in 1991. Yugoslav

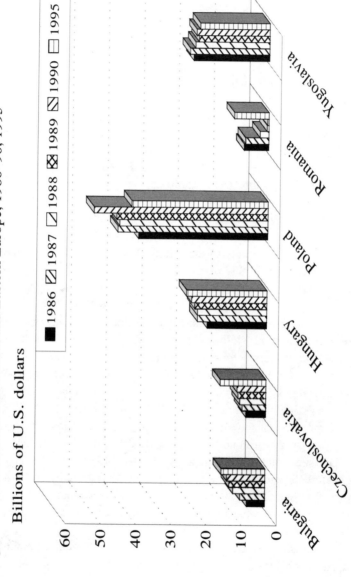

Figure 16. External Debt in Central and Eastern Europe, 1986–90, 1995

Billions of U.S. dollars

■ 1986 ▨ 1987 ▨ 1988 ▨ 1989 ▨ 1990 ☐ 1995

Source: See table 5. The 1995 figures are forecasts by PLANECON (Washington, July 1991).

Table 5. External Debt and Financial Indicators: Central and Eastern Europe, 1986—90[a]

Billions of U.S. dollars unless otherwise specified

| Country | Total external debt | | | | | | 1990 (percent) | | |
	1986	1987	1988	1989	1990	1995	Total external debt/exports	Total external debt/GNP	Total debt service/exports
Bulgaria	5.2	7.1	9.1	10.2	10.9	12.5	136.0	56.9	16.7
CFSR	5.6	6.7	7.4	7.9	8.2	13.0	55.6	18.6	10.4
Hungary	16.9	19.6	19.6	20.4	21.3	22.8	242.2	65.6	48.7
Poland	36.7	42.6	42.1	43.0	49.4	38.7	251.5	82.4	4.9
Romania	7.0	6.6	2.5	0.5	0.4	9.8	5.5	1.1	0.4
Yugoslavia	21.5	22.5	21.0	20.0	20.7	19.7	67.1	23.7	13.7
Total	92.9	105.0	101.8	102.0	110.9	116.5	125.0	40.2	13.9

Sources: World Bank, *World Debt Tables, 1991-1992: External Debt of Developing Countries*, vol. 1 (Washington, 1991), pp. 42, 102, 182, 322, 330, 442. The 1995 figures are from PLANECON, *Review and Outlook* (Washington, July 1991), pp. 55,83,111,143,116,189.

a. The total external debt figures include long-term and short-term debt, as well as use of IMF credits. International reserves have not been subtracted from the total external debt figure. International reserves are the sum of the country's authorities holdings of special drawing rights (SDRs), its reserve position in the IMF, its holdings of foreign exchange, and holdings of gold.

authorities also seek to refinance the $4.6 billion in principal and interest owed in 1992 to commercial banks. These negotiations are complicated by the fact that the six republics hold a share of the external debt, and an agreement must be reached on how it will be repaid.

Hungary's foreign exchange reserves rose to $4 billion during 1991, and, according to the deputy chairman of the Hungarian National Bank, the net foreign debt declined from $16 billion to $14 billion in 1991.[159] The country has maintained its payments to international creditors and so far has not attempted to negotiate any debt relief to avoid a loss in its good reputation in the international capital markets.[160] At the same time, it cannot be overlooked that in 1990 Hungary ranked highest among the countries of Central and Eastern Europe, with a $2,050 debt per capita. In addition, Hungary spends about 49 percent of its export earnings to service its debt, thereby blunting the pace and quality of economic reform.[161] This has led Hungary to reconsider its strategy with its Western creditors and to call for a debt accord similar to that obtained by Poland.[162]

Although Czechoslovakia ranks low in terms of indebtedness among the countries of the region, it will require additional capital imports to transform the economy. This is likely to increase Czechoslovakia's external indebtedness, since exports will not be able to balance the new credit needs. The Czechoslovak government expected its foreign debt to increase by 40 percent during 1991.[163] The Romanian case is difficult to assess because the country had no external debt until late 1989. But this changed rapidly after the fall of the Ceaucescu regime. Romania had accumulated an external debt of $2.3 billion by the end of 1990. The Romanian parliament quickly approved a government proposal to borrow $2 billion for the first half of 1991.[164] In April 1991 Romania reached an agreement with the Paris Club that allows for the postponement of trade credits guaranteed by national governments. In May 1992 the first such bilateral agreement was signed between Germany and Romania, rescheduling its $82.2 million debt.[165] Similar agreements can be expected with other countries in the future, and the request for further international credits is likely to increase at an even faster rate given the state of Romania's economy and the early stage of the transformation process there.

To add to all these problems, Western banks have reduced their net exposure to Central and East European countries. Until the second half of 1989, lending by commercial banks to Central and Eastern Europe and the Soviet Union continued to expand. Although up by $3.3 billion, the increase was less than the $5.3 billion recorded in the first half of 1989.[166] This picture changed drastically in 1990. The same banks that had been lending money to the Communist bloc for the preceding two decades were now either unable or unwilling to support the transformation process toward a market economy and democracy.

During the first half of 1990, banks reduced their lending by $5.1 billion.[167] Much of this drop ($3.5 billion) is accounted for by the Soviet Union, but outstanding claims on Hungary and Czechoslovakia also contracted (by $0.8 billion and $0.3 billion, respectively), as did claims on Bulgaria (-$0.4 billion) and Poland (-$0.2 billion). With the exception of Poland, where the situation stabilized, banks continued to decrease their exposure to Central and Eastern Europe. In the second half of 1990 total claims declined by another $3.3 billion, raising the total for 1990 to $8.4 billion. The largest decline in claims was recorded for the Soviet Union ($2.0 billion), Hungary ($0.8 billion), and Bulgaria and Czechoslovakia ($0.2 billion each). Thus, following a 43 percent expansion over the last five years, Western banks' total identified claims vis-à-vis Central and Eastern Europe and the Soviet Union fell by $9.9 billion, or 11 percent, between April 1990 and March 1991. This trend continued in the second quarter of 1991.[168]

The Worsening Situation

While the situation varies across individual countries in Central and Eastern Europe, the debt situation is likely to worsen in the coming years. One estimate reckons that the overall debt for the five Central and East European countries will rise to $105 billion by 1995, from a level of $66.4 billion in 1990.[169] Another estimate arrives at $116.6 billion for 1995.[170] This would amount to an interest burden of $10–11 billion by 1995.[171] This interest burden may increase even more if interest rates rise as a result of an international capital shortage, or if private financial institutions resume their lending to Central and Eastern Europe. In turn, this would enlarge the overall debt. Moreover, the transformation toward market economies in Central and Eastern Europe and the associated economic contraction are likely to discourage exports over the years to come.[172] The associated decline in foreign exchange earnings may exacerbate the external indebtedness if countries are forced to incur new indebtedness solely for the purpose of servicing their increasing debt. If, however, countries are unwilling or unable to increase their external indebtedness, they will have to reduce imports that are essential to the system transformation, and the reform process will be undermined further.

The debt situation in Central and Eastern Europe suggests that countries there will have difficulty in mastering the system transformation and in getting through the long transition phase, unless official and private creditors agree to write off or postpone the repayment of a large part of their external debt. The external debt burden is inimical to the economic and political transformation of Central and Eastern Europe. If countries have to use a substantial amount of their export earnings for interest payments, they will not be able to import the capital goods they need to modernize their infrastructure and industry.[173] Foreign companies are less willing to invest in heavily indebted countries. Investments become worthless if a country's exchange rate collapses once its foreign reserves are exhausted. Central and East Europeans themselves will have little incentive to save and pay taxes if these serve primarily to pay for a debt that the former Communist governments accumulated.

A strategy of system transformation must ensure that newly accumulated savings are invested domestically. "Cold War debts" have been accumulated under a political system and regime that no longer exists and whose demise was encouraged by the West. Without doubt the Western nations would have accepted a "debt-for-democracy" swap in 1988 had they been offered the democratic revolutions in return for debt relief. When compared with the political and economic costs of a failure of the transformation process in Central and Eastern Europe, the costs of a concerted debt relief effort by the West are small.

Poland's Agreement with the Paris Club

Poland's agreement with the Paris Club was a clear sign that official creditors have an interest in the stability and success of the transformation process.[174] The agreement contains several elements that may be helpful in thinking about similar arrangements for other countries.[175] One central element of any debt relief agreement should be that it supports the goal of long-term economic growth and does not just avoid a balance-of-payments crisis. Thus, in addition to reducing the official net present value of the debt by 50 percent, the Polish agreement with the Paris Club reduces the country's annual debt service by 80 percent over the next three years. This is a crucial measure because it supports the difficult transition phase and is contributing to the revitalization of the economy.

A second element of the agreement is that countries are free to cut Poland's debt even further on a bilateral basis. So far the United States and France have taken advantage of this option and reduced their share of the debt even further.[176] A third element is that 10 percent of each country's share in the overall debt write-off can be swapped into zlotys and used for improvements in Polish environmental protection installations or infrastructure.[177]

More recently, the Polish government made another proposal for a debt-for-nature swap under which 10 percent of its debts would take the form of a domestic fund aimed solely at combatting pollution. According to the Polish government, environmentally beneficial schemes could be designed to reduce acid rain, global warming, and the emission of pollutants into the Baltic Sea, but the creditor governments themselves could determine the nature of the concrete projects.[178] The fund's activities would be monitored by an advisory panel composed of representatives from the creditor nations and would be audited by an international company. If all sixteen creditor nations agree, the fund would have to spend $3.1 billion over the next twenty years. So far the plan has the strong personal support of Norway's prime minister, Gro Harlem Brundtland. Given their geographic proximity, other Scandinavian countries are expected to back the initiative. The United States and France have also approved the idea.[179]

The basic structure of Poland's agreement with the Paris Club and the recent proposal of a large debt-for-nature swap may be a prototype of future debt relief for other countries in Central and Eastern Europe, but the nominal debt relief would be minor in comparison. The structure of Polish long-term debt distribution among public and private creditors is exceptional. In 1989 the share of public and publicly guaranteed debt was almost 70 percent. The creditor profile for the other Central and East European countries is the opposite.[180] For example, 85 percent of Hungary's outstanding debt in 1990 was owed to private creditors. Thus a 50 percent reduction of Hungary's debt owed to the Paris Club would be of minor significance to Hungary in stabilizing the transition phase and supporting the system's transformation. As can be seen from figure 17 (table A-12), this is also true for most other countries of Central and Eastern Europe.

As Poland has discovered, private creditors are unlikely to be equally forthcoming in providing debt relief as their public counterparts. The main point of contention between Poland and its private creditors is whether it should pay part of its outstanding interest payments before the London Club starts negotiating a debt relief package.[181] The Paris Club agreement has

Figure 17. Creditor Profile: Outstanding Long-Term Debt in Central and Eastern Europe, 1990

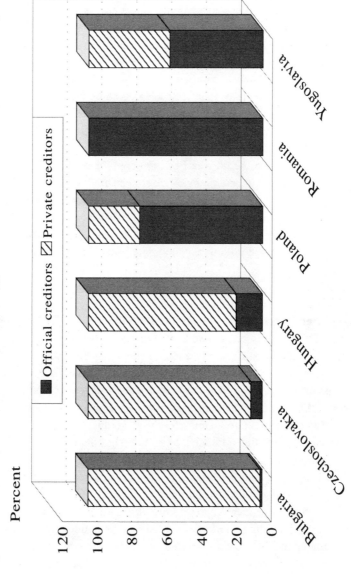

Source: See table A-12.

increased pressure on the banks to deal with the issue of debt relief.[182]   In addition, on July 26, 1992, Poland paid $100 million to the London Club for interest due on its debt.   This was after the banks had indicated that they were willing to cut at least 50 percent of the outstanding debt and generate a scheme similar to that developed in Paris, whereby the burden of payments would fall in those years in which Poland has regained its economic stability.[183]   So far Poland has failed to conclude an agreement on the $12 billion it owes to private banks.   In March 1992 Poland's finance minister at the time, Andrzej Olechowski, met with representatives of the creditor banks to explore the possibility of resuming negotiations.   But negotiations have been further delayed for two reasons: Poland has refused to begin to pay back some of the overdue interest ($1.8 billion) that it owes until an agreement on the overall debt problem is reached, and the London Club has stated that talks would not resume until the IMF board had accepted the Polish letter of intent outlining the government's economic reform program.[184]

Ways to Lessen the Debt Burden

The experience of Poland makes clear that various options exist to ensure that the burden of foreign indebtedness will not greatly hinder the transformation of the economies of Central and Eastern Europe.   First, Western governments could increase their pressure on private creditors to take their share of the burden of debt relief.   Indeed, several banks have indicated that they are prepared to write off a substantial part of Poland's debt, but divisions in the steering committee representing the 400 creditor banks have so far prevented a deal.[185]

Second, official creditors should use their leverage over the market value of privately held debt to pressure other creditors into coming to an agreement. As a result of the Paris Club agreement, the market value of outstanding Polish debt to private creditors rose by 12 percent, from 18 percent to 30 percent.[186] The Paris Club could negotiate an agreement with the London Club whereby 50 percent of the appreciation in the secondary markets, as a result of official debt relief, would be written off by private creditors.   This would allow them to reap the benefits of the other 50 percent of the appreciation in the secondary market.   In addition, the Paris Club member governments should use their political weight to sway commercial banks to resume their lending activities to the Central and East European countries.   It is counterproductive to encourage countries to transform their centralized economic systems to a market-based system while at the same time refusing to actively support the transformation with new loans. This behavior has raised doubts in the minds of many Central and East Europeans about the sincerity of Western support. If the market-based system is indeed superior, the safest and *only* way to recover some of the outstanding loans is to support its creation.

Third, another way to reduce the debt burden would be for the banks and the debtor countries to reach an agreement on large-scale debt-equity swaps. The outstanding debt would be converted (at the discount reflecting the secondary market value) into shares of the countries' soon-to-be privatized industries. Apart from creating some debt relief, such a move would also provide additional incentive for these countries to move ahead with the privatization of their industries.[187] In addition, it would bring foreign experience and know-how into the domestic industry. If the transformation process is successful, these shares might soon have a higher value than at the time of conversion.[188]

Fourth, if banks are unwilling to reduce their claims and to adjust the time profile to alleviate the burden arising from interest rate payments during the critical transition phase, Western governments—as a last resort—should step in. Interest rate payments by the debtor countries could be postponed by a fund that would bridge the gap between the different time profiles of the creditors and of the debtors, to reflect the length and difficulty of the transition period. In this context, it is doubtful whether a three-year "grace period" to reduce Poland's annual debt service during the crucial years of transition will be sufficient. As argued earlier, system transformation aimed at putting Central and Eastern Europe on a path toward long-term sustainable economic growth will take more than three years. This point should be remembered in any future debt relief agreements that include postponement of interest rate payments. As to the principal, some of it could be assumed—at a considerable discount—by individual governments or a group of countries. Upon assumption of the debt, part of it could be written off, as in the case of Poland.

In addition, the new creditors should consider swapping some of the debt into the local currencies of the debtor nations and investing the money in projects that promote the transformation process in Central and Eastern Europe.[189] This would not be confined to debt-for-nature swaps but could encompass the other issues addressed by the aid programs provided by the Group of 24 (G-24), as well as those coordinated by the European Community under the PHARE program.[190] "Debt-for-education," "debt-for-health," and "debt-for-infrastructure" swaps should be considered long-term investments in the infrastructure of a market economy. Such investments will almost certainly improve the absorptive capacity of those economies and consequently attract more foreign investors.[191] Also, public authorities could act as intermediaries and facilitators by offering "debt-for-equity" swaps to private investors who plan to invest in Central and Eastern Europe.

One argument raised against debt deferral or relief is that it will lead countries to lose their borrowing capability in international financial markets. However, the history of foreign indebtedness provides little evidence that debt reduction hurts the ability of countries to borrow in the future, especially if the reduction is achieved through negotiations. Countries that have recently received reduction under the Brady plan are finding that they can raise funds in national and international bond markets. Thus a concerted debt reduction package, combined with a program of system transformation that promises to be politically and socially sustainable, is more likely to improve a country's international creditworthiness, as attested by price movements of outstanding debt in secondary markets after debt relief.

The European Community should spearhead the debt relief effort, because it has the central role in coordinating the aid effort to Central and Eastern Europe and because its members and their banks account for by far the largest share of the outstanding debt. In fact, the Community has been very outspoken about the need to address the problem of external indebtedness in the countries of Central and Eastern Europe.[192] At the same time, it must be remembered that the debt problem is global in scope, and that it needs to be solved at the global level. On the debtor side, geographic concentration on Central and Eastern Europe, and possibly the former Soviet Union, would amount to a blatant disregard of the poorest countries in Africa. Similarly, on the creditor side, debt relief by some countries opens the possibility for other countries to get a free ride, which poses the familiar problems of collective action that can only be solved by global cooperation on behalf of *all* creditors. Still, the experience in Central and Eastern Europe and the political urgency of these problems may ultimately help to solve them on an international scale.

II. WESTERN EUROPE: THE CHALLENGE OF SYSTEMIC REFORM

The consequences of the historic developments in Central and Eastern Europe and the Soviet Union since the fall of 1989 have reached far beyond the borders of Central and Eastern Europe. They have altered the political and economic geography of the entire European continent in a profound way. Developments in Western Europe, therefore, cannot be decoupled from the process of system transformation in Central and Eastern Europe. On the contrary, as mentioned in the introduction, Western Europe itself will have to adjust to the changes in the East. However, the depth of change needed is not as comprehensive (though it may be more difficult to achieve) as that needed in the former centrally planned economies. West European markets, and in particular the Single European Market, will have to undergo systemic reform in response to the developments in Central and Eastern Europe. That kind of reform will play a decisive role in facilitating and shortening the process of system transformation in Central and Eastern Europe, and thus cannot be separated from an overall strategy of European unification.

Systemic reform in this context means adjusting the economic, political, and social institutions and the norms and principles that govern those institutions to allow a system to cope with change exogenous *to it and to improve its performance. Reform differs from system transformation, which addresses issues* endogenous *to the system and requires a total overhaul of the institutional framework and a radical change in its norms and standards. The principal challenge to policymakers in Western Europe is to ensure that this systemic reform does not undermine what West Europeans have achieved since the end of World War II in the context of the European Community. That is to say, the Community must be at the helm of the systemic reform.*

In section 8, I develop a strategy of systemic reform, with particular emphasis on debate over broadening versus deepening; *in section 9, I present a three-stage strategy of integrating Central and Eastern Europe into the European Community.*

8. The EC and Central and Eastern Europe: Common Concerns and Conflicting Interests

A number of common concerns have led the Community to become engaged in the system transformation in Central and Eastern Europe. First, as discussed in section 2 of this paper, the European Community has a historic responsibility to embrace the countries of Central and Eastern Europe. Although many political and economic conditions have to be met before this can take place, Article 237 of the treaty that established the Community opens the possibility of membership to every democratic European state.

Second, in many ways the Community can serve as a model of economic and political integration necessary to replace the traditional state system in Central and Eastern Europe. Greater regional and local autonomy, combined with a transfer of power and authority in the macropolitical and economic sphere, may well be the only policy response capable of overcoming ethnic and national rivalries smouldering in many Central and East European countries.

Third, over the past two years it has become clear that the present members of the Community are unwilling to risk undoing their own political and economic integration process, or to consider alternative structures for a future European architecture, in the light of the transformation of the Eastern bloc.[193] As Italy's foreign minister, Giannni De Michelis, stated, "It is basically up to the Europeans to manage the establishment of peace and restoration of their continent, and the European Community will be the core around which the new balance is fashioned."[194] Therefore, an alternative intergovernmental or supranational organization is unlikely to emerge in Europe in response to the change in the East. The agreement between the Community and the EFTA countries concerning the formation of a European Economic Area (EEA) along with the membership applications of Austria, Sweden, Finland, and Switzerland to the Community indicate that an alternative organization that acts as an integrating pole in Europe is no longer viable. According to the Commission president Jacques Delors, "It is difficult to see what would be gained from wasting more than 30 years of successful experience to create a completely new organization."[195]

Fourth, the European Community has a strong political interest in supporting the system transformation in Central and Eastern Europe. The formation of democratic political regimes based on market economies will contribute to the stability and prosperity of the *entire* European continent by giving rise to valuable export markets and investment opportunities. Furthermore, if the transformation were to fail, it would have considerable negative consequences for the Community. A lengthy interruption or even breakdown of market formation in the countries of Central and Eastern Europe would create a political vacuum that could threaten the security of the neighboring EC and its members. Moreover, large economic and welfare disparities or civil unrest could set off an uncontrollable flow of emigration from East to West.[196] Such a flow might be difficult to stop and thus might precipitate a nationalistic counter-reaction in the EC member countries, and threaten the process of political and economic integration among the current members themselves. In addition, the Community has a vital interest in controlling and eventually reducing the pollution generated in Central and Eastern Europe and in ensuring the safety of nuclear power plants in the former Eastern bloc.

Fifth, for the countries of Central and Eastern Europe the European Community is *the* anchor of political and economic stability on the continent. The Common Market acts like a magnet in the new European architecture and has become the central focus for Central and East European countries in establishing foreign relations. The Community's geographic proximity, its success in managing interstate relations in a peaceful manner, and the possibility of political and economic aid as well as open markets for exports—all these factors make the Community the primary system of reference. As a result, Central and East European countries have structured their transformation program in anticipation of an eventual membership in the Community, adhering closely to the *acquis communautaire*. If transformation fails, not only will the region be destabilized, but the European Community will be delegitimized as the center of political and economic authority in the emerging new European political economy.[197] A collapse of the reform process may also threaten the continued political and economic integration of Western Europe as individual members might differ on how to respond to such a crisis.

It is thus in the interest of the Community and its members to develop a policy course that will allow it to cope with the political, economic, and social challenges the Western part of the continent will face as a result of system transformation in the states of Central and Eastern Europe. Three factors, however, have complicated the debate over the exact nature of that course.

First, the European Community was caught by surprise by the developments in the fall of 1989. It was even more surprised than its member states, which to varying degrees had established bilateral relations with Central and East European countries. Second, the Common Market is itself in the midst of a fundamental transformation begun long before the dramatic changes in Central and Eastern Europe and the former Soviet Union. Third, the current twelve members of the Community differ in the degree to which they are willing to grant the countries of Central and Eastern Europe political and economic access to the Community. The last two factors in particular have generated some conflict among member countries.

Problem of Unpreparedness for Change in the East

Turning to the first complication, official contacts between the Community and the CMEA were not established until the late 1980s.[198] Until then, their relationship was primarily conditioned by the Cold War. The Soviet Union considered the Community to be the hybrid of American capitalism, and economic integration was considered the ultimate form of it. In 1962 the Soviet Union published an ideological critique of the Community entitled "32 Theses on the Imperialist Integration of Europe." The EC's strategy was to insist on concrete agreements with individual countries rather than with the CMEA. Such bilateral treaties, the Community hoped, would strengthen the political and economic independence of the Soviet satellites and undermine the cohesion of the Eastern bloc. However, no treaties were concluded. This climate of no interaction changed somewhat during the 1970s, when the Soviet Union opted for a more pragmatic approach by allowing the CMEA to hold talks.with the Community. In 1974 the EC Council of Ministers reiterated its willingness to conclude bilateral trade agreements with individual CMEA members but continued to refuse to settle trade questions in a framework agreement with CMEA, since it had no common trade policy.[199]

Negotiations resumed in 1984 and were given a strong stimulus in a 1985 speech in which Mikhail Gorbachev officially recognized the Community by calling for "favorable relations" between the two organizations. In June 1988 a joint declaration on the establishment of official relations between the EC and the CMEA was signed. From the Community's perspective, the centerpiece of the treaty was the opening of official diplomatic relations between the Community and the individual countries, allowing for the establishment of bilateral agreements between the Community and individual countries from the CMEA.[200] Hungary and Poland were the first to sign commercial and economic cooperation agreements in 1988 and 1989, respectively. Similar trade and cooperation agreements were concluded with other countries of Central and Eastern Europe. In late 1989 treaties were signed with the Soviet Union and Czechoslovakia, followed by agreements with Romania and Bulgaria in 1990.

By the fall of 1989 the European Community had established official relations with CMEA members for little more than a year. Nonetheless, the fact that the Community had little or no experience in dealing with Central and Eastern Europe and was institutionally unprepared proved to be a short-lived hindrance.[201] The EC was fully aware of its special political and economic responsibility to provide a general and stable frame of reference for the countries of Central and Eastern Europe, while the Soviet Union remained a powerful force with great military influence in the Eastern half of Europe. Given that, the Community quickly became the leader in the development and coordination of the international assistance designed to support the system transformation of Central and Eastern Europe. First, the Community was entrusted with the task of coordinating G-24 assistance implemented through the PHARE program, which is the Community's largest aid program.[202] PHARE sets five priorities in its aid program: improved access to Western markets, food supply, training, the environment, and investment and economic restructuring.[203] So far 60.2 percent of the ECU 30.5 billion pledged by December 1991 has come from the Community and its members (table A-13).[204] Second, the Community and its member countries hold the largest share of the capital of the European Bank for Reconstruction and Development, giving it a leadership role in devising lending policies toward the East.[205]

Problem of a Changing Common Market

The second factor mentioned, however, continues to have a strong influence in shaping the Community's response to the countries of Central and Eastern Europe. As indicated, the Common Market is itself in the midst of a fundamental adjustment, whose scope and direction were laid out long before the democratic revolutions in Central and Eastern Europe had begun. The two Intergovernmental Conferences (IGCs) on economic, monetary, and political union, which were concluded at the Maastricht summit in December 1991, could no longer be separated from the developments in Central and Eastern Europe. What once was considered an effort to lay the institutional foundation that would govern the current twelve members of the European Community beyond the completion of the Single Market program had turned into an interim stage on the road toward a new European architecture. The exact shape of that structure remains to be determined as Community members grope to reassess and redefine their position in the emerging new Europe. The unification of Germany and its increasing political weight in Europe have undoubtedly influenced this assessment, as have the negotiations leading up to the Maastricht summit. The summit itself and the ratification process, as the Danish referendum of June 2, 1992, demonstrated, could no longer be separated from the reassessment. Indeed, it was the rapid progress toward German unity that prompted French President François Mitterrand to persuade German Chancellor Helmut Kohl to formally call for the intergovernmental conference on political union in the spring of 1990.

To date, the German government's official support for European political and economic integration has not changed. There is reason to believe, however, that it will use its new and more powerful position in the Community to influence the future architecture of Europe. This influence will reflect its own ideas and interests, possibly accentuating the differences that currently exist among the members regarding economic, monetary, and political union. From an economic perspective, Germany is already the most powerful economy in the Community, and in the area of monetary policy has an almost complete monopoly of decisionmaking power.[206] Although numerous short-run difficulties may weaken the German economy's position in the Community, unification will increase German economic dominance in Europe in the long run.[207] Germany has risen to the status of a dominant power in Europe politically as well. Not only has it regained its full sovereignty, but the collapse of the Soviet Union and its client regimes in Central and Eastern Europe have transformed Germany, within less than a year, into a powerful actor at the center of the new political and economic geography of Europe.

So far the consequences of Germany's new status are mixed. A manifestation of Germany's increased political weight was the debate among EC members over the timing and conditions attached to a recognition of the Yugoslav republics as independent states, as well as the nature of the compromise reached by the Community.[208] On other occasions, however, Germany has been more careful in applying its increased political power. For example, it accepted the fact that the outcome of the Maastricht summit did not live up to the original goals, especially in the areas of joint EC internal policies on such matters as immigration and security.

Note, too, that Germany failed to substantially expand the decisionmaking power of the European Parliament, for which the government was heavily criticized not only by the opposition Social Democrats (SPD) but also by its own party, the Christian Democrats (CDU), and its sister party, the Christian Social Union (CSU); and its coalition partner, the Free Democrats (FDP).[209] In addition, Germany failed to secure an increase of the membership in the European Parliament as a result of German unification. Referring to Germany's role in Europe and the importance of the Franco-German axis, Commission president Jacques Delors stated that Germany has made "more concessions than [it] received in the construction of Europe, particularly at Maastricht."[210]

But German unification has also led other members to reevaluate their positions on the issues negotiated at the two IGCs. Some see that one way to weaken Germany's newly gained powerful position is to accelerate the path toward political and economic integration. Doing so would strengthen the Community as an autonomous political entity and thereby prevent individual nation-states from gaining a dominant position, while reestablishing the lost political and economic influence of weaker states.[211] This option is particularly attractive to France, which is greatly concerned about Germany's future role in the Community.[212]

German unification, the events in Central and Eastern Europe and the Soviet Union, and the central role the European Community has taken in shaping these developments all had an impact on the Maastricht summit and on the way it was perceived by EC members. The strong security component of the current foreign economic policies toward the former Eastern bloc, as well as the political conditionality that the Community has set for the continued economic support for the system transformation in Central and Eastern Europe, amounted to an unprecedented EC coordination of foreign policy. To be able to constructively use its political and economic clout in the power vacuum created by the collapse of the Eastern bloc, the Community and many of its members now perceive a clear benefit in strengthening its internal cohesion and political capacity. This increased the pressure on individual member states to work toward a successful conclusion of the IGC on political union, and particularly on matters of joint foreign policy.[213]

Problem of Differences among Community Members

The third factor that has complicated the development of a strategy of European unity is the disagreement among the current EC members on the timing, format, and degree of Central and East European integration into the Community. From the beginning, France has considered the Community a mechanism balancing German power with that of other member states.[214] As mentioned, the internal power balance of the Community was already disturbed by German unification, and now threatens to destabilize the special relationship between France and Germany—in many ways the foundation of the Community itself. To maintain the traditional power balance on the European continent, France initially attempted to stop, and later to at least slow down, the process of German unification.[215]

As Central and Eastern Europe countries begin to join the Community, which is considered to be only a matter of time, the center of gravity will shift toward Germany even more, thus further weakening France's position in the EC.[216] So far the French response to this challenge has been mixed, and to outside observers it has at times even appeared confused.[217] Initially France publicly indicated its opposition to the rapid integration of these countries into the Community.[218] To escape criticism from the countries of Central and Eastern Europe, President François Mitterrand proposed the creation of a European Confederation. This scheme would link Central and Eastern Europe more closely to the West through a number of joint policy areas and thereby reduce the need to absorb these countries into the institutional framework of the Community, while binding them closer to it.[219] Although Central and East Europeans have responded favorably to the idea of a confederation, they have also indicated that they consider it to be a complementary measure to association and eventual integration into the Community, not a substitute.[220]

During 1991, however, France began to shift its policy. The French government has evidently now decided to diffuse Germany's newly gained strength in Europe by accelerating the integration process toward a European federation.[221] With the center of political and economic power in Brussels, individual states, particularly Germany, would have less influence on the decisionmaking process. This shift in France's position was most clearly expressed by Prime Minister Bérégovoy in the recent French debate over the ratification of the Maastricht Treaty: "If the treaty is not ratified by France, then Europe risks coming apart. Germany which is today integrated into Europe . . . could be at that moment left to follow its own free will."[222]

Furthermore, if the basic political and economic structure of Europe could be established before the entrance of new members, the political weight of the existing twelve during this decisionmaking process would not be diluted by new entrants. Although such a development is in the interest of all current twelve members, France is more threatened by enlargement than Germany. Germany might even benefit from the entrance of German-speaking countries such as Austria and Switzerland, or the entrance of Central and East European nations, which would be closely linked to Germany and thus be more likely to seek their *European* interests through an alliance with Germany. At the same time, the French government continues to push the idea of a European confederation, which would now also include some CIS member states, given the dissolution of the Soviet Union.[223] This idea could supply the opportunity for a compromise between France and Germany that would allow for a rapid integration of some Central and East European countries into the Community, while creating a looser confederation that would include parts of the former Soviet Union, whose membership in the EC has been rejected by the German government.[224]

Some members of the EC's "southern tier" have also expressed reservations about embracing the countries of Central and Eastern Europe. There are essentially three reasons for this reluctance. First, the southern members of the Community have profited from membership, and they fear that the benefits may be reduced if Central and Eastern Europe are closely linked to the Community. The 1980s, for example, was a period of economic expansion toward Southern Europe. Between 1980 and 1986, as these countries moved closer to the EC and eventually joined as full members, the sources of supply for the industrial imports of the then EC-member countries shifted from Central and Eastern Europe to Southern Europe, acting as a stimulus to economic growth. The entrance of Spain and the restructuring of the French economy with an increasing focus to the South enabled a new pole of economic growth and development to emerge. Closer political and economic ties between the Community and Central and Eastern Europe are likely to change this North-South emphasis of the EC's economic infrastructure. Southern European members justifiably fear that investment flows will, at least in part, be redirected to Central and Eastern Europe.[225]

Second, Southern member countries are still very much dependent on Community funds to facilitate the economic and industrial restructuring necessary to enable them to comply with EC laws and regulations. Financial support through the structural funds, which is designed to ease the adjustment burden and facilitate the transition process, is substantial and amounted to between 2 and 3.5 percent of their respective GNPs during the second half of the 1980s. Although the Community has pledged that these transfers will not change, Spain, Portugal, and Greece are concerned that in the future they will find it harder to enlist Community support for continued allocations at the same level.[226] The foreign minister of Portugal stated in December 1991 that the new circumstances in Central and Eastern Europe might be seen as harmful to the southern tier of the Community: "The countries of the South should in no way be penalized, especially the less advanced among them."[227] The debate over the EC's budget for 1992–97 clearly reflects this fear.

Third, the Mediterranean members—including France—consider migration from the Maghreb countries and political instability in the Middle East just as threatening as systemic instability in Central and Eastern Europe and a mass influx of refugees from that region. Consequently, rather than see most of the Community's attention and resources diverted to Central and Eastern Europe, they would prefer to see additional aid for, and closer economic cooperation with, North Africa, and greater attention to promoting peace in the Middle East.[228] According to Commissioner Cardoso e Cunha of Portugal, "Europe cannot simplistically shift its center of interest from the Third World to the East because there will be an increasing number of Nigerians and Moroccans and, for Portugal, more citizens from Cape Verde. This is another line of defence for Portuguese society."[229]

Germany, in contrast, has been a strong supporter of large-scale support and accelerated integration of Central and Eastern Europe into the Community.[230] This support is clearly reflected in its financial-aid commitments, in both credits and grants, to Central and Eastern Europe. At the end of December 1991, 20.4 percent (ECU 6.2 billion) of all G-24 assistance to Central and Eastern Europe came from Germany.[231] This amounts to 0.5 percent of GDP at 1991 prices, as against 0.1 percent of GDP and 0.08 percent for the United States and Japan, respectively (figure 18 and table A-13).[232] When the contributions of EC members alone are considered, ECU 11.4 billion at the end of December 1991, Germany's share amounts to 34.0 percent.

There are several reasons for Germany's position. First, if, as argued above, the integration of Central and Eastern Europe is likely to strengthen Germany's overall position in Europe, its support of such a move is not too surprising. Second, as an immediate neighbor, Germany is the country most threatened by political and economic instability in the East and by the possibility of large-scale emigration to the West.[233] Third, given Germany's historical links to the economies of Central and Eastern Europe and the fact that part of the new Germany's economy was once firmly embedded in the Eastern network, Germany is also likely to benefit most from Community support for the system transformation and the eventual revitalization of the Eastern economies.

Figure 18. G-24 Assistance for Central and Eastern Europe
Aid as a Percent of Gross Domestic Product

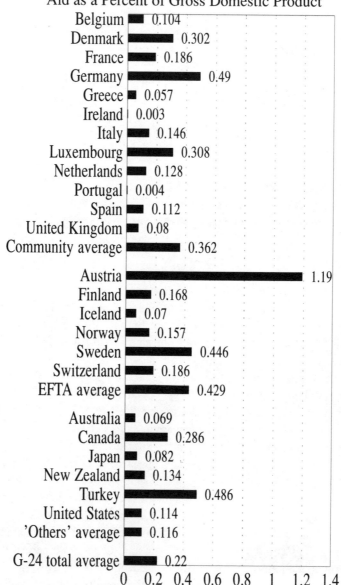

Finally, Germany has pledged to reciprocate the support it received from Hungary, Czechoslovakia, and Poland during the summer and fall of 1989 by publicly supporting their call for eventual membership in the European Community.[234] These countries either opened their borders to Austria, initiating a flood of East German emigrants, or in some instances refused to support the ailing East German state.

Although Germany is the most outspoken supporter of Community assistance for Central and Eastern Europe, it is not alone. Denmark, Italy, and Britain, each for its own reasons and interests, have also strongly supported the idea of broadening the Community.[235] Both Denmark and Italy, but less so than Germany, are also expected to gain from a political and economic power shift toward the center of Europe. The membership of the three Baltic states, along with that of Poland, will offer new economic and political opportunities to Denmark. Denmark's prime minister, in a speech to the Council of Europe, went so far as to suggest that membership negotiations with these countries should start soon after the conclusion of the Maastricht summit.[236] Britain, however, believes greater Community engagement in Central and Eastern Europe and a clear commitment to membership would slow down or even undermine the move toward a closer federation among the current twelve members. Prime Minister John Major has argued that the Community should not go forward with closer political and economic integration, because this would make it more difficult for other countries to join.[237]

These conflicting interests regarding the integration of Central and Eastern Europe are evident in the renewed debate over whether to broaden or deepen the Community, and they have dominated efforts to formulate a strategy for achieving European unity.[238] Thus the fundamental question in many minds is 'whether the Community should focus on geographic expansion, by allowing new countries to become full members, or whether it should continue on its present course toward further political and economic integration before it accepts any new members.

This question may have been relevant in the immediate aftermath of the democratic revolutions in the fall and winter of 1989, but today it is largely academic. As the economic legacy of more than four decades of central planning was exposed in 1990 and 1991, it became clear that full economic integration of the present Central and East European states into the Community would have catastrophic social, economic, and probably political consequences for those countries.[239] It is unlikely that any government in Central and Eastern Europe would survive the economic shock therapy currently being applied to the economy of the former German Democratic Republic. Neither the countries of Central and Eastern Europe nor the West has the resources to cushion these societies from the social consequences of a rapid opening to the world economy.[240] The vast structural differences between the economies in East and West would also threaten the process of economic integration among the current EC members. Moreover, it is often forgotten that the Community itself is a "moving target," as is clear from the decision of its current members to form an economic and monetary union by the end of the century. To join that union, EC members must fulfill stringent macroeconomic conditions, which at present only three of the current members can satisfy. Needless to say, they will be especially difficult for Central and East European countries to meet. From an *economic* perspective, therefore, the two concepts of deepening and broadening are *not* incompatible. Rather, they should be implemented sequentially.

9. A Three-Stage Response by the European Community

The concept of sequential broadening and deepening suggests a three-stage EC response to the challenges from Central and Eastern Europe. In the short term, the EC strategy must be geared toward *stabilizing* and facilitating system transformation in Central and Eastern Europe, because that will put the East on a path toward the long-term goal of integration into the Community. This short-term goal can be achieved only by strengthening the recently concluded association agreements. In the medium term, the Community must strengthen its own economic and political capacity if it wants to remain at the center of the new European political economy. That means further deepening, as well as broadening through the admission of the current EFTA countries as full members. In the long term, the Community has to embrace the countries of Central and Eastern Europe and fully integrate them into its institutional framework. This amounts to a substantial broadening of the EC, which will be hard to achieve without deepening the Community even further and raises difficult questions about its future institutional structure.

Short Term: Strengthening the Association Agreements

The recently concluded association agreements with the three East European countries currently provide the central mechanism through which the EC hopes to facilitate system transformation in Central and Eastern Europe and pave the way for its eventual integration into the Community. Although the agreements differ in their specifics, they are structured around a common framework made up of six components: (1) political dialogue, (2) the "four freedoms" (free movement of goods, services, capital, and labor), (3) economic cooperation, (4) cultural cooperation, (5) financial cooperation, and (6) the Association Council, Committee, and Parliamentary Commission.[241]

IMPORTANCE OF THE AGREEMENTS. The primary purpose of the association agreements is to support and stabilize system transformation in Central and Eastern Europe. Its centerpiece is a series of direct (economic aid) and indirect (trade) measures. Before these measures are implemented, the respective economic systems will be required to bring their laws and regulations in line with those of the Community. This process is referred to as *acquis communautaire*. In addition, these agreements offer the countries of Central and Eastern Europe a forum for political dialogue on bilateral and multilateral questions of interest to both parties and thus open the possibility for cooperation in matters of foreign policy through the Association Council. The establishment and continuation of the agreements is subject to a set of political and economic prerequisites: the rule of law, respect of human rights, the creation of a multiparty system, free and fair elections, and economic liberalization that encourages the creation of a market economy.

These agreements are without doubt unprecedented in the history of the Community's relations with third countries. They indicate the historical continuity, cultural affinity, and geographic proximity of Eastern and Western Europe and demonstrate the Community's support for the difficult task that lies ahead for the countries undergoing system transformation.[242] As Andrzej Olechowski, Poland's chief negotiator, has noted, the agreement "returns Poland to Europe and Europe to the Poles." Other signatories see in it a promise of "some real benefits on the political as well as the economic level."[243]

A central point of the agreements is that the Community and Central European countries will temporarily accept asymmetric access to their respective markets. The EC will liberalize its markets for imports from Central Europe before its three association partners open theirs. In the case of Poland, the Community will liberalize Polish imports over the next five years (or six years in the case of steel and textiles), while Poland will not start this process until 1995. According to one estimate, opening up the EC market should enable Poland to increase its exports of industrial goods to the EC by 20 percent. Similarly, Czechoslovakia hopes to increase its exports to EC markets by an additional $300 million over the 1990s.[244]

Under the agreements, national treatment and capital liberalization must proceed from a reciprocal basis. Investors from the Community, for example, will be subject to the same rules and regulations as their domestic counterparts. This condition is particularly important for the Central and East European countries, for they are likely to implement some transitory regulations to protect infant industries unable to compete with their West European counterparts. At the same time, West Europeans will benefit in that the principle of investment protection is included in the national treatment clause, which the

EC has already signed with Czechoslovakia, Hungary, and Poland. This protection is expected to increase the flow of investment capital from the Community to Central Europe. Capital liberalization includes such items as profits, proceeds from sales, and dividends. To avoid excessive capital outflow from the Central and East European economies, some restrictions will remain until a healthy balance of payments is restored.

The three Central European countries have agreed to bring existing and future legislation to EC standards or norms, and to adopt EC rules on competition and state aid. The improved and more predictable legislative framework that emerges from these actions should further stimulate the inflow of foreign investment. What has been lacking until recently, and what will be central in determining the success of the system transformation, is a political guarantee that new domestic and foreign businesses will be able to export easily into EC markets.[245] A provisional agreement covering the commercial part of the treaty, over which the Community enjoys jurisdiction, came into force on March 1, 1992. The full agreements will not come into effect for some time, pending ratification by national parliaments.[246]

The Community intends to conclude similar agreements with East European nations. It requested the authorization to negotiate such agreements in early September 1991, and in December 1991 an EC delegation visited Bulgaria to start the procedure by which Bulgaria will apply for associate membership. Bulgaria and the Commission believe that most obstacles to starting the negotiation of an association agreement have been removed. In the case of Romania, talks were suspended in September 1991 during the governmental crises, but negotiations reopened in 1992. The Community hopes to conclude agreements with Bulgaria and Romania by the end of 1992.[247] And Albania will undoubtedly also conclude an association agreement once the initial conditions set out in the framework treaty have been established.

THE HISTORY OF THE NEGOTIATIONS. Despite the generally positive character of the association agreements, there is some question whether they will get the necessary parliamentary support for ratification in their current form.[248] The history of the negotiations raises doubts about the sincerity and commitment of some EC member governments to the system transformation in Central and Eastern Europe. This lack of commitment was reflected in the deadlock that developed in the summer of 1991 between the Community and Czechoslovakia, Hungary, and Poland. Since the beginning of the negotiations, the three Central European countries had charged that the accords were unfairly biased toward the interests of the Community, and they insisted that the Community make greater concessions.[249] After six rounds, their talks with the Community were deadlocked, and Poland threatened to break off the negotiations. In light of its increasing domestic economic difficulties, the Polish government came under strong political pressure not to concede to the EC conditions.[250]

Only a political decision by the Council of Ministers to broaden the negotiating mandate of the Commission was likely to bring the negotiations to a conclusion. The opportunity to enlarge the mandate arose during the aborted coup in the Soviet Union. In the immediate response to the coup, the foreign ministers of the EC member states suddenly found a surprising consensus on their position toward Central and Eastern Europe. Realizing the symbolic effect that the association agreements would have on the Soviet Union, the ministers urged the Commission to bring the negotiations to a rapid conclusion, indicating their willingness to broaden the mandate.[251] The Commission reacted with irritation, since it had long demanded a larger negotiating mandate from the member states. Jacques Delors stated, "It's no good making fine speeches about solidarity with Eastern Europe on Sunday and the next day refusing their demands to import more of their goods."[252] Commissioner Karel van Miert concurred: "We have to do more, and more quickly. I think that is the political lesson from what has happened. It is a question of political will."[253]

The Central European countries then reiterated their desire to conclude the agreements in the hope of getting greater concessions, pointing out that "it took this drama to bring home to the Community how vital our link-up with the bloc is to the stability of Europe," and that "we expect real concessions, not purely political declarations of good will."[254] In early September the Commission presented the Council of Ministers new and improved proposals on market access for the three Central European countries in the areas of food and agriculture, textiles, and coal and steel.[255] These proposals were expected to bring that round of negotiation to a conclusion within four weeks.

But with the aborted coup in the Soviet Union and mounting domestic pressure in the West to resist further market opening, some countries retreated from their earlier positions. France, supported by Belgium, Greece, and Ireland, refused to accept an increase of 10 percent in meat imports over the next five years and caused yet another stalemate in the negotiations.[256] At first, Germany and Portugal also objected to increases in coal and textile imports, respectively, but later agreed to drop their demands if other countries were going to follow through with their concessions. In response to the French position, all three Central European countries announced they were suspending all future negotiations with the Community.[257]

In the hope that a final agreement could be signed before the end of the year, the Central Europeans had little choice but to resume the negotiations in late September. In view of France's refusal to change its position, the Commission developed a compromise solution whereby the Community would make available $600 million to buy additional Polish meat "imports," while then exporting the goods to the Soviet Union. This allowed the negotiators to resume their talks.[258] However, France's position, along with the stabilizing political situation in the former Soviet Union rekindled the concern of other countries, which once again delayed signing the agreements.[259] The Central Europeans also charged that the "EC bureaucracy" was trying to undermine the talks by annulling provisions that had been accepted in the main part of the treaty through appropriate annexes.[260] On one occasion, Spain submitted an appendix to the document regarding steel imports after it had already been initialled in late November. This document was submitted so late that some Central European countries did not have a chance to read it, and so there was another delay in the signing of the documents.[261]

OPPOSITION TO THE AGREEMENTS. These difficulties suggest that the national parliaments may be reluctant to ratify the agreements in their present form. The deteriorating economic situation in several EC member countries may stir up further opposition to ratifications. There will certainly be increased domestic political pressure against any market liberalization in the three sectors in which Central Europeans enjoy a comparative advantage.[262] Some Central European parliaments may also be reluctant to ratify the treaty. A hint of the possible problems appeared when Slovakia insisted throughout the negotiations that the accord contain a preamble specifying that Czechoslovakia's constituent republics would participate in fulfilling the agreement.[263] Slovakia wanted to maintain associative status even if the republics decided to separate, but its request was unacceptable to some EC member countries that are compound states themselves and feared the potential repercussions in their own countries. The Czechoslovak government accepted an EC proposal that it make a verbal declaration during the signing ceremony acknowledging that the CSFR is a compound state and that both republics were participating in the fulfillment of the agreement.[264] The Slovak government has accepted this solution for the time being, but the matter may be brought up again during the ratification debate.

Another criticism came from Poland's Council on Rural Development, which argued that the treaty puts some of Poland's agricultural production at risk. In response, acting prime minister Jan Krzystof Biliecki stated that "if the Sejm committees are not happy with the treaty, it may not be signed at all."[265] Just as in the European Community, domestic resistance to the agreements may flare up in Central Europe as economic conditions deteriorate and unemployment continues to rise. Central European societies, having just regained their independence from Soviet domination, may also resent giving up some of their sovereignty to the Community in return for associate status. To comply with the *acquis communautaire*, the Central European countries must pass about 8,000 EC laws and regulations.[266] Moreover, as the Maastricht summit demonstrated, the Community is moving forward with its own political and economic integration, which implies that Central Europeans may have to give up more sovereignty than they initially expected. Reacting to the summit, one Central European official commented, "We are now beginning to enjoy our freedom and independence. A deeper and more integrated Europe will either delay our entry [because of additional requirements] or, when we do finally join the Community our decision-making powers will be diluted."[267] Recently senior officials from all three associate members stated that the agreements may tip their countries' expanded trade with the Community into deficit, which could hamper ratification in the national parliaments.[268]

FOUR IMPORTANT ISSUES TO RECONSIDER. Even if the agreements are ratified by all parliamentary bodies, the Community should reconsider four particular issues if the association is to accomplish its principal goal—which is to facilitate the process of system transformation and to initiate the reintegration of Central and Eastern Europe into the West European market economy. Those issues are (1) the membership clause in the agreements, (2) the approach to trade with Central and Eastern Europe, (3) the financial support necessary to enact the agreements, and (4) the microeconomic, legal, and social aspects of transformation.

Membership clause. According to the initial mandate of the Community, the objective of the agreements is "to create a climate of confidence and stability favorable to political and economic reform and to establish political relations that reflect common values."[269] The initial draft does not make any reference to membership. Although the Community saw the agreements as an end in themselves, Czechoslovakia, Hungary, and Poland continue to consider the association agreements a means, a transitional stage, to full membership in the Community.[270] This gap was not reduced in any substantive way by the three Council decisions to broaden the Commission's mandate.[271] Poland, which has been the most outspoken critic of the Community's attitude toward the membership question, even threatened to walk out of the negotiations. All three countries argued that the stability of their fragile democracies would improve substantially if the West declared its commitment to eventual EC membership.[272]

But the Community did not change its position in any fundamental way. Although the agreement's preamble recognizes "the fact that the final objective of [Czechoslovakia, Hungary, and Poland] is to become a member of the Community and . . . this association, in the view of the parties, will help to achieve this objective," the Community has made no firm commitment to accept these countries once they meet the necessary political and economic preconditions.[273] Pablo Benavides, the Community's chief negotiator, has pointed out, "This is not an entrance ticket. It's a kind of trial run [to see] if they would like to become members."[274] Conversely, acting Polish prime minister Balcerowicz, speaking for the Central European countries, has noted, "For us the agreement is the beginning of the road to full EC membership."[275] In failing to constructively resolve the membership issue, some of the member countries indicate they still do not fully appreciate the symbolic importance of future membership to the transformation process itself. Furthermore, Community membership of some or all Central and East European countries is indeed a long-term reality, but it is certainly not a short-term threat.

First, for the societies of Central and Eastern Europe, the European Community offers an example to which they aspire. Linking their region to the Community helps to reduce the risk of political, social, and economic setbacks. It also provides an institutional anchor on the road to transformation, just as it did for Spain, Portugal, and Greece, for which the decision was primarily a political and not an economic one.

Second, the prospect of membership is also likely to reduce the centrifugal pressures that are currently growing in Central and East European societies. Membership in the Community and adherence to its rules and norms at the macropolitical and economic level will eventually allow a further decentralization at the national level. In addition, it may be the *only* way in which the reemerging ethnic and nationality conflicts in Central and Eastern Europe can be resolved.

Third, if the frame of reference is a firm commitment to EC membership, adjustment and the eventual harmonization of Central and East European laws, regulations, norms, and standards with those of the Community—through the *acquis communautaire*—can only act as a stabilizer.

Fourth, the promise of membership should provide the governments in Central and Eastern Europe with incentives to take the necessary internal steps to qualify for membership. Given the difficulties that the transformation process is generating, membership can act as an important domestic policy instrument to rationalize the social and economic hardships of transformation as well as present them as a temporary phenomenon rather than as a permanent state.

Fifth, a firm political commitment to eventual EC membership for Central and Eastern Europe is a central factor in attracting large-scale foreign investment to these countries. Unless European and other Western investors are assured that these countries will eventually belong to the single market—where goods, services, capital, and labor can flow freely—they are unlikely to commit substantial resources.

From the Community's perspective, membership should not be considered a short-term threat. Conditions for membership are such that new members will not threaten what has already been achieved by the existing Community members. In fact, previous decisions to enlarge the Community proved to be an impetus to further deepening. Offering Central and Eastern Europe membership in the Community is therefore likely to increase the disposition of present members to change the EC's internal decisionmaking structure. Also, as already mentioned, EC membership is a "moving target" that may be difficult to catch up with, and thus may further postpone eventual membership.

Of course, offering EC membership by no means implies a free entry ticket into the European Community. The Community should specify a list of targets that have to be met before Central and East European nations can become members. Once these targets have been met, however, entry should be automatic. Obviously, it would be difficult to agree on the nature and level of the economic targets. To bring such negotiations to a successful conclusion, the Community can use the experience it gained during the membership negotiations with Spain and Portugal.

Both parties would benefit from such a policy approach. Central and East Europeans would be provided with a clear perspective of their future status in Europe, and of the requirements they would have to meet to reach that status.

West Europeans would be forced to develop a more coherent and long-term strategy for the future architecture of the continent. At the same time, they would be reassured that integrating Central and Eastern Europe into the Community would not undermine what has already been achieved.

Trade with Central and Eastern Europe. The Community must open its markets to more exports from Central and Eastern Europe. Exports are an essential ingredient in the strategy of economic growth in Central and Eastern Europe. The West's post–World War II experience in this regard is instructive. Besides providing massive financial aid to Western Europe, the U.S.- administered Marshall Plan also ensured open markets in Europe and North America. These helped prevent the economic collapse of Western Europe.[276] Perhaps even more important, Western Europe was given improved terms of access for its exports to the U.S. market.[277]

Since the transformation process is going to take much longer than originally anticipated, the agreed-upon asymmetry in trade—currently expected to last from four to five years—will not give the economies of Central and Eastern Europe sufficient time to prepare for the competition of the European and world economy. If domestic industry is not strong enough to withstand foreign competition, it is likely to be swept aside in the fray with dire economic and social consequences for the Central and East European countries. The Community should therefore keep its options open on the length of the asymmetric opening for the countries of Central and Eastern Europe.

Most Central and East European countries have a comparative advantage in agricultural products, textiles, and coal and steel and thus would benefit from the ability to export these commodities freely to the Community's market.[278] The history of the Community's trade policy toward Central and Eastern Europe, however, shows a highly restrictive pattern that has not changed in any fundamental way as a result of the trade and cooperation agreements signed in 1989 and 1990, nor as a result of the association agreements.[279] Although the association agreements are asymmetric in the sense that the Community will open its markets at a faster rate than the three Central and East European economies, their access to EC markets will be restricted by and large to industrial goods, in which the competitive advantage of Central and East European enterprises is limited. Market opening is much slower in coal, steel, and textiles. In agriculture the process of liberalization is based on reciprocity.[280] As one Polish negotiator commented, "We cannot agree to the Community offering us concessions for commodities that we do not produce, for example, bananas, pineapples, or oranges."[281] While the

Figure 19. Agricultural, Coal and Steel, and Textile Exports to
the EC from Czechoslovakia, Hungary, and Poland as a
Percent of Total EC Imports of These Commodities, 1988

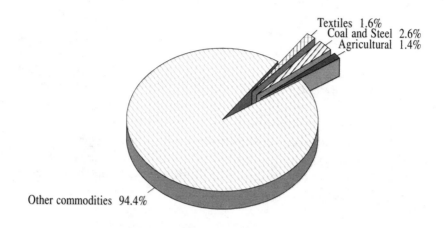

Textiles 1.6%
Coal and Steel 2.6%
Agricultural 1.4%

Other commodities 94.4%

Source: See table A-14.

Czechoslovak and Hungarian officials were less outspoken, they voiced the
same criticisms.[282] Central and East European disappointment over the extent
of this "hidden asymmetry" was best summarized by Vladimir Dlouhy,
minister of economics of the CSFR: "When we started our political changes
we had a lot of support from Western European circles. But now, when we are
really coming to the terms of that support, only cool blooded economic facts
are put on the table."[283]

Community members must therefore reconsider their position on market
access in the three product categories in which Central and East European
economies can compete. Since the market share of EC imports from Central
and Eastern Europe in these categories is small compared with total EC imports
in these product groups, the overall effect of liberalization on the EC is also
likely to be small. As figure 19 (table A-14) shows, the share of total EC
imports ranges from 1.41 percent in the case of agriculture to a mere 2.55
percent in the case of coal and steel. If the same quantities are measured as a

Figure 20. Agricultural, Coal and Steel, and Textile Exports to the EC from Czechoslovakia, Hungary, and Poland as a Percentage of All Commodity Exports from These Countries, 1988

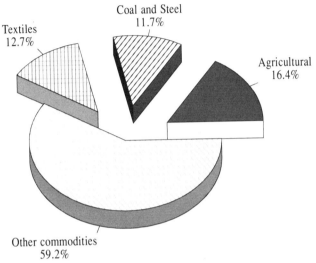

Source: See table A-14.

percentage of total Central and East European exports to the Community, the strategic importance of further market liberalization for those countries becomes even clearer (figure 20 and table A-14).

For example, Poland's 1990 agricultural exports to the Community amounted to 21 percent of its total exports there and were valued at approximately ECU 5.2 billion. The share for Hungary was even higher at 24 percent of total exports and amounted to ECU 4.42 billion. For the CSFR, which has a relatively small agricultural sector, the share was 7 percent of its total 1990 exports and was valued at ECU 2.7 billion. Similarly, textiles account for 11 to 16 percent of exports to the Community. Some of these shares have certainly increased since 1990, but they would rise even further if the Community were to open its markets.

Lower quantitative restrictions in these sectors are not the only answer to the East's problems, however. If standard EC anti-dumping and safeguard clauses continue to apply, exports from Central and Eastern Europe will most likely be subject to penalties. It is fair to assume that Central and East European economies will use undervalued exchange rates to increase the competitiveness of their exports in world markets. This will trigger Community anti-dumping actions that will affect all exports from the country being penalized and will reduce the likelihood of foreign direct investment. One representative of the German steel industry suggests it would be better for the countries of Central and Eastern Europe to maintain the old trade and cooperation agreements. The alternative would be anti-dumping suits "because in our perspective everything which comes from there is either being dumped or subsidized."[284] Similarly, safeguard clauses would almost certainly apply, given the sensitive nature of the EC's agricultural, textile, and steel and coal sectors—product categories important to Central and Eastern Europe.

Greater access to Western markets would help to improve living standards and build market economies in the East. Such access would not only reduce some of the painful costs of economic and social adjustments but would also protect Central and Eastern Europe from the more radical political forces that have an interest in undermining the current transformation effort. As Poland's negotiator Andzrej Olechowski has pointed out, "The accent should have been on helping us to go as quickly as possible to the *acquis communautaire*. What we wanted was a shield from wild politicians, but we really failed to achieve this."[285]

Instead, increased trade in agricultural goods during 1991 appears to have had a *destabilizing* effect on the Eastern countries. Poland and other former CMEA members have dismantled their central planning tariff structures and have only partly implemented new ones, with the result that Central and Eastern Europe was flooded with cheap agricultural products from abroad in 1990 and 1991, mostly from the European Community. Angry reactions by the farmers and the peasant parties in Poland have further destabilized the already fragile political landscape.[286] In Hungary and the CSFR, citizens charge that their governments are giving up too much to the European Community and are selling out domestic agricultural industry to the Community interests. All the while, the Community refuses to reduce its tariffs and quotas but floods the countries with cheap agricultural imports that further undermine their stability.[287]

Without doubt, fast and effective support for the still fragile democracies of Central and Eastern Europe requires considerable systemic reform in Western Europe in the areas of agriculture, textiles, and coal and steel. As a holistic approach to systemic reform would predict, and as the ongoing debate over the reform of the Common Agricultural Policy indicates, such reform will be politically difficult to secure. But rather than give in to well-entrenched interest groups and delay a politically inconvenient but economically inevitable step, the Community and its member states should consider the developments in Central and Eastern Europe as both an additional reason and a political opportunity to begin systemic reform.

The freedom advocated in the association agreement will be of limited or no value if the European Community is not willing to agree to the asymmetric opening of its markets in the European agreements for *all* products from Central and Eastern Europe. The Community cannot expect to be taken seriously if it advocates a free-market economy for Central and Eastern Europe and then fails to abide by the same principles.

It is true that full access to the EC agricultural market would merely expand the East's agricultural sector, which in an all-European context could not be sustained in the long run. But closing EC markets under the present social, economic, and political conditions in Central and Eastern Europe is not the right strategy to induce industrial restructuring. It would merely delay the unavoidable restructuring that the Community itself must undertake in these sectors, and it shuts out the few Central and East European producers that are able to compete in the EC market.

At the same time, Central European countries should avoid discriminating among their association partners in the West. As a reward for promises of investments with Polish partners, Poland has stated it would split the quota of 30,000 passenger cars to be imported free of duty between Fiat, GM (Opel), and Volkswagen. Because France and Britain strongly objected to such an arrangement, the full implementation of the interim agreement between Poland and the EC had to be delayed.[288] A similar agreement has been struck between Hungary and Voest-Alpine, the Austrian state-owned steelmaker.[289] Apart from further jeopardizing the eventual ratification of the association agreement with Poland, this development is another example of the different degrees of interest that current EC members have in Central and Eastern Europe and is the source of considerable tension among them. In addition, it is a first indication of the new industrial structures that are likely to emerge in the New Europe—structures that may radically alter the traditional West European industrial alliances and patterns of interest.[290]

Financial support. The Community has pledged financial support and economic help, but it has declined to include financial protocols in the general framework of the agreements.[291] Such measures would commit the European

Community to financial credits and grants, and it would set priorities for the financing of the various elements of the agreement.[292]

Once the associate status for Czechoslovakia, Hungary, and Poland has been ratified by the national and European parliaments, possibly during the fall or winter of 1992, financial support for the implementation of the agreement will have to be financed through the PHARE program. Although the association agreements apply to the Community only, PHARE is currently supported by the members of the G-24, and it applies to all Central and East European countries. This may create distributive problems. In addition, it is unlikely that other members of the G-24 will be willing to finance the association of Central and East European nations with the Community, with the result that some separation of the financing may take place.

In its five-year budget plan for 1992–97 the EC Commission has proposed to increase the funds for external action from ECU 3.6 billion to ECU 6.3 billion, a large share of which is earmarked for Central and Eastern Europe and the former Soviet Union (see table 7). In addition, the Commission plans to create a separate category for EC external action that will allow for a more independent allocation of funds.[293] If this part of the budget plan is approved in its current form, it represents a considerable improvement over the previous arrangement. Nonetheless, a direct link to the association agreements is still lacking, and considerable uncertainty remains. Even if the funds are approved, it remains to be seen whether they will be sufficient to meet the challenges ahead, especially in light of the fact that the number of associate members is likely to increase considerably in the next few years.

Microeconomic, legal, and social issues. In their current form the agreements place a disproportionate weight on the establishment of the "four freedoms," which would in effect set up free market conditions in Central and Eastern Europe, both in their internal and external relations. This effort is supported by financial assistance at the macroeconomic level, in the form of a stabilization fund, and by loans from the G-24 and international financial institutions. Except for the privatization programs, the agreements place less emphasis on the microeconomic aspects of system transformation, such as industrial restructuring and labor market reform. Less attention is also given to the legal and administrative, and social and psychological, dimensions of system transformation. Between January 1990 and December 1991, more than one-third (35.9 percent) of global cumulative commitments went toward macrofinancial assistance. Another 25.7 percent went to export credits and investment guarantees that have to be repaid in full. But only 2.0 percent was earmarked for social infrastructure and services and 7.9 percent for economic infrastructure and services, which includes such items as the environment and training.[294]

This is *not* to say that macroeconomic stabilization is unimportant to system transformation. Rather, there is a large imbalance in the financial assistance provided for the micro- and macroeconomic level of the hoped-for market economies. There is also an imbalance between the attention given to the economic dimension of the new market economies on the one hand, and its legal and administrative, and social and psychological, dimensions on the other. Before system transformation—*or the macroeconomic stabilization itself*—can succeed, this imbalance will almost certainly need to be corrected. Some of the resources need to be redistributed to the microeconomic level, and some to the legal and administrative and social and psychological areas of the emerging market economies.

More resources should therefore be spent on what the association agreements refer to as "economic and technical cooperation." Economic and technical cooperation is vital on both specific issues, such as investment protection and the implementation of industrial norms and standards, and broader questions such as the establishment of a modern transportation and distribution system, telecommunications, the protection of the environment, and the need for adequate health care and training.[295]

The negotiations between EFTA and the Community over the establishment of the European Economic Area demonstrate the complexity of integrating even two highly developed economic systems. It is a task that cuts across all three dimensions of a market economy.[296] For the Central European countries that have concluded association agreements with the Community, these issues must be resolved before the four freedoms can begin to generate real economic benefits. The fact that many Central and East European countries cannot even absorb all the financial assistance currently offered indicates that more emphasis needs to be put on helping them build the infrastructural elements of a market economy. These elements will strengthen the market's institutional capacity to efficiently absorb the aid that is provided.

The Community should also expand the role of the political dialogue in the association agreements so that market institutions in the West (legislators, regulators, administrative personnel, interest associations, and the like) can share their knowledge and experience with those in the East. Human capital is a central resource of the holistic approach being promoted in this exchange.

Political dialogue would serve other purposes, since a strategy of association that relies disproportionately on the establishment of a market economy as the *principal* stabilizing element in Central and Eastern Europe today is questionable. First, even under favorable circumstances, the Community, under pressure from individual member states, is unlikely to *radically* open its markets to exports from Central and Eastern Europe in the short term. It is also fair to assume that the vast amount of financial, technical, and human resources required to support the system transformation will not be raised in that interval. In addition, the social and psychological dimension to system transformation requires not only money but time, experience, and practice.

Second, differences in the economic structure, degree of economic development, and relative previous experience with systemic reform—as distinct from system transformation—will allow some Central and East European states to transform their economic systems at a faster rate than others. It is thus realistic to expect considerable variations in the degree of *economic* integration of Central and Eastern European nations into the Community to emerge over the next decade. The Community will soon be forced to emphasize the differences among Central and East European countries rather than their commonalities if it structures its new relationship with Central and Eastern Europe primarily around economic issues, as is now the case. The geographic distribution of assistance to Central and Eastern Europe demonstrates that point. So far, the allocation of financial support by the G-24 has been skewed toward Poland and Hungary. Excluding regional programs, 55 percent of the credits and grants by the G-24 were committed to Poland (39.1 percent) and Hungary (16.0 percent) by the end of 1991 (figure 21 and table A-15).[297]

This skewed distribution is in part explained by the fact that assistance to Poland and Hungary started as far back as 1989. Today the Community recognizes that it needs to reorient some of its aid toward the Balkans in order to avoid the further economic and political marginalization of the region. This is the region of Europe that has the greatest need for assistance, as well as the highest potential for political, social, and ethnic instability. In the short and medium term, however, continued differentiation among the countries of Central and Eastern Europe in the economic realm of association cannot be avoided and thus raises questions about the integrative and stabilizing attributes of that side of the association.

As for political dialogue and cooperation, however, countries could be integrated on an equal basis as soon as they have met the initial conditions set out in the association agreements. Since current EC members are less likely to resist intensified political dialogue and cooperation, this aspect of the association agreement could become the primary integrating mechanism to put *all* Central and Eastern Europe countries on an *equal* footing. Such

Figure 21. G-24 Assistance to Czechoslovakia, Poland, and Hungary as Percent of Total

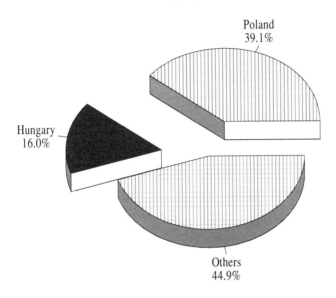

Poland
39.1%

Hungary
16.0%

Others
44.9%

Source: See table A-15. From 1st quarter of 1990 to end of 4th quarter of 1991.

cooperation would enable the Community to include countries such as Albania, Bulgaria, Romania, the Baltics, and the newly independent republics of the former Yugoslavia, some of which are not in a position to implement the four freedoms as currently offered in the agreements.[298]

AFFILIATE MEMBERSHIP. If the Community were to shift its focus from the rapid establishment of the four freedoms to economic and technical cooperation and political dialogue, the members should reconsider the idea of an *affiliate membership* proposed by the EC commissioner Frans Andriessen.[299] This concept provides a means of dealing with the contradictory circumstances facing the Community—the political urgency of embracing Central and Eastern Europe, on the one hand, and the economic impossibility of doing so in the immediate future, on the other. Affiliate membership would enable countries wishing to join the Community to start participating in such areas as common transport and communication policies, the development of a European energy and environmental agenda, and common research and development and cultural policies.[300] In addition, Central and Eastern Europe could participate in the foreign policymaking process of the European Community.[301]

In Andriessen's plan, affiliated countries would have an advisory voice that would be taken into account in the decisions of the Council of Ministers. Similar meetings of an expanded parliament could take place at regular intervals.[302] Central and East European nations could also participate in the European elections in 1994. Their precise status in Luxembourg would still have to be determined.[303] Besides strengthening the European identity of the new democracies, the Community could benefit from the knowledge and experience these countries have acquired in the Balkans and the former Soviet Union.

Some have also suggested that the Central and East European nations could associate themselves with the European Monetary System, which would provide a "monetary anchor" for domestic monetary policy, provide greater access to international financial markets, and give greater security to foreign investors.[304] Furthermore, affiliate membership could be used to create the economic conditions that would have to be met before a country could become a full member. In some ways, affiliate membership also deals with the fact that the Community itself is a moving train. The greater the number of issues the Central and East Europeans can begin to participate in today, the easier it will be for them to become full members in the future.

Initially, other members of the Commission and the European Parliament were rather cool to the notion of affiliate membership, and even the Central and East Europeans hesitated to endorse the idea. They feared that it was similar to the French proposal for a European confederation and designed to delay their entry into the Community.[305] This position has changed somewhat with the increasing realization that system transformation will take much longer than anticipated. Central and East European countries, too, look upon the idea more favorably now.[306] The initial rejection in Western Europe may also have come too soon, because the association agreements have underestimated the difficulties of system transformation in the East and systemic reform in the West, while facing the *political necessity* of embedding the Central and East European democracies into the larger European framework.

The principal advantage of an affiliate membership is that it brings a more flexible approach to the integration of the individual countries. It is, in fact, an evolutionary, progressive strategy that is better able to deal with the increasing number and diversity of potential applicants.[307] Of course, there are limits to how far economic and political integration can be separated. In the short term, however, such a separation may be the only way to produce some quick and visible examples of integration that have their intended stabilizing effect.

SUMMARY. To sum up, by concluding association agreements, the Community has demonstrated that it is aware of its central role as the anchor of political, social, and economic stability in all of Europe. At the same time, it is still not clear whether individual members are prepared to entrust the Community with the financial and political means to exercise that responsibility. To do so, member states first have to ratify the agreements. Second, those member states that have opposed it should periodically reconsider their current position, on both the issue of membership and the access of Central and East European states to West European markets. At present, the agreements do not send a symbolically powerful message of belonging to Europe ("trial run"), and they provide a limited amount of immediate help to the economies of Central and Eastern Europe. As long as the Community remains on the defensive with respect to the membership of these countries and remains hostage to small but powerful interest groups in individual member states, these agreements may not be able to fulfill their primary purpose—that purpose is to act as an anchor for political and economic stability. This defensive position is not in the interest of Central and Eastern Europe or the Community, which must recognize that it cannot separate itself—geographically, demographically, historically, and morally—from the developments in the region.

At the same time, the Community cannot risk its own political and economic cohesion by overextending itself. The present lack of financial resources, potential budgetary constraints, and economic slowdown in Western Europe make it difficult for the Community to take on a much larger role in Central and Eastern Europe. The Community cannot risk a domestic backlash against its own institutions and accomplishments.[308] The challenge for the Community is to find the right balance between what is necessary for the stability of Central and Eastern Europe and what is possible for the continued cohesion of Western Europe. Affiliate membership provides such a balance, delivers a satisfactory response to the membership issues, and would require a financial protocol allowing all participants to develop a comprehensive strategy of European unification. Such a strategy should begin by examining the amendments in the Treaty of Rome to determine what steps would be required to establish affiliate membership.

Medium Term: The First Phase of Deepening and Broadening

In the medium term, the European Community must strengthen its own economic and political capacity to respond adequately and constructively to the challenge that system transformation in Central and Eastern Europe poses to the continent. Two interrelated systemic reform steps are necessary. The EC must strengthen itself politically and economically by accepting the EFTA countries as full members as soon as possible. However, doing so will have its full effect only if the Community also reforms its own decisionmaking apparatus in the process of continued deepening, especially in the legal and administrative, and social and psychological, domains of the European market economy.

BROADENING THE MEMBERSHIP. While granting full membership to Central and Eastern Europe may be premature, this is not true for the EFTA countries.[309] Indeed, membership of the EFTA countries would increase the economic and political capacity of the Community and enable it to better face the challenges emerging from Central and Eastern Europe. Contrary to the rather limited coordination among the G-24 countries, EFTA and the Community could coordinate their assistance to the countries of Central and Eastern Europe by pooling the available resources. That would reduce the inefficiencies and waste in the initial stages of data gathering, fact finding, and project evaluation in Central and Eastern Europe.[310] EFTA is already negotiating trade agreements with Poland, Hungary, and Czechoslovakia that closely resemble the trade components of the association agreements.[311] In addition, the move toward the formation of a European Economic Area (EEA) and the rising number of membership applications by EFTA countries to the European Community have a logical counterpart in a closely coordinated move by the Community and EFTA toward system transformation in Central and Eastern Europe, as well as market access by Central and East European economies. Note that the EEA agreement also contains a section on "political dialogue," in which EC and EFTA member states express "the desire to strengthen their political dialogue in order to develop closer ties and to bring into line their viewpoints on foreign policy issues in areas presenting an interest for the two parties."[312]

Given the high level of economic development of the EFTA countries, EFTA membership would raise the average per capita GNP of the Community from $13,547 to $16,370 and thereby increase the Community's financial capacity to support system transformation.

The long-term viability of EFTA has been put into serious doubt by the applications for EC membership by Austria in June 1989, Sweden in July 1991, and Finland and Switzerland in March and May 1992, respectively, which may be followed by the application of Norway before the end of 1992.[313] In a recent declaration drafted by the Commission for the Council of Ministers, both Sweden and Austria are mentioned as countries whose accession negotiations can start as soon as the Community has settled the review of its five-year budget and farm reform in 1992.[314]

The initial difficulties during the negotiations on the EEA between the Community and the EFTA countries reflected the continued EC resistance to fully embrace these countries into the European economy. It is also a reflection of the members' opposition to some of the demands by the EFTA countries.[315] Some Community members tried to capitalize on the EFTA weakening, but at the same time individual EFTA countries have refused to yield to some of the EC's demands.[316] After the treaty was finally initialed in October 1991, yet another hurdle had to be overcome.[317] The European Court of Justice (ECJ) called the treaty's system of jurisdiction into question and asked for further clarification. It then rejected the treaty, indicating the increasingly powerful role of the court in shaping the future European architecture.[318] The court and at least two member countries objected to the establishment of a parallel EEA Court, which would be allowed to interpret EC law by virtue of its power to settle disputes between the EC and EFTA.[319]

These obstacles, however, could not derail the conclusion of the agreement. Rather than establish an EEA court, members agreed to a procedure used in legal disputes. Under the agreement differences over judicial interpretation of EEA laws would go to a joint EEA political committee rather than to a joint court. If there was no agreement, and if one side chose to invoke retaliatory measures, then the other side could demand binding arbitration. In a major concession to the European Community, EFTA agreed to let the Commission and the European Court deal with virtually any significant competition case.[320] This time the Commission submitted the treaty to the court before presenting it to its members for initialing, and the court approved the compromise.[321] In early May 1992 the treaty was signed, establishing the world's largest market and free-trading zone.[322]

When it was first proposed in early 1989 by Jacques Delors, the EEA was conceived to stave off any immediate enlargement of the Community. EFTA members, however, soon realized they were becoming members of an economic club, the rules of which they did not have the ability to establish.[323] Moreover, since Central and East European countries are pressing for membership as well, EFTA countries now consider the agreement to be the first and decisive step toward their speedy integration into the EC.

Several obstacles, however, remain before the EEA can become fully effective on January 1, 1993. First, the agreement is "mixed," and thus has to be ratified by nineteen national parliaments.[324] Although this does not appear to be a major obstacle in most cases, the agreement may be rejected as a result of referendums in Switzerland and Iceland. If that should happen, then another governmental conference has to be called to renegotiate the treaty. Second, the European Parliament, which also has to approve the agreement, has expressed reservations.[325] These reservations have become even greater since the Maastricht summit failed to give the Parliament any significant new powers, and the members now fear that "outsiders" may have greater influence in shaping EC law, as they do. The Parliament tried to use the ECJ's disagreement with the treaty, as well as the subsequent compromise agreed upon by the court, to derail the entire treaty. The committee charged that the new solution was inadequate, and it reiterated the fact that the European parliament has been granted only a modest role in the decisionmaking process.[326]

The consequences of failing to ratify the agreement are not entirely clear. Although it might accelerate the formal application for membership by the other EFTA members, it could also delay the actual integration, since many of the delicate compromises in the EEA regarding membership would have to be renegotiated. Therefore, it is in the interest of all parties to ratify the agreement so that it can go into force in 1993, in conjunction with the establishment of the Single Market. If successfully concluded, the EEA agreement should be considered the first and decisive step toward rapid integration. Negotiations for full accession could start early in 1993 and be completed by 1995. The prospects for such a timetable are realistic. By creating the EEA, the Community and EFTA have already resolved approximately half the negotiating points that would arise during membership negotiations.[327]

Nonetheless, some difficult issues remain to be negotiated, including those concerning the agricultural sector, tax harmonization, and border controls. Compared with the countries of Central and Eastern Europe, however, the EFTA countries have minimal structural and institutional differences from the EC in their political-economic systems. Similarity should allow for a smooth and rapid integration into the Community that benefits all countries, while at the same time strengthening the Community's pan-European and global position.

Merely accepting the membership of the EFTA countries, however, will not be sufficient to strengthen the political and economic capacity of the Community. In fact, the Community will be weakened by this first round of enlargement unless it reforms its own decisionmaking apparatus by continuing the process of political and economic deepening. Just as with system transformation in the East, systemic reform of the West European market economy will succeed only if it follows a holistic approach.

ESTABLISHING THE EMU. Efforts to reform the Common Market are by no means new. As already mentioned, the challenge to develop a strategy of European unification has been complicated by the fact that the Community itself has been undergoing systemic reform. This challenge was most clearly reflected in the signing of the Single European Act in 1986, which provided a blueprint for the deep integration of the national economies of the member states. But the prospect of continued deepening in the economic realm calls for similar reforms both in the legal and administrative and in the social and psychological spheres of the emerging Single Market.[328]

The two intergovernmental conferences (IGCs) on political and economic and monetary union, which began in December 1990 and concluded a year later at the Maastricht summit, were convened to move the Community along these dimensions. The principal goal of the conference on Economic and Monetary Union (EMU) was to agree on an institutional and administrative structure and to establish some of the macroeconomic policy principles by which the Single Market would be governed. Such an agreement, in principle, was reached at Maastricht.

The most important conditions for membership set out in the Maastricht Treaty are (1) the budget deficit must be 3 percent of GDP or less one year before the commencement of EMU; (2) public debt cannot exceed 60 percent of GDP; and (3) inflation cannot exceed the average of the lowest three countries by 1.5 percent.[329] In practice, however, it seems unlikely that all current EC members will be able to join such a union even by 1999.[330] As table 6 shows, only France, Luxembourg, and Denmark qualified to join the EMU in the spring of 1992. Germany, while remaining just below the inflation average, would have had to make use of the exception rule in the Maastricht Treaty that allows for temporary divergence of the deficit ratio.[331] Britain also would have failed to qualify because its inflation rate of 5.9 percent was above the critical value, which at the time was 4.4 percent. Although both countries are likely to meet the necessary conditions (the British annualized inflation rate is currently 4.2 percent), others may have greater difficulty satisfying the criteria, and in some cases may do so only at the price of lower growth and higher unemployment.[332] Belgium, for example, would have to reduce the current government debt of 130 percent of GDP by more than 50 percent in the next six years. A similar situation exists in Ireland and the Netherlands, where government debt is 110 percent and 80 percent of GDP, respectively. If they meet the other conditions set out in the treaty, there is little doubt that the exemption clause will be used in these cases to justify their entry.

The situation in the southern tier is more complicated. Both Spain and Portugal are close to meeting the requirements regarding state indebtedness and the budget deficit. One way these countries plan to improve the indebtedness ratio is to sell off government-owned enterprises and, in the case of Portugal, state-owned banks.[333] Portugal, however, with an inflation rate of 11.4 percent during 1991, may have greater difficulty meeting the standard of price stability.[334] The situation in Italy is also difficult. Although there is a large privatization potential to reduce the government indebtedness, to reduce the current deficit and inflation rate would be a great political challenge. For Greece, the outlook is probably the bleakest, with the current inflation rate at 18 percent and a 1991 budget deficit of 17.5 percent. At the same time, as table 6 shows, the EFTA countries would have little difficulty meeting the macroeconomic indications. As a result, assuming the Maastricht Treaty will come into effect, the possibility of a "two-speed" Europe by the end of the century, with a group of core countries forming a European Monetary Union, can no longer be discounted. On the other hand, as table 6 indicates, most of the potential members from the EFTA countries would easily qualify for EMU membership, which would argue for their speedy inclusion into the Community and EMU.

IMPLICATIONS OF THE EMU. But even for those countries that will be able to join the monetary union, the implications of this decision, if fully implemented, will be profound. For the union to be operational and effective, member states will have to trade their capacity to manage their *national* economies for a share in the collective management of the *European* economy. The principal reasons that members are likely to agree to this arrangement is that, from an economic perspective, it represents a logical extension of the Single European Act.[335] Politically, the decision could be rationalized by the fact that in the area of monetary policy most states have already lost their policymaking autonomy and sovereignty to Germany. Economic and Monetary Union, therefore, would allow them to regain some of that autonomy by allowing them to share sovereignty in the newly created European Central Bank.

But the implications of the Maastricht decision reach far beyond the issue of monetary policy, especially in the fiscal domain. For the union to be credible and effective, states will also have to lose much of their individual capacity to influence the level of employment in their economies. More specifically, macroeconomic intervention geared to the reduction of unemployment will have to be decided upon at the European level. This presupposes a common "European position" on the necessity, purpose, effectiveness, and timing of such interventions before an agreement can be fully implemented. Taking the discongruent political business cycles in EC member states into account, the harmonization of a position on macroeconomic intervention may be difficult to achieve. In addition, the escape clause negotiated by Britain has opened the possibility for all countries to renege on their commitment, even though Britain is likely to be the only country to use this option. This escape clause has given the agreement a provisional flavor.[336] Both examples indicate that the real challenge of implementing the agreement is much greater than perceived today, and it penetrates deeply into the politics of the individual member states and the emerging European market economy as a whole.

The holistic approach can illuminate these complex dynamics of European integration and point to some of the policy steps that are necessary to succeed in the continued deepening of the Community. The Community and its member states have reached such a high degree of integration largely because the implications of specific reform steps are often considered in isolation, while the close interdependence of all three dimensions of a market economy is neglected. Thus the full implications of systemic reform are not always immediately apparent. According to the holistic concept, a decision to move forward with systemic reform in one particular domain of a market economy is likely to require systemic adjustments in its other constituent elements. For the European Community, economic integration at one particular level of the economy should lead to pressures for integration at other levels in the economic realm, as well as in other dimensions of the emerging European market economy. Indeed, from a holistic perspective these systemic reforms are considered a necessary condition, a logical extension designed to support initial adjustments toward economic integration.

EC policymakers, member states, and domestic interest groups advocating the initial integrative steps are likely to support these additional reforms. This follows from the holistic argument that unless systemic reform in one sphere

Table 6. Convergence Situation of Potential EMU Members
Percent unless otherwise specified

Country	Inflation rate[a] 1991	Inflation rate[a] January 1992	Budget deficit as percent of GDP[b] 1991	Budget deficit as percent of GDP[b] 1992	Debt as percent of GDP 1991	Debt as percent of GDP 1992	Unemployment, 1991
Convergence criteria[c]	4.4		-3.0	-3.0	60.0	60.0	. . .
Denmark	2.4	2.1	-1.7	-1.5	66.7	65.8	9.5
France	3.1	2.9	-1.9	-1.6	47.2	47.5	9.5
Ireland	3.2	3.6[d]	-4.1	-4.1	109.3	106.7	16.8
Luxembourg	3.2	2.9	1.9	2.0	6.9	6.4	1.6
Belgium	3.2	2.3	-6.3	-6.2	129.4	129.6	8.6
Germany[e]	3.5	4.0	-3.9	-4.6	41.4	43.5	4.6
Netherlands	3.9	4.1	-4.4	-4.1	78.4	79.5	7.2
United Kingdom	5.9	4.2	-2.3	-4.5	36.7	38.4	8.4
Spain	5.9	5.9	-4.4	-4.5	45.6	46.4	15.8
Italy	6.4	6.1	-10.8	-9.9	101.2	103.9	9.4
Portugal	11.4	8.6	-6.3	-5.5	64.7	62.7	4.0
Greece	18.9	18.1	-17.5	-13.7	96.4	99.0	8.8
Number meeting criteria	7	5	4	3	5	5	. . .

Potential EC members
(to join before 1997)

Austria	3.3	3.9	−2.2	−1.5	54.4	53.5	5.8
Norway	3.4	2.4	−1.0	−0.5	43.8	45.3	5.5
Finland	4.1	2.9	−3.6	−7.0	18.6	25.5	13.5f
Switzerland	5.9	4.9	−1.5	−1.9	27.6	28.2	1.3
Sweden	9.3	5.3	−0.3	−1.5	44.8	45.8	2.7
Number meeting criteria	3	3	4	4	5	5	. . .

Sources: From a presentation on June 1, 1992, in Washington, D.C., with Horst Tietmeyer and Transatlantic Futures, and our own calculations. For unemployment figures the source is the Commission of the European Communities, "European Community," no. 50 (December 1991), p. 216. The unemployment figure for Austria is from the Austrian Embassy Press Information Office (Mr. Pacher); the figure for Finland is from the Finnish Embassy Press Attache (Mr. Lansi Turo); the figure for Norway is from the Norwegian Embassy Press Cultural Section (Ms. Anne Bjellend); the figure for Sweden is from the Swedish Embassy Labor Counselor's Office (Ms. Brita Cromquist); the figure for Switzerland is from the Swiss Embassy Commercial Section (Mr. Hauser).

a. Annual average.

b. Public sector borrowing requirement (general government).

c. For inflation rate: average of three best rates plus 1.5 points. For budget deficit: public sector budget deficit not exceeding 3 percent of GDP. For debt: total public sector debt not exceeding 60 percent of GDP.

d. Inflation in Ireland is for the fourth quarter 1991.

e. Inflation is only for West Germany, and the budget deficit excludes off-budget items and special budgets; unemployment figure is for West Germany only.

f. The unemployment figure for Finland is as of January 21, 1992. Unemployment in Finland had doubled from the same time in the previous year because of a virtual collapse of trade with the former Soviet Union. Finnish exports to the former Soviet Union were primarily labor intensive, and were essentially protected industries because of the longer-term trade agreements with the former Soviet Union. Once that trade ended, these industries were forced to compete in global export markets.

or level is accompanied by similar adjustments in other spheres and levels, initial reform measures will stall and possibly even be reversed, with substantial economic and political costs to society as a whole. Thus, by targeting those narrow areas in which systemic reform can be initiated without considerable political resistance, policymakers can set in motion a process that is more far-reaching than initially perceived.

The European Commission and other forces supporting European integration have consistently made use of such a strategy. The dynamics of European integration during the 1980s and early 1990s support this perspective. With the signing of the Single European Act, member states committed themselves to partial systemic reform. They pledged to integrate their market economies primarily at the microeconomic level, and to include reforms in the legal and administrative spheres. Also, it took only a few years before advocates of closer European union proposed and found increasing support for closer macroeconomic integration. A complete economic and monetary union, once considered a fiction, now seemed an almost logical and even a necessary extension of the "1992" program, and it received support among most member states.[337]

This is not to say that different countries and their domestic constituents had different interests in this process. Rather, the ensuing debate was not over whether the Single Market should be governed by a common macroeconomic policy but about what principles such a policy should follow, and how these principles should be implemented. The Maastricht agreement has resolved that problem to some degree. Nevertheless, many obstacles to economic and monetary union have not been overcome with the Maastricht agreement. In essence, they have been postponed. Moreover, new problems resulting from conflicting political, economic, and social interests are likely to emerge in the future. In particular, the implications of European macroeconomic management for individual countries is likely to create political obstacles to economic deepening, or to increase the pressure for changing the conditions that were set at Maastricht. This concern has been expressed most strongly by the Bundesbank's Central Bank Council. According to the council, "The Maastricht decisions do not yet reveal an agreement on the future structure of the envisaged political union and on the required parallelism with monetary union. Future developments in the field of the political union will be of key importance for the permanent success of the monetary union."[338] Note that political union, in this instance, refers to centralized fiscal control rather than matters of joint foreign or security policies.

POLITICAL, SOCIAL, AND PSYCHOLOGICAL ISSUES. The Commission's new five-year budgetary plan is one area in which the political ramifications of the Maastricht Treaty have been in the foreground, almost since the signing. This plan has pitted the more prosperous members of the Community against the poorer partners of Greece, Ireland, Portugal, and Spain. The plan has also been labeled the Delors II package, in reference to the previous five-year budget plan (Delors I), which covered the years 1987 to 1992. The Delors I plan provided the financial means to implement the Single Market program, to be completed in early 1992. The Delors II plan, also referred to as the Bill for Maastricht, calls for an increase of ECU 21 billion (about US$27.5), or 31.5 percent in spending over the next five years (table 7). This would increase the Community's resource ceiling from 1.2 percent to 1.37 percent of its combined GNP.[339] Half of this increase (ECU 10.7 billion) would go to structural operations, which include the newly created cohesion fund that will help those countries enter the EMU at the end of the decade.[340] Germany remains the Community's largest net contributor, with DM 11.7 billion and DM 19 billion in 1990 and 1991, respectively. Germany, which has experienced financial strains as a result of unification and its aid commitments to Central and Eastern Europe and the former Soviet Union, has rejected the initial budget proposal.[341] Other countries—including Belgium, Britain, France, Italy, and the Netherlands—have also expressed reservations, which point in particular to the parallel demand of the Maastricht Treaty to shrink their public debt.[342] The conflict that has erupted over this issue will test the members' political will to move ahead with the Maastricht agenda and to initiate the negotiations over enlargement, which the poorer members have made conditional on the conclusion of the Maastricht agreement.[343]

The social and psychological aspects of European integration will also become obstacles to deeper economic integration. The intergovernmental conference on political union aimed to secure some specific advances in these areas of systemic reform. Its outcome, however, did not fully live up to that goal. In the field of social policy most members agreed to establish a European Social Charter. The charter would assure the population in the member states that further integration would not lead to competition among different national social policy networks, eroding long-established labor market principles and rights of individual workers. Of particular importance is the introduction of majority voting in some areas of social policy. But Britain's refusal to join the agreement forced the other eleven member states to conclude a separate agreement.[344] This procedure is unique, and it raises questions about the future

Table 7. European Community Budgets, 1987, 1992, 1997[a]
Amounts in billions of 1992 ECUs and percent of total unless otherwise specified

Commitment appropriations	1987		1992		1997	
	Amount	Percent	Amount	Percent	Amount	Percent
1. Common agricultural policy	32.7	64.1	35.3	53.1	39.6	45.3
2. Structural operations (including the cohesion fund)	9.1	17.8	18.6	28.0	29.3	33.5
3. Internal policies (other than structural operations)	1.9	3.7	4.0	6.0	6.9	7.9
4. External action	1.4	2.7	3.6	5.4	6.3	7.2
5. Administrative expenditure (and repayments)	5.9	11.6	4.0	6.0	4.0	4.6
6. Reserves	0.0	0.0	1.0	1.5	1.4	1.6
Total	51.0	100	66.5	100	87.5	100
Payment appropriations required	49.4	...	63.2	...	83.2	...
As percent of GNP	...	1.05	...	1.15	...	1.34
Own resources ceiling as percent of GNP	...	None[b]	...	1.20	...	1.37

Sources: Commission of the European Communities, *From the Single Act to Maastricht and Beyond: The Means to Match our Ambitions*, COM(92) 2000 (Brussels, 1992).
a. Average annual GNP growth: 1987-92 (actual) 3.1%; 1992-97 (projected) 2.5%.
b. Except VAT - 1.40.

of a common European legal space. Future policy will clarify to what degree the British position on the social charter was more the result of internal pressures in the Conservative party than genuine opposition to the concept of a social charter. In this context it is interesting to note that even British employers have cast some doubt on the value of remaining outside the social charter.[345]

In the psychological domain, the decision to establish a "Citizenship of the Union" is an important step toward generating both higher awareness and a better understanding, at *all* levels of society, of what European integration is about.[346] Among other things, it confers the right on every citizen of the member states to vote, and to stand as a candidate at municipal elections in the member state in which he or she resides. The idea of European citizenship was based on the belated recognition that by the early 1990s European economic integration had reached a point where the general public and public decisionmaking procedures could no longer be excluded from the integration process itself. Whereas the lack of awareness and the resultant lack of interest in European integration by many Europeans may have helped to overcome earlier obstacles to integration, the continued lack of public interest and involvement now works to the detriment of the Community and its goals.

European citizenship, however, must not only generate greater interest in Europe itself; it must also be accompanied by the right to translate those interests into policy decisions. To ensure European popular representation, another goal of the conference on political union was to strengthen the legislative power of the European Parliament at the expense of the Council of Ministers, where most of the legislative power is currently located. In this respect Maastricht failed, for the European Parliament continues to be excluded from many central decisionmaking areas. Its role is merely to issue positions and to call for hearings.[347] Real co-decisionmaking remains limited and is a complicated and lengthy process.[348] The European Parliament's control over the appointments to the Commission remains restricted and now merely consists of a vote of approval.[349]

The various national structures and means of aggregating and representing interest, including an effective legislature, must be replaced or at least complemented by European ones. If they are not, the Community will lack the political support and social cohesion to proceed with further economic deepening. The European Parliament gave its approval to the Maastricht agreement in order to ensure continued progress on the road to European integration.[350] But it also sharply criticized the failure to reduce the democratic deficit.[351] As a sign of its dissatisfaction, the Parliament presented a long list of improvements.[352] Although the Parliament was not in a position to veto the Maastricht agreement, it has indicated that it is likely to reject the ratification of any new international treaty. In particular, it will reject the incorporation of new members unless some of its concerns are addressed in a new intergovernmental conference.[353]

Most government leaders hailed the Maastricht summit as a resounding success, and some went so far as to describe its outcome as an "irreversible process towards a European Union."[354] Implicitly, such a statement relies on the holistic approach to systemic reform, for it stresses the economic and political costs that each country and the Community as a whole would incur if the process came to a halt or was even reversed. But European integration is not some inevitable, fully determined process. Just as with system transformation in Central and Eastern Europe, systemic reform in the Community is unstable during the transition phase and is vulnerable to political forces trying to undermine it. These forces have found their expression in the recent success of nationalist, mostly right-wing movements and political parties in member states of the European Community. They have taken a clear anti-European position. Their popularity and success will continue to rise if European citizens are not given the right to participate in the decisions that shape political, economic, and social union. Europeans will reject deeper economic integration unless they believe they can exchange their social contract at the national level for a European social contract, especially during difficult economic times as currently prevail in many EC member countries. For the European market economy to act as the principal mode of social organization, people have to understand how the Community works, they have to identify with it, and they have to benefit from it. Only then can the market economy have the integrating force that it has at the national level.

To make such a judgment, however, the European public must also gain a better understanding of what European integration is about. The outcome of the Danish referendum on June 2, 1992, shows that efforts by policymakers to address the social and psychological dimension of European integration at the Maastricht summit were *too little* and came *too late*. The unfavorable vote in the referendum defied an 84 percent majority in the Danish Parliament; the major industrial associations that favored the treaty; the unions that campaigned that a No vote would mean more unemployment, falling investment, and higher interest rates; and the powerful agricultural lobby that feared Denmark's exclusion from the Common Agricultural Policy (CAP). CAP has brought economic benefits to Denmark, making it a big agricultural exporter to third countries. As such, the Danish vote was at least as much a reflection of the individuals' rejection of the political elite out of protest, confusion, and insecurity, as it was a collective decision against the goals of European integration. This points to the importance of the social and psychological dimension of European integration and supports the holistic approach to systemic reform. In the first instance, therefore, the compromise of Maastricht failed because its architects disregarded the multidimensional and multilayered nature of systemic reform. European economic integration will advance only as far as legal and administrative, and social and psychological, aspects of integration will support it by advancing as well.

Even before the Danish referendum, the debate on the implications of Maastricht in other European countries indicated that insufficient attention to the social and psychological aspects of European unification was not just a Danish problem but a European one. The German public's sudden weariness regarding the agreement on economic and monetary union points to fact that German popular support for closer European integration does not run very deep. It can easily be shaken in a country usually considered among the most supportive of European integration. Germans are particularly concerned about the future of the deutsche mark, which, despite the difficulties encountered during the process of German unification, has remained the symbol of German economic strength and political power.[355]

Furthermore, the budgetary implications of the Maastricht agreement for Germany, which is by far the largest net contributor in the Community, may be too overwhelming. The country has strained its resources to the limit as a result of unification and in its commitment to support system transformation in Central and Eastern Europe and the CIS states.[356] The political backlash against the costs of German unification, most vividly expressed in the strikes during the spring of 1992, could easily repeat itself during the debate over the cost of European unification.[357]

Seen from the holistic perspective, the debate about the benefits *and* costs of European integration that has erupted in many member states is beneficial for the process of European integration, whatever the particular concern in each individual country.[359] If successful, the debate will eliminate many of the suspicions and insecurities among Europe's citizens, and it will clarify the purpose, scope, and limits of European union. It will also not only force all political parties to clearly define their position, but will require those political forces that oppose European integration to develop realistic alternative scenarios—scenarios that can deal with the challenges emanating from Central and Eastern Europe and the former Soviet Union as well as with the process of global economic integration. To simply suggest that Europe could return to a nineteenth-century system based on interstate rivalry is not only misleading but dangerous, given the challenges the continent and the world will face in the years to come.[360]

The countries that continue to support European integration in the wake of such a debate can thus rely on the popular support of the majority of their citizens and can consider it a mandate to implement the decisions taken at Maastricht. The governments that decide not to ratify the treaty and that have followed democratic principles should be respected by other Community members. Their constituents will have carefully considered the potential costs and benefits of the treaty, including the country's future relationship to the union itself.[361] Obviously, this raises a difficult question about the future structure of Europe, (briefly discussed below). But this cannot deflect from the fact that in the long run deeper political and economic integration under democratic principles is not sustainable without broad social support.

FOREIGN AND SECURITY POLICY. This broad social support will also be required to develop a common European foreign and security policy, most often referred to when explaining the negative outcome of the Danish referendum. Pressure for systemic reform in this area has heightened over the past three years. In fact, the issue of a common foreign and security policy was pushed to the top of the agenda of the conference on political union, once it became clear that the United States was either unable or unwilling to take on a leadership role in the system transformation of Eastern Europe. The pressure on the Community to take on such a role was heightened by the Yugoslav civil war and by the possibility of similar crises elsewhere in Central and Eastern Europe and the former Soviet Union, as large-scale immigration from Central and Eastern Europe would almost certainly encourage nationalist retrenchment.

In its initial phase, the Community's less than successful intervention in the Yugoslav civil war was understandable, given its lack of institutional and technical mechanisms to deal with such crises. But while the EC's handling of the Yugoslav crisis can be considered a foreign policy failure, it does not mean there is no EC foreign policy, nor does it mean that EC foreign policy has failed to meet other challenges in Central and Eastern Europe and the Soviet Union. In response to the developments in Central and Eastern Europe and the former Soviet Union, member states have taken the unprecedented step of establishing common political criteria or standards that states seeking associate status must meet. Common EC criteria have also been established for the recognition of newly independent states in the former Soviet Union. And despite some of their deficiencies, the association agreements are a clear indication of the willingness of member states (including Denmark) to cooperate closely in matters of foreign and security policy.

Nevertheless, the civil war in the former Yugoslavia has demonstrated that the current institutional design and practice of foreign policy formation in Europe is inadequate to meet the more serious challenges posed by system transformation in Central and Eastern Europe and the Soviet Union. More specifically, it has pointed to the weakness of the concept of European political cooperation, which, in requiring that decisions be based on unanimity, encourages the dominance of national interests and leads to decisions based on the lowest common denominator. The same weakness of the unanimity principle was exposed by the negotiations over the association agreements, which were dominated by narrow national economic interests rather than guided by an overall strategy to unify the now economically and socially divided Europe.

To some, the Maastricht summit also fell short of its original goal to establish a framework for a common foreign and security policy. Policy issues related to the CSCE-process, arms control and disarmament, nuclear nonproliferation, and economic aspects of security, including export controls, will become subject to a procedure that may lead to decisions based on a qualified majority.[362] But there is a question of whether the new procedure is more likely to block common action than to encourage it.[363] Although the member countries demonstrated their willingness to cooperate closely in these matters, each member state can still block common action, an outcome that has been openly criticized by the Commission president Jacques Delors.[364]

At the same time, the treaty has opened the possibility of creating a European Community defense organization embedded in the Western European Union (WEU): "The Union requests the Western European Union (WEU), which is an integral part of the development of the Union, to elaborate and implement decisions and actions of the Union which have defence implications." This clause creates a strong institutional link to the Community "which might in time lead to a common defence." The treaty also invites "states which are members of the European Union . . . to accede to the WEU . . . or to become observers if they so wish." Furthermore, "other European Members of NATO are invited to become associate members of the WEU in a way that will give them the possibility of participating fully in the activities of WEU."[365] The two previous statements open the possibility of a successively expanding future European defense that includes Central and Eastern Europe and Turkey. The intergovernmental conference planned for 1996 has been asked to address the possibility of further changes in this arrangement.

The commitment by the European Union to having a common foreign and security policy, with some limited provision for majority voting, turned out to be one of the principal explanations for the outcome of the Danish referendum.[366] The debate that revolved around Denmark's independence on issues of foreign and security policies was fueled by a parallel discussion over Danish membership in the WEU.[367] Denmark, currently not a member of the WEU, wants to preserve the Community's civilian image. But the Maastricht declaration of its nine members indicating their desire to develop the WEU into the defense component of the European Union strengthened Danish suspicions, and ultimately its resistance to transferring more power to Brussels.

THE NEED FOR CHANGE. This question of how much policymaking authority should be transferred to Community institutions is one of the most politically sensitive issues in the debate over systemic reform. But so far it has been by and large avoided by the member states. Policymakers tend to refer to the principle of *subsidiarity* as a solution to this problem. The Maastricht agreement has attached increased importance to the concept of subsidiarity by including it under the basic principles of the treaty. According to Article 3b of the Principles, "In areas which do not fall within its exclusive competence, the Community shall take action, in accordance with the principle of subsidiarity, only if and in so far as the objectives of the proposed action cannot be sufficiently achieved by the Member States and can therefore, by reason of scale or effects of the proposed action, be better achieved by the Community."[368]

Although this principle sounds convincing in theory, it does not work in practice. As the Danish referendum shows, national constituencies may differ on the question of what should or should not be solved at the domestic level.

Determining under what circumstances Community action should override the principle of subsidiarity is thus not a technical matter but a highly political question that often depends on domestic political circumstances and is sometimes influenced by historical legacies. In addition, what action the Community can initiate under the principle of subsidiarity is also open to interpretation, since such action "shall not go beyond what is necessary to achieve the objectives of this treaty."[369] These objectives, however, are defined in such a broad manner that they do not provide any clear guideline on policy competence.[370]

This is not the first time that a signatory to the Maastricht Treaty has refused to transfer sovereignty in a particular policy domain to the institutions of the Community. The unwillingness of Britain to join its EC partners in including a European social charter in the treaty is in many ways a predecessor to the Danish referendum. The difference, however, is that the British concern was raised before the conclusion of the treaty, and a compromise could be worked out by appending the Agreement on Social Policy. In contemplating the implications of the Danish referendum, it became apparent that this "solution" cannot be used as a guideline for future conflicts resulting from the Maastricht Treaty. In legal terms the agreement is an amendment to the Treaty of Rome, which, according to Article 236, requires unanimous consent by all member states. But if the treaty is opened for renegotiation, it will soon be reduced to a series of bilateral and multilateral protocols reflecting the preferences of individual EC members.

The Danish referendum points to the urgent need for an operational definition of subsidiarity and for a set of criteria that would trigger its application. In developing such criteria, governments must take advantage of the current debate and engage their constituents in a discussion that weighs the potential costs and benefits of further integration or disintegration. In doing so, however, they must consider not only the economic aspects of European integration but also the legal and administrative and the political implications of continued integration, in particular the required systemic reforms.

Broadly speaking, it is necessary to distinguish between two sets of systemic reforms: structural and institutional, and functional and operational. As regards structural and institutional reform, the policy outcomes of both IGCs showed that European integration has reached the stage where continued progress on the basis of intergovernmental negotiations is increasingly limited, and the results are vague and open to different interpretations. Even though a compromise was reached, the intergovernmental nature of the ratification process, which requires unanimity, allowed 0.65 percent (50.7 percent of the Danish electorate) of eligible voters in the European Community to block the treaty in its present form (see table A-16 for a geographic distribution of the EC electorate).

To serve the public good, any political decisionmaking authority will *have* to take policy steps that some of its constituents oppose. If member states continue to structure the Community's policymaking process around the principle of unanimity, they defy this most basic axiom of politics and undermine the Community's capacity to serve the European public good. This result cannot be in any of the members' interest.

The principle of unanimity has consistently distorted the Community's policy agenda and weakened its domestic (European) and global policy output. If the Commission knows in advance that a member will make use of its veto right, the issue in question will not be put on the agenda, even though that issue may be of great importance.[371] Those issues that do get on the agenda subsequently undergo a long bargaining process, in the course of which the unanimity requirement can bias the policy output in several ways. It may be necessary to omit some aspects of a policy measure over which no agreement can be found. This will alter the original policy mandate and postpone its full implementation. Or it may be necessary to permit individual countries not to join the agreement or to allow them to opt out at a later date, as was the case at the Maastricht summit. Rather than exclude some aspects of a policy measure or allow a country to choose the option of exit, member countries may negotiate "away" any obstacles to a unanimous agreement, so that all member countries eventually can agree. Even though unanimity was adhered to in all of the examples mentioned, the original objective of the policy has been distorted in substance, significance, and participation.

If the Community is to develop into an efficient and effective center of decisionmaking that promotes the common good of its members and its European interests at home *and* abroad, it has to increase its collective and cooperative decisionmaking power in two ways. First, member states have to relinquish their veto power in more policy areas. Qualified majority voting must become the principal decisionmaking mechanism in the Council of Ministers.[372] Furthermore, the Council of Ministers should delegate some of its executive power to the Commission to strengthen the Commission's ability to initiate policy. The Commission should also be given the power to make policy decisions and subsequently implement them.

One could conceive of the following division of labor between the Council and the Commission: having decided on the general purpose and direction of a policy, and having set the principal parameters in which such a policy can be pursued, the Council could refer the matter to the Commission. The Commission would then be empowered to work out the technical details of policy design and to subsequently implement it. Transferring a substantial amount of power from the Council to the Commission would, however, increase the democratic deficit of the Community and reduce the meaning of European citizenship even further. Thus the shift in the balance of power toward the Commission *must* be matched by a substantial strengthening of parliamentary control. The European Parliament must receive full legislative powers in the European policymaking process, which so far had been monopolized by the Council of Ministers. And to ensure greater accountability of the Commission to the European electorate, the Parliament must also have direct influence over the appointment of the president and the commissioners.

Structural and institutional reform alone, however, will not suffice. To enable the Community to meet the challenge, both at home and abroad, its functional and operational capacity must be enhanced as well. Two steps need to be taken to achieve such institutional enhancement. First, in those policy areas over which the Community currently has partial authority, jurisdiction should be absolute, and additional policy areas should come under EC jurisdiction. Unless this transfer of autonomy takes place, the institutional reform is of little real significance. Second, the Community can become fully operational in these policy areas only if it has control over the financial resources that national budgets have allocated to them. This requires a transfer of budgetary and taxing authority in these areas from the national to the European level. In the medium term these reform efforts will ensure that the Community can transform the decisionmaking at Maastricht into practical policy and establish a more efficient, effective, *and* democratic decisionmaking process.

Long Term: The Second Phase of Deepening and Broadening

In the long term, further consideration of systemic reform is required. Until the fall of 1989 the Community's policymaking agenda was dominated by the goal of continued deepening among member states and possible EC enlargement by some EFTA states. As argued above, this agenda should not change; rather, it should be intensified. Although the goal of West European integration used to be considered an end in itself, that is no longer true. In the long term, systemic reform in the Community must be geared toward the new policy goal, namely the unification of Europe with the EC at its core.

If the EFTA countries join the European Community by the second half of the 1990s and Central and Eastern Europe join, even though full integration may be more than a decade away, the number of members will rise from the current twelve to twenty, and possibly to thirty countries. If the Community wants to meet this challenge of increased membership and remain *the* political and economic nucleus of the new Europe, thereby avoiding "the risk of being geographically marginalized and to become somewhat like an enlarged Benelux,"[373] it must undergo even greater systemic reforms to cope with the doubling of its membership.

Even if the systemic reforms suggested here are implemented, decisionmaking within a Community of more than fifteen members, anticipated sometime after 1995, will most likely remain slow and difficult. In some cases it may even get worse. For example, a second round of enlargement will increase the number of commissioners and their staff to levels that would render the Commission unwieldy and inefficient. If the Community is broadened further, member states must consider ways to keep the number at present levels, perhaps by reducing the number of commissioners for large members from two to one. Countries below a certain population size could form groups that would share a commissioner whose nationality rotates. This is just one of many possible ways to consolidate the Commission as the number of members increases. Similarly, with twenty or more members the European Parliament would be an institution so large that it would become inoperable under the current distributional key. A new formula for allocating European members of Parliament has to be found. The greatest challenge to policymakers will be to ensure that smaller countries will continue to be adequately represented in the new institutional design.

The debate in the Community on how to cope with its eventual enlargement has only just begun. To this end, members must demonstrate their willingness to take on the challenge of enlargement by calling for a new intergovernmental conference to be concluded by the end of 1995—when some or all EFTA countries may join the Community, and Central and East European countries will begin to submit their applications. The purpose of this conference would be to develop and agree on a European architecture that can accommodate the realities of the New Europe. In some respects, the conference would be a continuation of the last two ICGs, which focused on further deepening the Community. This time, however, the emphasis would be on European unification, particularly the stepwise integration of Central and Eastern Europe into the Community, as outlined earlier.

Although most countries are open to discussing a new European architecture, not all of them are likely to subscribe to the strategy outlined above. Britain, which currently holds the EC presidency, and Denmark, which should take on the presidency in January 1993, both support broadening the Community, not the least because they hope that it will prevent other countries from deepening the EC. As the debate over the Danish referendum has shown, however, both countries consider further deepening an unacceptable threat to their nation's sovereignty. A conference to achieve both goals is thus unlikely to be sponsored by Britain or Denmark.[374]

But the argument that further deepening compromises a country's sovereignty is not well founded, and it defies one of the most basic principles of the Community: *sovereignty is divisible.* Even if the Community receives complete jurisdiction in some policy areas, as suggested here, and takes on the function of a federal state, this does not imply that the member states cannot retain their autonomy in other areas.[375] In fact, the concept of "L'Europe des regions" —which has gained in popularity in recent years and has gained quasi-institutional standing with the formation of the Committee of the Regions at the Maastricht summit— suggests that in some cases sovereignty may actually be devolved to lower levels of social organization than the nation-state in a more deeply integrated Europe.[376] In this context, it is interesting to note that the British government strongly opposes any move toward the further independence of Scotland within the European Community.[377] That raises the question whether the British government's campaign against Brussels is based on a genuine belief in the decentralization of political decisionmaking, or whether this belief stops at the level of the nation-state and thus serves to solidify and protect the British government's own power. The divisibility of sovereignty is also the analytical foundation of the concept of subsidiarity, which relies on the presence of multiple layers of autonomy. Policy matters, therefore, must urgently move forward by enhancing the institutional role of the committee of the regions.

Sovereignty is defined as "freedom from external control," which implies that the nation-state does not have a monopoly on this concept.[378] On the contrary, increasing interdependence of national economies has left the nation-state increasingly incapable of providing this freedom from external control. Seen from this perspective, European integration in some policy areas does not imply a loss of control. Rather, it allows countries to regain some of the freedom they lost as a result of interdependence in the European and international economy. In the European context, EC member states will regain some control over the conduct of monetary policy, which over the past decade had been dominated by Germany. On a global scale, where an ever-increasing number of important economic and political decisions are being taken, no single European country, not even a unified Germany, could equal the United States or Japan. By pooling their sovereignty, therefore, EC members will be able to collectively preserve some of the effective control they have lost individually. It is this projection of external strength that will allow for greater diversity within the Community.

How many countries will continue to subscribe to the notion that sovereignty is divisible and press ahead with deeper integration is an open question, but it is almost certain that countries will differ. One response to the possibility that some countries will prefer a greater degree of integration than others in a specific policy domain, and one that has gained renewed momentum in light of the Danish referendum, is the concept of "L'Europe à deux vitesses" or "Europe à la carte."

Europe à la carte would allow countries to choose from a menu that offers differential degrees of integration within various policy areas. Clearly, this appears to be an attractive policy option because it resolves one of the most divisive policy issues in the Community. In fact, I have already alluded to the concept of Europe à la carte twice in this discussion, when I advocated the notion of affiliate membership by Central and East European countries, and when I suggested that not all current EC members may be able to join the EMU by January 1, 1999. In both cases, however, this choice of menu would be a transitory stage. In the case of Central and Eastern Europe, affiliate members would eventually join the EC. In the case of EMU, it would make little sense to allocate an additional ECU 10.7 billion to the structural and cohesion funds if it were not for the purpose of facilitating the eventual EMU membership of all members. Thus, as long as L'Europe à la carte is understood as a dynamic concept, in which the different menus are considered transitory, it may well be an ingenious response to the multiple challenges that Europe faces, particularly the dual pressure for broadening and deepening.

To consider the concept a lasting structure, however, would contradict a holistic approach to European integration, as it permanently divorces economic from legal and administrative and from social and psychological integration. This has been understood by the EFTA countries, which have recognized that their status not only is untenable in the long run but may even be disadvantageous. They have responded by agreeing to form the EEA and are pressing ahead with their drive toward full membership. Ironically, now that these countries are applying for membership, one option that was suggested for Denmark in response to the referendum was to return to an EEA status.

III. CONCLUSION AND EPILOGUE

10. Conclusion

Today the European Community and its members again face the fundamental question whether they will be able to overcome the divisive system of European interstate rivalry and pool their sovereignty in an increasingly global economy. There is clearly no blueprint for the formation of the new European political economy. Indeed, one reason the European Community has been so successful in the past is that it has not developed a fixed master plan geared toward one single and ultimate goal. Given the cultural, ethnic, and linguistic diversity of the European continent, and the powerful political and economic interests that would feel threatened by some grand European design, a scheme that would finalize any future structure of the Community would be doomed to failure. At the same time, the challenges brought forth by the end of the Cold War require at least a structural and well-balanced response.

This discussion has outlined some of the policy parameters that should guide a European response to these challenges. First, it is important to recognize that both Eastern *and* Western Europe will have to adjust if Europe is to become politically and economically integrated, with the Community at its core. It is possible to examine the nature and extent of these changes using a holistic concept of a market economy. There is no doubt that the market economy is the primary integrating mechanism that will shape the new European political economy. It is the principal form of social organization that Central and Eastern Europe are aspiring to, and that Western Europe derives much of its prosperity from. However, to fully understand the complexity of the changes required, one must apply a holistic definition of the market economy.

This approach has important policy implications. It conditions policy choices not only along the lines of economic rationality but also along the lines of political and social rationality. The holistic approach has revealed the complexity of creating a market economy in Central and Eastern Europe and of reforming the West European market economy. It forces policymakers to evaluate their policy choices not just for their economic feasibility but also for their political and social sustainability. It exposes the risks of developing strategies of system transformation based strictly on economic rationality. The holistic perspective applied in this analysis has revealed that systemic reform in Western Europe also faces numerous obstacles, and that it requires institutional realignment in the European Community that may be difficult to achieve without the strong support of the member states.

The challenge facing the societies of Central and Eastern Europe is unprecedented. At present, the benefits of transformation continue to outweigh the costs, but the margin has narrowed considerably since the spring of 1991. If the transformation were to break down, it is unlikely that Central and Eastern Europe would return to the status quo ante, but the outcome would most likely destabilize the entire region and precipitate crises that would threaten the stability of the continent, including the cohesion of the European Community.[379] As a result, the Community has been propelled into a powerful but precarious position. To avoid regressing to the traditional system of balance of power, it will have to form the core of the new European political economy. As such, the Community, particularly its member states, bear a considerable responsibility for the success or failure of establishing democracy and a market economy in Central and Eastern Europe. Judging from the response to date, the Community and its members, and for that matter all Western nations, have yet to publicly acknowledge the enormous magnitude of the challenge, as well as the potential implications for both East and West of a failure of system transformation.

It is generally agreed that the German government erred politically by initially concealing the actual resource transfers necessary to prevent a collapse of the social and political condition in the former German Democratic Republic.[380] The Community and the member countries should not repeat that mistake by creating the illusion that system transformation will not require considerable sacrifices by the West. Only then will the Community be able to generate the necessary political support for resource transfers to Central and Eastern Europe as well as for the institutional reform of its own market economy, which remains the foundation of a new European political economy.

It is difficult to fully comprehend the momentous change that individual countries and the international system have undergone over the last three years—and the change they will continue to experience. Thus the issues discussed in this paper constitute only the "first round" effects, with many more to follow. In responding to this change and the challenges that emanate from it, the debate and subsequent policy response have, for the most part, focused on how to modify existing institutions, sometimes building new ones, to cope with the rapidly changing international environment. Indeed, these institutions and their member countries often find themselves competing with one another when addressing the challenge of system transformation. The lack of cooperation and coordination among them and the mounting inefficiencies have begun undermining the entire effort.

But the goals and policy outputs of institutions, though important and powerful in their own right, should do little more than reflect the ideas, norms, and principles of their members. Thus, before we can adjust the institutions and develop new ones, we have to adjust our own thinking and concepts on how to deal with this change. Only then can we determine which institutions are best suited, and when and for what purpose new institutions are required. Institutions should not determine our policy response; they should execute them.

As stated at the beginning of the paper, one central concept that has influenced much of the thinking and policy in East-West relations over the past decades is continuity. Indeed, it has conditioned many of the West's policy responses to the end of the Cold War by structuring these responses around "points of stability," if not the status quo. Such a response is costly and could even be risky. It overlooks the fact that the status quo no longer exists and that under the present circumstances "points of stability" can be no more than temporary phenomena, sooner or later undermining whatever has been built around them.

The reality is that change, and not continuity, will dominate political and economic relations among states and the international system for many years to come. Thus the challenge to policymakers is not to preserve continuity but to induce change. As a result, change should become the guiding principle for policymaking. Accepting change as a given and making it the basis of policy will allow policymakers to control and guide it, turning it into an important source of stability.

11. Epilogue

As with the Danish vote, the outcome of the French referendum (held September 20, 1992) confirmed that the ambivalence and insecurity about the path and speed of European integration is more widespread and deeply rooted than most observers imagined. The French vote—only marginally in favor of the Maastricht Treaty—reinforces the proposition that the formation of a European market economy goes beyond the economic sphere and can be understood only by adopting a holistic approach to integration that recognizes the different dimensions and multiple levels of a modern market economy.

The turbulence in European currency markets following the French referendum has led to the withdrawal of both the British pound and the Italian lira from the European exchange rate mechanism (ERM), to a 5 percent devaluation of the Spanish peseta, and to the introduction of exchange rate controls in Ireland, Portugal, and Spain. Furthermore, additional realignments cannot be ruled out, as some EC members have to contend with the relative appreciation of their currency vis-à-vis the currencies of those countries that devalued or chose the option of exit.

These developments have reinforced the notion that the structural differences among some EC member economies may be too large to be overcome in the time period envisioned in the Maastricht Treaty and with the funds allocated in the Delors II package—let alone whether the required austerity measures are politically feasible. Unfortunately, the fact that the structural differences have been exposed in the context of a currency crisis that imposed realignments has damaged the political relations among some of the member countries.

To be sure, the actual crisis in the Community during the last two weeks of September was to a large extent precipitated by domestic developments in the individual member countries. In France, a serious strategic miscalculation has led President François Mitterrand to turn the debate over European Union into a popularity contest over the performance of his presidency. In Britain, the exchange rate at which the pound entered the ERM, the economic policy crisis, the differences within the Conservative party over Britain's role in Europe, and

Britain's disagreement with its European partners over the emerging structure of Europe itself have created one of the weakest EC presidencies in the history of the Community at a time when strong leadership was most needed. In Germany, the continuing struggle with the political, economic, and social consequences of unification has caused increasing strain among the institutions responsible for economic policymaking and has resulted in fiscal pressures whose repercussions can no longer be confined to Germany alone.

This primacy of domestic politics in times of stress reminds us that in many ways the Community remains an intergovernmental alliance of nation-states, where national interests are not yet equivalent to the European interest. Two factors have reinforced the national element in the Community over the last two years. First, though not publicly acknowledged, all members are being tempted to reassess and even redefine their role in a Europe whose political, economic, and geographic structure continues to change. Second, economic slowdown and stagnation in Europe have weakened the cause of European integration as governments and elected officials turn inward to preserve their political fortunes, and blame the failure of their policies on others.

One is therefore inclined to conclude that Europe's integration has come to a standstill and may well be reversed. Such a conclusion, however, would put too much emphasis on short-term developments and overlook the fact that the European Community is a hybrid that has evolved over the past decades, reflecting and responding to both the internal developments of its members and the external environment in which it is embedded. From the longer-term perspective, grounded historically as outlined in section 2 of this paper, it is clear that the Community faces a serious challenge because of the rapidly changing external environment and its repercussions at each member's national level. But this challenge does not invalidate the underlying purpose of European integration. To the contrary, as argued throughout the paper, it reinforces it.

To meet the challenge, policymakers should respond forcefully by reiterating their commitment to continued European integration while at the same time allowing the Community to adjust to the changing external environment. On both accounts, however, their response has been weak. With respect to the future course of integration, the concept of subsidiarity has become an all-purpose remedy for solving the Community's problems. But, as discussed, subsidiarity is not just a technical concept but a political one as well. British efforts to enforce EC competition rules while France tries to formulate an EC industrial policy is just one example. Broad application of subsidiarity therefore requires not only a technical discussion by the European Commission but also a political compromise among the member states, which may sometimes mean abandoning economic principles that have had a long history and tradition in each of these countries.

Furthermore, in the economic sphere of the single market the transfer of rule-making authority to lower levels is likely to create regulatory disparities among different economic jurisdictions. From a private sector perspective these differences amount to competitive inequalities and encourage regulatory arbitrage as enterprises search for the least-regulated environment. Local, regional, or national authorities faced with the exit of businesses and investment capital will be forced to adjust their own regulations as they compete with other decisionmaking centers in a single market. Thus, though formally still in place, authorities will lose much of their autonomy in a single market, which will reinforce the need for a common regulatory framework. Finally, subsidiarity assumes the existence of a well-functioning bureaucratic and administrative apparatus, not just at the national but also at the state and local levels, and few member countries currently have such structures in place. To broaden the applicability of the concept of subsidiarity, it is useful to distinguish between *functional* and *structural* subsidiarity. Though subsidiarity is limited from a functional perspective, as just explained, national, regional, and local decisionmaking centers could be engaged more actively both when common market rules are developed and when they are subsequently implemented and applied. By making use of the multilayered structures, the Community could decentralize the management of its political and budgetary power to levels of authority that are closer to the intended recipient or are managed by the recipient itself, subject to a regular review process.

Finally, subsidiarity is only one of several responses to the criticism that Community decisions are too far removed from the individual and the public at large. Instead of relocating political power at levels where democratic decisionmaking structures are in place and functioning, the member states could also agree to reduce the Community's own democratic deficit by introducing more transparency into the Council of Ministers and by strengthening the legislative component in Community decisionmaking procedures. Such a response of course assumes that member states are actually willing to give up some of their power and points to the fact that the debate over subsidiarity is as much a turf battle between and among EC institutions and national governments as it is an attempt to bring democracy to every European citizen.

As for the Community's ability to adjust to its changing external environment, EC member states so far have categorically rejected the notion of a two-speed Europe and clung to a fixed and rigid structure. This was understandable immediately after the French referendum and the ensuing currency crisis, since it demonstrated their firm commitment to the ratification of the Maastricht Treaty. But if the timetable for economic and monetary union among the twelve will have to be postponed because of the crisis in the ERM, the probability of a two-speed Europe has increased. The resultant gap between political rhetoric and economic reality is convenient for some member states. First, adhering to the notion of a one-speed Europe puts off the need to develop a response to the fact that some countries may not be able to join EMU. Second, for the time being the gap allows the continuation of the negotiations over enlargement which the Southern tier has threatened to boycott if other members consider a two-speed Europe. Third, and most important, it shifts the burden of failure away from the Maastricht Treaty, which under present circumstances has set conditions that cannot be met by all members, to those individual countries that will be unable to meet the convergence criteria.

If, on the other hand, member governments truly believe a single-speed Europe remains a real possibility, they will have to contend with those forces that fear it can be realized only by softening the convergence criteria set out in the Maastricht Treaty and the process by which those criteria are evaluated.

Either of these scenarios promises renewed conflict among member states that will hurt the integration process and should be avoided. In the first instance, as the gap between rhetoric and reality gets smaller approaching 1997 or 1999, a confrontation between those that can join EMU and those that cannot will arise, leaving some countries feeling deceived after all the efforts they have made and the commitments they were given. In the second instance, those that oppose a softening of the conditions will try to enforce the establishment of a two-speed Europe through market mechanisms, in particular through financial markets, which as the September 1992 crisis showed is economically costly and politically damaging to Europe as a whole.

Thus, rather than deny the prospect of a two-speed Europe, member states should openly discuss its probability and present their ideas on how to institute it. Indeed, several scenarios were developed in late 1989 in response to the turmoil in Germany and Central and Eastern Europe. These scenarios could be used as a point of departure. Moreover, in many policy areas of the Community some form of multi-speed Europe is a reality. The European Monetary System, the Schengen agreement (which will remove all border controls among eight of the twelve members), and the long transition periods granted the Southern EC members in preparation for full membership (some of which are still in effect as the application of foreign-exchange controls during the September crisis has shown) are all examples of a multi-speed Europe. In fact, the Maastricht agreement itself, with the opt-out clause on EMU negotiated by Britain but available to all countries and the protocol on the social charter, embraces the two-speed concept even though the treaty does not refer to it as such. Finally, the relationship between the Community and the European Free Trade Association now entering a new phase with the formation of the European Economic Area, and the EC's relations with Central and Eastern Europe organized around the association agreements, are manifestations of a Europe at different speeds.

The greatest asset of the multi-speed concept of Europe is that it can respond to the many, sometimes conflicting, demands the Community faces today, a situation that is not likely to change in the near future. So long as the concept is understood as a dynamic one, in which—as argued in the paper—the various stages are considered transitory, it will not cause some members to fear being permanently left outside the inner circle. To allay such fears, member states that belong to the core should demonstrate their goodwill by continuing to pledge their financial support of the convergence process. A multi-speed Europe also enables some countries, such as Denmark, to pause and reconsider their role in the new Europe before they make a firm commitment to join the European Union. This would appear to be a more stable solution than joining the union subject to a time limit, which, because it may result in a withdrawal from the arrangement, creates an insecure environment for investment, business, and coherent economic policy.

But though some countries may remain outside the European core in the early years, this core can respond to the countries that want to go ahead with the Union and to the EC members that want to see the unified Germany firmly embedded in a set of European political and economic institutions. Neither of these results can be achieved by weakening the Maastricht Treaty through renegotiation or the attachment of additional protocols. Finally, establishing an inner core will also provide a stable point of reference for the countries of Central and Eastern Europe. Their current plight and future role in Europe went almost unmentioned in the deliberations of the member states after the French referendum and the turmoil in currency markets, even though Central and Eastern Europe represents the very changing external environment with which the Community is trying to cope.

IV. APPENDIX TABLES

Table A-1. Distribution of Europe's Trade by Major Country Groups, 1928, 1938

Percent share

Exporting area and year	Western Europe (industrialized)[a]		Mediterranean countries[b]		Scandinavia[c]		Germany		Central and Eastern Europe[d]		USSR[e]	
	Exports	Imports	Exports	Imports	Exports	Imports	Exports	Imports	Exports	Imports	Exports	Imports
Western Europe (industrialized)[a]												
1928	30.6	24.3	6.3	27.8	3.4	25.9	11.0	30.5	2.6	14.2	0.7	10.3
1938	28.5	20.4	4.3	21.4	6.7	30.4	8.0	23.5	3.8	18.2	3.1	44.2
Mediterranean countries[b]												
1928	35.8	4.7	9.4	6.8	1.4	1.8	12.0	5.5	6.6	5.9	0.9	2.3
1938	19.1	2.4	7.1	6.1	3.0	2.4	23.4	12.1	9.1	7.5	1.1	2.8
Scandinavia[c]												
1928	48.6	5.5	3.6	2.2	12.0	13.2	16.2	6.4	2.2	1.7	2.3	5.3
1938	47.6	7.7	3.0	3.4	13.1	13.5	17.5	11.7	3.1	3.3	1.3	4.2
Germany												
1928	35.3	9.5	7.8	11.7	10.2	26.7	...	...	17.1	31.6	4.8	25.8
1938	27.6	8.3	12.7	26.4	12.5	23.9	...	...	15.3	30.4	2.2	13.3
Central and Eastern Europe[d]												
1928	13.7	2.2	10.3	9.0	3.6	5.6	24.2	13.4	37.8	41.2	2.0	6.4
1938	22.1	3.8	10.5	12.6	5.1	5.6	23.0	16.3	23.0	26.2	1.4	4.7
USSR[e]												
1928	32.7	1.6	5.5	1.5	3.4	1.6	26.6	4.6	3.1	1.0	10.5	10.3
1938	51.4	2.6	4.6	1.6	5.7	1.9	14.4	3.0	1.9	0.6	3.0	3.1

Source: United Nations Economic Commission for Europe, Research and Planning Division, A Survey of the Economic Situation and Prospects of Europe (Geneva, 1948).
a. United Kingdom, Ireland, Iceland, France, Netherlands, Belgium, Luxembourg, and Switzerland.
b. Italy, Greece, Spain, Portugal, Turkey, and miscellaneous continental Europe.
c. Denmark, Sweden, Norway, and Finland.
d. Czechoslovakia, Austria, Poland, Romania, Hungary, Yugoslavia, and Buglaria.
e. USSR, including independent Estonia, Lithuania, and Latvia.

Table A-2. European Trade by Commodity Classes, 1928[a]

Percent

Country	Imports					Exports				
	I	II	III	IV	V	I	II	III	IV	V
Austria	8.1	22.6	28.3	38.7	2.3	1.0	2.4	22.5	72.3	1.8
Belgium	0.2	21.1	53.4	24.9	0.4	0.5	8.2	33.7	57.4	0.2
France	0.5	20.9	50.9	16.8	10.9	0.7	11.9	18.7	67.9	0.8
Germany	1.0	28.0	48.2	16.4	6.4	0.1	5.2	19.9	74.5	0.3
Italy	1.9	27.5	46.2	24.0	0.4	0.1	23.1	14.4	62.4	n.a.
United Kingdom	1.7	41.3	32.0	19.9	6.0	0.3	5.7	14.4	69.0	10.6
Bulgaria	n.a.	5.4	20.5	74.1	n.a.	4.2	28.4	60.9	6.5	n.a.
Hungary	0.2	7.3	39.6	51.6	1.3	11.6	50.5	14.7	22.7	0.5
Poland	0.1	16.2	34.9	40.4	8.4	9.2	21.0	55.3	14.5	n.a.
CSFR	3.7	18.2	47.7	30.3	0.1	0.3	13.7	17.2	68.6	0.2
Yugoslavia	n.a.	13.0	16.4	70.3	0.1	13.8	25.9	50.3	10.0	n.a.

Source: League of Nations, *Statistical Year-Book of the League of Nations 1930/31* (Geneva: League of Nations Economic Intelligence Service, 1931). Share calculations are by the author.

n.a. Not available.

a. The commodity classes are as follows: I for animals, II for food, III for materials, IV for manufacturing, and V for gold and silver.

Table A-3. National Income Per Capita in Europe, 1937, 1988

U.S. dollars

Country	1937	1988
Western Europe		
Great Britain	440	14,477
Sweden	400	21,155
Germany	340	19,743
Belgium	330	15,394
Netherlands	306	15,421
France	265	17,004
Regional average	347	17,199
Central and Eastern Europe		
Czechoslovakia	170	2,737
Hungary	120	2,625
Poland	100	1,719
Romania	81	1,374
Yugoslavia	80	2,279
Bulgaria	75	2,217
Regional average	104	2,158

Sources: Iván T. Berend and Gyorgy Ránki, *Economic Development in East-Central Europe in the 19th and 20th Centuries* (Columbia University Press, 1974); *The Economist, Book of Vital Statistics* (London: Random House, 1990); and author's own calculations.

Table A-4. Industrial Output in Central and Eastern Europe and the Soviet Union, 1986–91

Percent change over same period of preceding year

Country	1986	1987	1988	1989	1990	1991 Jan.-March	1991 Jan.-June	1991 Jan.-Sept.	1991 Jan.-Dec.
Bulgaria	4.7	6.0	3.2	-0.3	-12.6	-21.0	-29.1	-28.1	-27.3
CFSR	3.2	2.5	2.1	0.8	-3.5	-10.5	-14.3	-19.8	-23.1
Hungary	1.9	3.5	-0.3	-2.5	-4.5	-8.7	-14.2	-16.6	-19.1
Poland	4.7	3.4	5.3	-0.5	-24.2	-5.5	-9.3	-11.0	-11.9
Romania	7.3	2.4	3.1	-2.1	-19.0	-17.0	-16.6	-17.7	-18.7
Yugoslavia	3.9	0.6	-0.7	0.9	-10.3	-21.1	-17.4	-18.3	-20.7
Eastern Europe	4.6	3.2	3.3	-0.1	-18.9	-13.7	-15.6	-17.7	-19.1
USSR	4.4	3.8	3.9	1.7	-1.2	-5.0	-6.2	-6.4	-9.0[a]

Sources: United Nations Economic Commission for Europe, *Economic Survey of Europe in 1991-1992* (New York, 1992), tables 3.2.6, B.11, pp. 64, 302; United Nations, *Economic Bulletin for Europe*, vol. 43 (Geneva, November 1991), table 1.3.2, p. 26; OECD *Short-Term Economic Statistics: Central and Eastern Europe* (Paris, February 1992); various issues of Foreign Broadcasting Information Service, *Daily Report: East Europe*, Radio Free Europe/Radio Liberty, *Daily Report and Research Report*, *Financial Times*, and *Neue Zuricher Zeitung* (December 25, 1991), p. 11.

a. Goskomstat projection (*Izvestiya*, July 18, 1991).

Table A-5. Unemployment in Central and Eastern Europe, 1989–92

Numbers in thousands; percent of labor force

Date	Bulgaria	Czechoslo-vakia	Hungary	Poland	Romania	Yugoslavia
December 1989						
Number	0.0	0.0	13.0	9.7	n.a.	1,248.0
Percent	0.0	0.0	0.3	0.1	n.a.	12.2
December 1990						
Number	65.1	76.7	79.5	1,126.1	150.0	1,386.5
Percent	1.7	1.0	1.7	6.1	1.3	13.6
January 1991						
Number	72.2	119.5	99.1	1,195.7	200.0	n.a.
Percent	1.8	1.5	2.1	6.5	1.8	n.a.
February 1991						
Number	103.1	152.0	130.0	1,258.9	n.a.	1,430.0
Percent	2.6	2.0	2.5	6.8	n.a.	13.8
March 1991						
Number	134.8	184.6	144.8	1,321.1	79.2	1,455.0
Percent	3.5	2.3	3.0	7.1	0.7	14.2
April 1991						
Number	160.0	219.0	164.0	1,370.1	92.4	n.a.
Percent	4.0	2.8	3.3	7.3	n.a.	n.a.
May 1991						
Number	205.9	255.6	165.0	1,434.5	138.9	1,489.0
Percent	5.1	3.2	3.4	7.7	1.2	14.6
June 1991						
Number	233.7	300.8	185.6	1,574.1	169.9	1,498.8
Percent	6.0	3.8	3.9	8.4	1.6	14.7
July 1991						
Number	282.1	362.7	216.6	1,749.9	217.1	n.a.
Percent	6.7	4.6	4.5	9.4	2.0	n.a.
August 1991						
Number	302.0	405.6	251.0	1,854.0	237.8	n.a.
Percent	6.9	5.1	5.2	9.8	2.2	n.a.
September 1991						
Number	343.3	446.2	292.8	1,970.9	260.5	1,540.4
Percent	8.8	5.7	6.1	10.4	2.4	15.2
October 1991						
Number	n.a.	474.4	318.0	2,044.9	256.5	n.a.
Percent	n.a.	6.0	6.6	10.8	2.4	n.a.
November 1991						
Number	402.1	500.2	351.0	2,145.0	325.0	n.a.
Percent	10.0	6.3	7.3	11.1	3.0	n.a.
December 1991						
Number	419.0	523.7	406.1	2,155.6	337.5	2,000.0
Percent	10.7	6.6	8.3	11.5	3.1	19.6
December 1992[a]						
Number	75.0	1,000.0	600.0	3,000–3,500	n.a.	n.a.
Percent	17.8	12.6	13.0	16–18	n.a.	n.a.

Sources: United Nations Economic Commission for Europe, *Economic Survey of Europe in 1990–91* (New York, 1991), table 2.2.14, p. 59; UNECE, *Economic Survey of Europe in 1991–1992* (New York, 1992), table 3.2.9, p. 68; UNECE, *Economic Bulletin for Europe,* vol. 43 (Geneva, November 1991); *OECD Economic Outlook 50* (Paris, December 1991); OECD, *Short-Term Economic Statistics: Central and Eastern Europe* (Paris, February 1992); various issues of the Foreign Broadcasting Information Service, *Daily Report: East Europe;* Radio Free Europe/Radio Liberty, *Daily Report; Financial Times; Handelsblatt;* and *Neue Zuricher Zeitung.*

n.a. Not available.

a. Forecasts based on government projections.

Table A-6. Inflation in Central and Eastern Europe, 1989–91

Period or month	Bulgaria	Czechoslovakia	Hungary	Poland	Romania	Yugoslavia	USSR
			Percent change from same period in preceding year				
1989							
Jan.–Dec.	6.2	1.4	17.0	244.1	n.a.	1,256.0	n.a.
1990							
Jan.–March	n.a.	3.4	23.3	1,110.7	n.a.	2,990.0	2.6
Jan.–June	13.5	3.7	25.3	1,091.2	2.2	2,137.0	2.8
Jan.–Sept.	n.a.	7.2	26.6	920.4	n.a.	702.0	3.6
Jan.–Dec.	20.0	10.0	28.9	584.7	13.0	587.6	5.0
1991							
Jan.–March	n.a.	n.a.	34.3	n.a.	n.a.	n.a.	n.a.
Jan.–May	293.7	59.5	34.8	78.1	139.8	63.4	n.a.
Jan.–June	316.9	61.5	35.7	77.1	144.5	74.0	55.5
Jan.–July	351.9	61.1	36.0	75.6	167.7	74.1	61.4
Jan.–Aug.	385.8	60.4	35.8	74.5	197.6	79.5	n.a.
Jan.–Sept.	404.0	55.0	36.0	73.6	219.0	85.8	70.6
Jan.–Nov.	n.a.	n.a.	n.a.	n.a.	350.0	183.6	n.a.
Jan.–Dec.	249.8	57.9	35.0	70.3	344.5	118.1	650–700[a]
1992							
Jan.–Dec.[a]	n.a.	15–20	35.0	45.0	n.a.	590.0	n.a.

Percent change from preceding month

1990							
July	−0.6	n.a.	2.6	0.2	n.a.	n.a.	n.a.
Aug.	10.9	n.a.	2.9	1.8	n.a.	1.9	n.a.
Sept.	4.5	n.a.	1.5	4.6	n.a.	7.1	n.a.
Oct.	4.1	n.a.	1.5	5.7	n.a.	8.1	n.a.
Nov.	4.9	n.a.	2.1	4.9	23.4	3.0	n.a.
Dec.	10.4	n.a.	1.7	5.9	11.6	2.7	n.a.
1991							
Jan.	13.6	25.8	7.5	12.7	8.6	5.6	4–6[a]
Feb.	122.9	7.0	4.9	6.7	7.0	9.2	n.a.
Mar.	50.5	4.7	3.7	4.5	6.6	3.2	n.a.
Apr.	2.5	2.0	2.4	2.7	26.5	4.9	110.0
May	0.8	1.9	2.2	2.7	5.1	10.9	2.0
June	5.9	1.8	2.1	4.9	2.0	10.3	−0.1
July	8.4	−0.1	0.9	0.1	9.5	5.8	0.1
Aug.	7.5	0.0	0.2	0.6	11.2	8.0	0.0
Sept.	3.8	0.3	1.5	4.3	7.3	14.4	1.5
Oct.	3.3	−0.1	1.3	3.2	10.4	18.8	n.a.
Nov.	5.0	1.6	1.4	3.2	10.9	18.9	n.a.
Dec.	4.9	1.2	1.6	3.1	13.7	18.2	n.a.
1992							
Jan.	4.8	1.0	3.2	7.5	n.a.	26.1	n.a.

Sources: United Nations Economic Commission for Europe, *Economic Survey of Europe in 1990–1991* (New York, 1991), table 2.2.11, p. 54; UNECE, *Economic Bulletin for Europe* (Geneva, November 1991), table 1.3.5, p. 28; UNECE, *Economic Survey of Europe in 1991–1992* (New York, 1992), tables 3.4.3, 3.4.4, p. 93; OECD, *Short-Term Economic Statistics: Central and Eastern Europe* (Paris, February 1992), pp. 69, 300, 372; Foreign Broadcast Information Service, *Daily Report: East Europe*, December 10, 1991, p. 39, and January 16, 1992, p. 39; Radio Free Liberty/Radio Liberty, *Daily Report*, November 21, 1991, p. 3, December 3, 1991, p. 6, and January 8, 1992, p. 5; Radio Free Liberty/Radio Liberty, *Research Report: Economic and Business Notes*, December 14–27, 1991, p. 36; and *Neue Zuericher Zeitung* (Zurich, Switzerland), December 25–26, 1991, p. 11.

n.a. Not available.

a. Estimate.

155

Table A-7. Public Opinion on the Economic Situation
in Czechoslovakia, Hungary, and Poland, 1990, 1991

Percent

Country and opinion	Past 12 months		Next 12 months	
	1990	1991	1990	1991
Czechoslovakia				
Better	12	23	26	36
Same	13	13	14	21
Worse	72	61	51	36
Don't know	3	3	8	7
Hungary				
Better	[a]	20	11	33
Same	[a]	16	11	26
Worse	[a]	61	74	31
Don't know	[a]	3	4	10
Poland				
Better	52	17	41	24
Same	14	14	23	25
Worse	29	64	14	30
Don't know	5	5	22	21

Source: European Commission, *Eurobarometer*, no. 34 (Brussels, November 1990);
and EC, *Central and Eastern Eurobarometer*, vol. 2 (Brussels, January 1992).
a. The polling for this question did not include Hungary in 1990.

Table A-8. Public Opinion on Household Finances
in Czechoslovakia, Hungary, and Poland, 1990, 1991

Percent

	Past 12 months		Next 12 months	
Country and opinion	1990	1991	1990	1991
Czechoslovakia				
Better	6	13	9	21
Same	27	20	17	37
Worse	66	66	66	34
Don't know	1	1	8	8
Hungary				
Better	a	9	6	20
Same	a	24	18	31
Worse	a	66	74	39
Don't know	a	1	2	10
Poland				
Better	18	10	24	17
Same	34	25	31	33
Worse	46	64	24	32
Don't know	2	1	21	18

Source: European Commission, *Eurobarometer*, no. 34 (Brussels, November 1990); and EC, *Central and Eastern Eurobarometer*, vol. 2 (Brussels, January 1992).
a. The polling for this question did not include Hungary in 1990.

Table A-9. Public Opinion on the Development of Democracy in Czechoslovakia, Hungary, and Poland, 1990, 1991

Percent

Country and opinion	1990	1991
Czechoslovakia		
Satisfied	30	28
Not satisfied	55	66
Don't know	15	6
Hungary		
Satisfied	19	30
Not satisfied	75	60
Don't know	6	10
Poland		
Satisfied	38	27
Not satisfied	37	50
Don't know	25	23

Source: European Commission, *Eurobarometer*, no. 34 (Brussels, November 1990); and EC, *Central and Eastern Eurobarometer*, vol. 2 (Brussels, January 1992).
a. The polling for this question did not include Hungary in 1990.

Table A-10. Public Opinion in Central and Eastern Europe, 1991

Percent

Country and opinion	Economic situation		Household finances	
	Past 12 months	Next 12 months	Past 12 months	Next 12 months
Bulgaria				
Better	24	48	10	35
Same	18	18	20	27
Worse	50	19	66	23
Don't know	8	15	4	15
Czechoslovakia				
Better	23	36	13	21
Same	13	21	20	37
Worse	61	36	66	34
Don't know	3	7	1	8
Hungary				
Better	20	33	9	20
Same	16	26	24	31
Worse	61	31	66	39
Don't know	3	10	1	10
Poland				
Better	17	24	10	17
Same	14	25	25	33
Worse	65	30	64	32
Don't know	4	21	1	18
Romania				
Better	15	46	26	36
Same	23	17	34	22
Worse	57	18	39	24
Don't know	5	19	1	18
Russia (European)				
Better	6	25	16	16
Same	8	20	25	24
Worse	84	44	58	46
Don't know	2	11	1	14

Country and opinion	Economic reform
Bulgaria	
Too slow	48
Right speed	26
Too fast	5
Don't know	21
Czechoslovakia	
Too slow	34
Right speed	32
Too fast	22
Don't know	12
Hungary	
Too slow	49
Right speed	21
Too fast	13
Don't know	17
Poland	
Too slow	40
Right speed	11
Too fast	26
Don't know	23
Romania	
Too slow	17
Right speed	41
Too fast	28
Don't know	14
Russia (European)	
Too slow	64
Right speed	4
Too fast	5
Don't know	27

Country and opinion	Political views
Bulgaria	
Left	23
Center	29
Right	23
Don't know	25
Czechoslovakia	
Left	20
Center	27
Right	31
Don't know	22
Hungary	
Left	15
Center	49
Right	13
Don't know	23
Poland	
Left	15
Center	34
Right	20
Don't know	31
Romania	
Left	18
Center	33
Right	16
Don't know	33
Russia (European)	
Left	25
Center	21
Right	9
Don't know	45

Country and opinion	Frequency of thinking of oneself as European
Bulgaria	
Often	15
Sometimes	30
Never	41
Don't know	14
Czechoslovakia	
Often	12
Sometimes	39
Never	46
Don't know	3
Hungary	
Often	22
Sometimes	37
Never	38
Don't know	3
Poland	
Often	12
Sometimes	33
Never	46
Don't know	9
Romania	
Often	39
Sometimes	34
Never	18
Don't know	9
Russia (European)	
Often	6
Sometimes	25
Never	62
Don't know	7

Country and opinion	Prospect of emigrating to W. Europe
Bulgaria	
Will or may go	10
Will not or may not go	8
Have not considered it	75
Don't know	7
Czechoslovakia	
Will or may go	13
Will not or may not go	18
Have not considered it	62
Don't know	7
Hungary	
Will or may go	9
Will not or may not go	19
Have not considered it	70
Don't know	2
Poland	
Will or may go	13
Will not or may not go	20
Have not considered it	62
Don't know	5
Romania	
Will or may go	12
Will not or may not go	8
Have not considered it	77
Don't know	3
Russia (European)	
Will or may go	4
Will not or may not go	17
Have not considered it	71
Don't know	8

Source: EC, *Central and Eastern Eurobarometer*, vol. 2 (Brussels, January 1992).

Table A-11. Intra-Group Trade among Central and Eastern Europe and the USSR, 1988–90

Percent annual growth

Reporting country and trading partners	Exports			Imports		
	1988	1989	1990	1988	1989	1990
Bulgaria						
Eastern Europe	1.1	−10.1	−32.5	1.9	−15.6	−21.5
Soviet Union	6.8	−1.4	−24.2	−7.5	−9.7	−15.2
Czechoslovakia						
Eastern Europe	5.8	0.7	−26.5	7.9	3.5	−2.7
Soviet Union	4.8	−7.0	−18.5	−6.3	−1.9	−19.4
Hungary						
Rouble transactions	1.4	−4.4	−24.4	1.4	−9.2	−18.5
Eastern Europe	15.0	−2.7	−24.6	6.0	−6.6	−8.6
Soviet Union	−1.2	−5.0	−12.8	−6.1	−10.1	−7.6
Poland						
Rouble transactions	6.4	2.3	−7.0	−2.4	−6.5	−35.0
Eastern Europe	5.8	4.3	23.5	3.2	−1.9	−27.1
Soviet Union	6.5	2.0	31.9	−7.9	−7.2	−28.3
Romania						
Rouble transactions	7.7	−7.3	−42.0	0.2	6.8	−14.7
Eastern Europe[a]	1.5	−8.2	−51.1[b]	1.0	−1.0	12.8[b]
Soviet Union[a]	7.8	−4.2	−36.8[c]	−3.8	10.0	−22.3[c]
Soviet Union						
Socialist countries[d]	−3.0	−1.5	−19.2	3.0	3.0	−2.4
Eastern Europe	−3.7	−4.1	n.a.	2.6	1.7	n.a.

Source: United Nations Economic Commission for Europe, *Economic Survey of Europe in 1990–91* (New York, 1991), table 3.2.1, p. 75.

n.a. Not available.

a. Part of the trade with Eastern Europe and the USSR was transacted in convertible currencies. In 1990 this trade was significant; hence the divergence between the growth rates of the "rouble trade" and total trade with Eastern partners.

b. Trade with E. Europe is estimate based on trade partner data for the full year.

c. Trade with USSR estimated from trends in January–September 1990 relative to January–September 1989, as shown in Soviet data for that period.

d. Includes Asian socialist countries, Cuba, Yugoslavia, and European CMEA.

Table A-12. Creditor Profile: Outstanding Long-Term Debt, Central and Eastern Europe, 1990

Percent share

Country	Official creditors			Private creditors			
	Multi-lateral	Bilateral	Total	Total	Commercial banks	Bonds	Other
Bulgaria	1.2	0.0	1.2	98.8	41.3	3.0	54.6
CFSR	5.0	1.5	6.5	93.5	41.4	12.3	39.9
Hungary	14.2	0.9	15.0	85.0	53.0	26.5	5.4
Poland	1.3	69.3	70.7	29.3	26.1	0.0	3.3
Romania	0.0	100.0	100.0	0.0	0.0	0.0	0.0
Yugoslavia	22.9	30.8	53.7	46.3	45.4	0.0	0.9

Source: Values were calculated using figures from World Bank, *World Debt Tables, 1991-92: External Debt of Developing Countries*, vol. 1 (Washington, 1991), pp. 42, 102, 182, 322, 330, 442.

Table A-13. G-24 Assistance for Central and Eastern Europe, 1990–91[a]

Millions of ECUs unless otherwise specified

Country	Total assistance	Grants Amount	Grants Percent of total	Credits Amount	Credits Percent of total	GDP[b] (billions of ECUs)	Total assistance/ GDP (percent)
EC/CECA/EIB[c]	6,994.20	1,521.7	21.8	5,472.50	78.2	. . .	. . .
Belgium	165.88	0.00	0.0	165.88	100.0	159.1	0.104
Denmark	320.77	268.67	83.8	52.10	16.2	106.3	0.302
France	1,798.36	215.98	12.0	1,582.38	88.0	966.4	0.186
Germany	6,224.48	2,477.57	39.8	3,746.91	60.2	1,271.1	0.490
Greece	31.56	6.19	19.6	25.37	80.4	55.7	0.057
Ireland	0.90	0.90	100.0	0.00	0.0	34.6	0.003
Italy	1,345.38	424.66	31.6	920.72	68.4	921.4	0.146
Luxembourg	22.50	2.10	9.3	20.40	90.7	7.3	0.308
Netherlands	296.39	77.07	26.0	219.32	74.0	232.3	0.128
Portugal	2.00	0.00	0.0	2.00	100.0	56.0	0.004
Spain	476.92	4.41	0.9	472.51	99.1	426.4	0.112
United Kingdom	671.40	39.61	5.9	631.79	94.1	836.3	0.080
Total, Community	18,350.74	5,038.86	27.5	13,311.88	72.5	5,072.9	0.362

162

Austria	1,366.66	613.44	44.9	753.22	55.1	114.8	1.190
Finland	175.58	82.58	47.0	93.00	53.0	104.8	0.168
Iceland	3.30	3.10	93.9	0.20	6.1	4.7	0.070
Norway	128.54	62.47	48.6	66.07	51.4	81.9	0.157
Sweden	768.54	151.74	19.7	616.80	80.3	172.4	0.446
Switzerland	298.39	71.99	24.1	226.40	75.9	160.8	0.186
Total, EFTA[d]	2,741.01	985.32	35.9	1,755.69	64.1	639.4	0.429
Australia	177.96	7.26	4.1	170.70	95.9	256.3	0.069
Canada	1,417.80	1,204.24	84.9	213.56	15.1	495.1	0.286
Japan	2,203.53	523.49	23.8	1,680.04	76.2	2,696.9	0.082
New Zealand	50.86	0.62	1.2	50.24	98.8	37.9	0.134
Turkey	351.34	10.42	3.0	340.92	97.0	72.3	0.486
United States	5,185.42	3,629.07	70.0	1,556.35	30.0	4,556.6	0.114
Total, others	9,386.91	5,375.10	57.3	4,011.81	42.7	8,115.2	0.116
Grand total, G-24	30,478.66	11,399.28	37.4	19,079.38	62.6	13,827.5	0.220

Sources: Commission of the European Communities, "Scoreboard of G-24 Assistance, Summary ECU Tables and Graphics," Meeting of the Group of 24 at senior official level (Brussels, April 8, 1992). GDP figures for the EC, Japan, and the United States are from Commission of the European Community, *European Economy*, no. 50 (December 1991), p. 218. The GDP figures for the EFTA countries, Australia, New Zealand, and Turkey are from *OECD Economic Survey* (August 1991). The ECU exchange rates for the former group of countries is from the Commission of the European Communities, *European Economy*, no. 50 (December 1991), p. 262.

a. Cumulative commitments from the beginning of the Coordinated Assistance Programme for the period from the 1st quarter of 1990 to the end of the 4th quarter of 1991.
b. The GDP figures are for 1991, with the exception of 1989 figures for the EFTA countries, Australia, Canada, New Zealand, and Turkey.
c. European Community, European Coal and Steel Community, European Investment Bank.
d. European Free Trade Association.

Table A-14. Trade between the EC and Central and Eastern European Countries with Association Agreements, 1988

Exports in millions of U.S. dollars

Item	Czechoslovakia	Hungary	Poland	Total	Total EC imports by commodity
Total exports to EC	2,611.5	2,571.9	3,970.9	9,154.3	...
Agricultural exports to EC	174.1	620.2	707.1	1,501.4	106,183.8
As percent of total EC imports	0.16	0.58	0.67	1.41	
As percent of total exports to EC	6.7	24.1	17.8	16.4	
Coal and steel exports to EC	377.9	130.0	567.4	1,075.3	42,092.5
As percent of total EC imports	0.90	0.31	1.35	2.55	
As percent of total exports to EC	14.5	5.1	14.3	11.7	
Textile exports to EC	314.4	408.0	439.1	1,161.5	73,028.6
As percent of total EC imports	0.43	0.56	0.60	1.59	
As percent of total exports to EC	12.0	15.9	11.1	12.7	

Source: OECD, Department of Economics and Statistics, *Foreign Trade by Commodities*, vol. 5 (1989), pp. 240–41, 266, 289, 291, and 308. Agriculture includes SITC category 0; coal and steel includes SITC categories 32 and 67; and textiles include SITC categories 65 and 84.

Table A-15. Geographical Distribution of G-24 Assistance for Central and Eastern Europe, 1990–91[a]

Millions of ECUs unless otherwise specified

Country	Investment projects	Sector aid	Technical cooperation	Official export credit	Official support for private investment	Other and unspecified	Total Amount	Total Percent of country total	Grants Amount	Grants Percent
Albania	0.78	102.83	1.30	77.97	12.51	214.70	410.09	0.98	206.32	50.31
Bulgaria	0.00	327.88	37.12	79.16	38.90	1,078.84	1,561.90	3.75	183.33	11.74
Czechoslovakia	34.59	468.17	72.33	896.55	2.32	2,353.70	3,827.66	9.19	228.53	5.97
Hungary	2.50	1,412.78	57.24	1,346.04	41.79	3,816.22	6,676.57	16.02	293.97	4.40
Poland	31.03	2,496.19	163.79	2,000.45	168.61	11,445.76	16,305.83	39.13	7,158.60	43.90
Romania	0.03	492.07	74.07	657.98	1.55	1,869.43	3,095.13	7.43	413.13	13.35
Yugoslavia	0.00	917.48	8.43	656.48	0.00	1,489.70	3,072.09	7.37	115.75	3.77
Estonia	0.00	5.25	5.98	7.33	0.00	19.80	38.36	0.09	31.04	80.92
Latvia	0.00	5.71	2.43	7.33	0.00	22.51	37.98	0.09	26.73	70.38
Lithuania	0.00	6.47	3.21	7.33	0.00	21.66	38.67	0.09	27.42	70.91
Regional or unspecified	10.41	201.64	937.30	900.49	926.29	3,630.62	6,606.75	15.85	2,714.47	41.09
Country total	79.34	6,436.47	1,363.20	6,637.11	1,191.97	25,962.94	41,671.03	100.00	11,399.29	27.36

Source: Commission of the European Communities, ''Scoreboard of G-24 Assistance, Summary ECU Tables and Graphics,'' Meeting of the Group of 24 at Senior Official Level (Brussels, April 8, 1992).
a. From 1st quarter of 1990 through 4th quarter of 1991.

Table A-16. Eligible Voters in the European Community, by Country[a]

Millions unless otherwise specified

Country	Population	Percent of population under 18[b]	Number of eligible voters
Belgium	9.98	22.99	7.68
Denmark[c]	5.15	22.49	3.99
France	56.61	36.97	35.68
Germany	79.11	23.61	60.44
Greece	10.27	24.50	7.75
Ireland	3.52	34.31	2.31
Italy	57.75	22.57	44.71
Luxembourg	0.38	21.24	0.30
Netherlands	14.94	23.42	11.44
Portugal	10.29	26.93	7.52
Spain	39.32	26.53	28.89
United Kingdom	57.24	24.42	43.26
Total	344.56	25.83	253.98

Sources: Population figures from *Europa World Handbook* (1991 and 1992). Figures for percent of population under 18 are European Commission, *Eurostat: Demographic Statistics* (Brussels, 1990), pp.118-19. Number of German eligible voters is from their Embassy, Barbara Hellman (June 9, 1992), corresponding to the last national election on December 18, 1990. Number of British eligible voters is from the British Information Library in New York, Janet Bacon (June 9, 1992), corresponding to the last national election on April 9, 1992.

a. Number of eligible voters is an estimated based on latest population figures, in addition to the number of people below voting age (18 years) in each country.

b. Figures for the population below 18 years old are dated January 1, 1989, a date different from the population figures cited in the *Europa World Handbook*.

c. The Danish referendum (June 2, 1992) resulted in 1.607 million Yea votes, and 1.653 million Nay votes. The number of Danish Nay votes is only 0.65 percent of the total number of eligible voters in the EC, based on these estimates.

Notes

1. Unification refers to transforming two systems, divided during the Cold War, into a common political, economic, and security system, but not necessarily into a single state.

2. Dieter Senghaas, *Europa 2000 Ein Friedensplan* (Frankfurt am Main: Suhrkamp Verlag, 1990).

3. Central and Eastern Europe refers to Albania, Bulgaria, Czechoslovakia, Hungary, Poland, Romania, and Yugoslavia and its successor states, and the three Baltic republics. It does not refer to the successor states of the former Soviet Union.

4. John J. Mearsheimer, "Back to the Future: Instability in Europe after the Cold War," *International Security*, vol. 15 (Summer 1990), pp. 5–56; and Ferry Hoogendijk, "There is No European House," *European Affairs*, vol. 1 (Spring 1990), pp. 36–40.

5. Harold Macmillan, *Tides of Fortune, 1945–1955* (Harper and Row, 1969), p. 151; and A. L. Kennedy, *Salisbury, 1830–1903: Portrait of a Statesman* (London, Murray 1953), p. 273.

6. See Walter Lipgens, *Europa-Föderationspläne der Widerstandsbewegungen, 1940–1945* (München: Olenbourg Verlag, 1968); and Lipgens, "European Federalism in the Political Thought of Resistance Movements during World War II," *Central European History*, vol. 1 (March 1968), pp. 5–19.

7. Churchill indicated, however, that Britain could support but not participate in this union, since it belonged to the British Commonwealth of Nations.

8. The Schuman Plan, which led to the creation of the European Coal and Steel Community (ECSC) in April 1951, saw Franco-German reconciliation as the keystone of a new European order, with the explicit aim of creating conditions so that "war between France and Germany becomes not merely unthinkable, but materially impossible." In addition, the ECSC "should immediately provide the setting up of common foundations for economic development as a first step in the federation of Europe." *Declaration of May 1950*, reprinted in Pascal Fontaine, *Europe—A Fresh Start, The Schuman Declaration 1950–90* (Luxembourg: Office for Official Publications of the European Communities, 1990), p. 44. The failure of the European Defence Community, which was rejected by the French National Assembly in August 1954, did not undermine the European idea. At the Messina Conference in 1955, a new start was made that culminated in the Treaty of Rome, signed in March 1957, and established the European Economic Community and Euratom.

9. See, for example, Macmillan, *Tides of Fortune, 1945–1955*, esp. pp. 151–227. See also Fontaine, *Europe—A Fresh Start*.

10. *Treaties Establishing the European Community* (Luxembourg: Office for Official Publications of the European Communities, 1987), p. 1.

11. *Treaty Setting up the European Economic Community*, Rome, 25th March, 1957 (London: Her Majesty's Stationery Officer, 1967), article 237, paragraph 1. In 1978 this article was expanded by the word "democratic."

12. Walter Hallstein, *Europe in the Making* (Norton, 1972), p. 305.

13. George Lichtheim, *The New Europe* (Praeger, 1963), p. 77.

14. Press Release "Conclusions of the Presidency," European Council, Dublin, April 28, 1990. See also *The European Community and Its Eastern Neighbors* (Luxembourg: Office for Official Publications of the European Communities, 1990), esp. p. 5; and William Wallace, *The Transformation of Western Europe* (New York: Council on Foreign Relations, 1990).

15. Economic Commission for Europe, Research and Planning Division, *A Survey of the Economic Situation and Prospects of Europe* (Geneva: United Nations, 1948).

16. Paul F. Douglas, *The Economic Independence of Poland: A Study in Trade Adjustments to Political Objectives* (Cincinnati: Rutter Press, 1934).

17. Leopold Wellisz, *Foreign Capital in Poland* (London: George Allen and Unwin), 1938.

18. For further details of these differences, see Alexander Gerschenkron, *Economic Backwardness in Historical Perspective* (Cambridge, Mass.: Belknap Press, 1962); Barrington Moore, *Social Origins of Democracy and Dictatorship* (Beacon Press, 1966); Perry Andersen, *Lineages of the Absolutist State* (London: Verso, 1979); and Gianfranco Poggi, *The Development of the Modern State* (Stanford University Press, 1978). On the periphery relationship, see, for example, Roland Döhrn and Ullrich Heilemann, "Sectoral Change in Eastern Europe—The Chenery Hypothesis Reconsidered," *RWI-Papiere*, no. 25 (June 1991) (Essen: Rheinisch-Westfälisches Institut für Wirtschaftsforschung). This center-periphery relationship was particularly pronounced in the case of Germany; see Albert O. Hirschmann, *National Power and the Structure of Foreign Trade* (University of California Press, 1945).

19. Throughout the 1960s and 1970s several Central and East European countries attempted to diversify their export markets by establishing closer relationships with the countries of Western Europe. In most cases, however, these efforts failed because of the resistance of the Soviet Union. Statistisches Bundesamt, EUROSTAT, *Country Reports, Central and Eastern Europe 1991* (Luxembourg: Office for Official Publications of the European Communities, 1991).

20. András Inotai, "Economic Impact of German Reunification on Central and Eastern Europe," June 1991. The collapse of trade is occurring not only with the Soviet Union's East European trading partners, but also, for example, with Finland where trade with the Soviet Union declined substantially over 1991. That, too, has elevated Germany to the position of most important trading partner.

21. With $5.1 billion (10.4 percent), Italy is the second largest exporter, closely followed by the United States ($4.2 billion, or 8.5 percent). Total exports amounted to $49.3 billion in 1990. See "UK Stays Away from E Europe," *Financial Times*, March 2, 1992.

22. "Wachsende Kluft zwischen Ost und West," *Neue Zürcher Zeitung*, December 12, 1991.

23. As quoted in Don Cook, *Floodtide in Europe* (Putnam, 1965), pp. 14–15.

24. See, for example, Marc Granovetter, "Economic Action and Social Structure: The Problem of Embeddedness," *American Journal of Sociology*, vol. 91 (November 1985), pp. 481–510; and Fred Block and Margaret Sommers, "Beyond the Economistic Fallacy: The Holistic Social Science of Karl Polanyi," in Theda Skocpol, ed., *Vision and Method in Historical Sociology* (Cambridge University Press, 1984). See also Albert O. Hirschman, "Against Parsimony: Three Easy Ways of Complicating Some Categories of Economic Discourse," *Economics and Philosophy*, vol. 1 (April 1985), pp. 7–21; and Hirschman, "Rival Interpretations of Market Society: Civilizing, Destructive or Feeble?" *Journal of Economic Literature*, vol. 20 (December 1982), pp. 1463–84; and N. Kaldor, "The Irrelevance of Equilibrium Economics," *Economic Journal*, vol. 82 (December 1972), pp. 1237–55. For an idea of how economic theory has invaded other disciplines such as law, political science, and sociology, see George J. Stigler, "Economics—The Imperial Science?" *Scandinavian Journal of Economics*, vol. 86, no. 3 (1984), pp. 301–13.

25. See James S. Coleman, "Introducing Social Structure into Economic Analysis," *American Economic Review*, vol. 74 (May 1984), pp. 84–88.

26. For more on holism as a scientific method, see Paul Diesing, *Patterns of Discovery in the Social Sciences* (Chicago: Aldine-Atherton, 1971); and George Dalton and Jasper Kocke, "The Work of the Polanyi Group: Past, Present and Future," in S. Ortiz, ed., *Economic Anthropology* (New York: University Press of America, 1983). The concept of holism was originally used by the South African leader Jan Christian Smuts in a book entitled *Holism and Evolution*. Economists later adopted the notion of holism for their work. According to Alan Gruchy, "the term 'holistic' has been selected because it called attention to what is most characteristic in the new economics: Its interest in studying the economic system as an evolving, unified whole or synthesis, in the light of which the system's parts take on their full meaning." Alan Gurchy, *Modern Economic Thought: The American Contribution* (Prentice Hall, 1947), as cited in Philip A. Klein, "A Reconsideration of Holistic Economics," in John Adams, ed., *Institutional Economics, Contributions to the Development of Holistic Economics* (The Hague: Martinus Nijhoff, 1980), pp. 46–47.

27. See, for example, Karl Polanyi, *The Great Transformation: The Political and Economic Origins of Our Time* (Beacon Press, 1944); and Fernand Braudel, *Civilization and Capitalism, 15th–18th Century*, 3 vols. (Harper and Row, 1981–84). For an analysis of how social norms began to change with the introduction of capitalism and the market economy and how this affected the political debate, see Albert O. Hirschman, *The Passions and the Interests: Political Arguments for Capitalism before Its Triumph* (Princeton University Press, 1977).

28. To characterize the challenge to Central and Eastern Europe as *reform* is inadequate, if not misleading. When one speaks of systemic reform, one thinks of adjustments made to improve the performance of a system. But one assumes that the basic structure of the system is in place and that the people that man these structures

have sufficient experience and know-how to operate the system even though they themselves will have to adjust their operational skills periodically.

29. A similar but opposite change is required for the transformation of the polity in which close *horizontal* relationships existed among the bureaucratic and political elites, which enabled them to exercise vertical control over the economy. They now must be replaced by *vertical* organizational forms in order to transmit and aggregate the interests of all factions of society.

30 .This is not to imply that these countries have no vocational training systems, but that their systems will have to be restructured to become effective mechanisms of support for the creation of a market economy. For an overview of vocational training in the former Eastern bloc, see CEDEFOP, *Vocational Training, Our European Neighbours*, no. 2 (1989) (Berlin: European Centre for the Development of Vocational Training).

31. A total of $22.5 billion (or $6 billion more than in 1991) will be available in 1992 for use in the labor market of the new *Länder*. See "1992 Training, Job Creation Funds in East," Foreign Broadcasting Information Service, *Daily Report: West Europe*, December 6, 1991 (hereafter *FBIS-WEU*). See also "Job Creation Measures Relieve Unemployment," *FBIS-WEU*, January 3, 1992.

32. The opening of the societies in Eastern Europe has given rise in some countries to many groups and organizations. These groups could become vehicles for the transmission of ideas and interests to government as well as the basis for society's self-organization. However, such groups have not yet formed an organic entity; on the contrary, they are contributing to the social disintegration occurring in the region. Moreover, they constitute only a narrow segment of the society. Many people previously forced to participate in social life now refuse to engage in it. See Lena Kolarska-Bobinska, "Civil Society and Social Anomy in Poland," *Acta Sociologica*, vol. 33, no. 4 (1990), pp. 277–88.

33. Many Central and East European countries still lack comprehensive commercial codes.

34. Some have gone so far as to argue that the market dictates political decisions just as political considerations dictated the economy under socialist systems. See Charles Lindblom, "The Market As a Prison," *Journal of Politics*, vol. 44 (1982), pp. 325–36.

35. Tadeusz Mazowiecki, "Polens schwieriger Weg in die Normalität," *Frankfurter Allgemeine Zeitung*, August 24, 1991.

36. On culture, see "Freed from Censorship, Culture in Hungary Now Suffers Lack of Security," *New York Times*, December 11, 1991. Preliminary studies in the former German Democratic Republic describe people as "shaken and lacking self confidence." External coercion during Communist rule was translated into internal repression. The former republic is described as a nation of "repressed, inhibited and chronically dissatisfied victims of dictatorship." The studies also warn that "if one ignores the state of the psyche in the former GDR, then things will go awry here. They will end in uproar, violence, and chaos." See "Slow Harmonization of Workplace Psychology," *FBIS-WEU*, September 11, 1991; and Ingrid Stratemann, *Psychologische Aspekte des wirtschaftlichen Wiederaufbaus in den neuen Bundesländern* (Göttingen,

1991). See also "Lädiertes Selbstwertgefühl der Ostdeutschen wieder aufbauen," *Handelsblatt*, August 3, 1991.

37. George Dalton, *Primitive, Archaic and Modern Economies: Essays of Karl Polanyi* (Beacon Press, 1968).

38. Even though unemployment may not be considered excessively high in absolute terms, it is in relative terms, after years of full employment.

39. Few Central and East European countries have yet implemented new educational structures. A new law is being discussed in Poland. Hungary began educational reform in 1985, advocating decentralization and autonomy for the system, but the reform was not very effective. A new law is being planned for 1992. See Gerhard Huck, "Neudefinition der Bildungsinhalte," *Das Parlament* (August 16 and August 23, 1991). Besides setting up new structures and laws that may replicate Western systems, these countries need to train staff in curriculum development and the management of educational systems at both the school and university level so that each country can develop its own system, based on its own history and tradition.

40. See, for example, "Den Reformen fehlt oft die letzte Konsequenz," *Handelsblatt*, December 31, 1991. Even in the United Kingdom, the European country most committed to private ownership, major corporations and services have been supported with huge injections of public funds and have been carefully prepared for sale.

41. "Poland Outlines Mass Privatization Scheme," *Financial Times*, June 28, 1991. Much greater progress has been made in privatizing trade and retail outlets. Nearly 80 percent of Poland's shops have been privatized, and more than 46 percent of its imports in 1991 were handled by the newly privatized trade sector. "Warsaw Looks West for a Fast Track into Private Hands," *Financial Times*, February 25, 1992.

42. See "Slow Down in Polish Privatization," *RFE/RL Daily Report*, October 11, 1991; "Polish Privatization Program Scaled Back," *RFE/RL Daily Report*, October 17, 1991; "Die Umsetzung marktwirtschaftlicher Prinzipien bei den Unternehmen steht aus," *Handelsblatt*, May 28, 1991; "Korrekturen am Balcerowicz-Plan," *Handelsblatt*, September 25, 1991; "Newly Capitalist Poland Meets Underside of Free Market," *Journal of Commerce*, December 3, 1991; and "Economic Problems Frustrate Polish Government's Plans," *Financial Times*, February 7, 1992. One important aspect of Poland's new program is that 50 percent of the revenues will be kept by the privatization ministry to restructure some of the companies before they are sold off. See "Polish Government Gives Top Priority to Mass Privatization," *Financial Times*, February 15–16, 1992.

43. "Warsaw Looks West for a Fast Track into Private Hands," *Financial Times*, February 25, 1992.

44. "Gerüchte über Strohmänner geben in Prag Rätsel auf," *Handelsblatt*, October 21, 1991; "Increase in Failure of Privatized Shops Reported," Foreign Broadcasting Information Service, *Daily Report: East Europe*, August 5, 1991 (hereafter *FBIS-EEU*); "Prague Sell-off Disrupted," *Financial Times*, January 21, 1992.

45. Investment funds are bound only by a few paragraphs on joint-stock companies in the business code that Parliament adopted in November 1991. A new law is under preparation; see "Privatization Free-for-All Worries Czechoslovaks," *Financial Times*, February 13, 1992.

46. "Czechoslovaks Queue to Cash in on Capitalism," *Financial Times*, January 29, 1992; "Czechoslovakia's Coupon Privatization," *RFE/RL Daily Report*, January 22, 1992; "Czechoslovak Privatization Update," *RFE/RL Daily Report*, January 24, 1992; "Coupon Book Registration Not to Be Interrupted," *FBIS-EEU*, January 24, 1992; and "Czech Official Urges Care in Coupon Privatization," *FBIS-EEU*, January 27, 1992.

47. "Klaus Explains Investment Coupon Registration," *FBIS-EEU*, January 28, 1992; and "Ministry Seeks Ways to Pull Privatization Licenses," *FBIS-EEU*, January 28, 1992. A law that cleared the way for reestablishing stock exchanges was passed in April 1992. See "Parliament Passes Stock Exchange Law," *RFE/RL Daily Report*, April 22, 1992; and "Prague Plods On towards a Regulated Stock Market," *Financial Times*, May 15, 1992.

48. "In Poland, Red Tape Knows No Ideology," *Washington Post*, February 23, 1992.

49. This is not to say that an organic balance among the various market domains can be maintained at all times. Such fine tuning would be too difficult, given the unpredictability of this evolutionary process. However, by recognizing the multidimensionality, we can avoid major systemic disjunctures during the creation of a market economy and thus avoid severe setbacks.

50. Charles E. Lindblom, *The Intelligence of Democracy: Decision Making Through Mutual Adjustment* (New York: Free Press, 1965).

51. In fact, the high levels of state ownership and control in France, Italy, and several other West European countries suggest that large-scale privatization is not even a necessary condition for the establishment of an effective market economy.

52. See Adam Michnik, "The Two Faces of Europe," *New York Review of Books*, July 19, 1990, p. 7.

53. Wolfgang H. Reinicke, "Divergence between Expectations and Economic Reality Could Lead to Politically Explosive Situation in Former Eastern Bloc," *Europe in Washington*, vol. 1, no. 4 (1990).

54. United Nations, Economic Commission for Europe, *Economic Survey of Europe, 1989–1990* (New York, 1990); and United Nations, *World Economic Survey, 1991* (New York, 1991).

55. "Corruption Still a Problem in Poland," *RFE\RL Daily Report*, no. 150 (August 8, 1991), p. 3.

56. From January to June 1990 the main statistical office reported 91 strikes in Polish factories. This number rose to 159 during the second part of 1990. During the first six months of 1991, 271 strikes were registered. See "GUS Releases Data on Production, Deficits and Pay," Warsaw PAP, July 23, 1991, in *FBIS-EEU*, July 24, 1991, p. 18.

57. Most recently, Solidarity rejected a government proposal to suspend the valorization of wages in the second half of 1991, calling such a move a step that would deepen "the situation of chaos and uncertainty." See "Government, Unions Differ on Wages," *FBIS-EEU*, July 16, 1991.

58. "Modzelewski Hits Government Economic Policy," *FBIS-EEU*, August 1, 1991.

59. "Poles Losing Interest in Elections," Warsaw PAP, July 23, 1991, in *FBIS-*

EEU, July 23, 1991, pp. 22–23. A close aide of Lech Walesa commented on this trend as follows: "People feel more and more threatened by the future . . . support for the reforms is falling continuously. Eventually this might reach a critical point and turn into a general strike or such a level of apathy that people will stop taking part in public life." See "Walesa Advisor Najder on Threat to Reform," Warsaw ZYCIE WARSZAWY, July 26, 1991, in *FBIS-EEU,* August 2, 1991, pp. 27–29. For an analysis of the Polish elections, see Henrik Bischof, "Nach den freien Wahlen in Polen," *Kurzpapier* , no. 15, Abteilung Aussenpolitikforschung, Arbeitsbereich "Sowjetunion und Osteuropa," Bonn: Friedrich-Ebert-Stiftung, December 1991.

60. The strongest party received only 12 percent of the vote, and there are currently twenty-nine parties represented in the Sejm. On the crisis and the internal disagreements, see "Wenig Spielraum für einen Kurswechsel in Polen," *Neue Zürcher Zeitung,* December 25–26, 1991; "Walesa Denies Responsibility for Current Crisis," *FBIS-EEU,* January 16, 1992; "Economic Problems Frustrate Polish Government Plans," *Financial Times,* February 7, 1992; "Polish Minister Resigns over Rift," *Financial Times,* February 18, 1992; "Polish Budget Vote Casts Doubt on Government," *Financial Times,* March 6, 1992; "Bielecki Stands by Washington Remarks," *FBIS-EEU,* January 16, 1992. On Poland's conflict with the IMF and the World Bank, see "Poland Asks IMF to Ease Monetary Restrictions," *Financial Times,* June 17, 1991; "IMF Suspends Credits for Poland," *Morning Press,* IMF, September 27, 1991; "Polnische Angriffe gegen den IMF," *Neue Zürcher Zeitung,* December 4, 1991; "IMF Asks Poland to Cut Consumption," *Journal of Commerce,* February 21, 1992; "Poles Announce IMF Pact," *Financial Times,* March 18, 1992.

61. "Somber Mood Grips Hungary," *Journal of Commerce,* January 15, 1991, p. XX; "The Dilemmas of Freedom," *Financial Times,* December 27, 1990, p. 10.

62. "Hungarian By-Election Marked by Apathy," *RFE/RL Daily Report,* August 12, 1991; Peter Falush, "Hungary's Reform in Low Gear," *The World Today,* vol. 47 (April 1991), pp. 57–59.

63. "Schmerzhafte Reformen gefährden die Stabilität," *Handelsblatt,* January 3, 1992.

64. "Meciar Wants Restrictive Economic Policy Halted," *FBIS-EEU,* February 10, 1992; "Eine tschechisch-slowakische Vernunftehe," *Neue Zürcher Zeitung,* November 20, 1991; and "Czech Prime Minister Criticizes Federal Finance Minister," *RFE/RL Daily Report,* January 16, 1992.

65. "Czechs Lead Slovakia in the Economic Stakes," *Financial Times,* June 9, 1992; and "A State Well Worth Saving," *Financial Times,* June 9, 1992.

66. See, for example, Institute for International Finance, *Financial Sector Reform in Central and Eastern Europe* (Washington, January 1991).

67. For the role of the financial system in economic development, see Rondo E. Cameron, ed., *Banking in the Early Stages of Industrialization: A Study in Comparative Economic History* (London: Oxford University Press, 1967), and *Banking and Economic Development: Some Lessons of History* (London: Oxford University Press, 1972); and Charles Kindleberger, *A Financial History of Western Europe* (Allen and Unwin, 1984). For the role of financial markets in the post-World War II economies see Jacques Polak, *Financial Policies and Development* (Paris: Organization for Economic Cooperation and Development, 1989); and "Financial Systems and Devel-

opment," Policy and Research Series, no. 15 (Washington: World Bank, October 1990).

68. E. Gerald Corrigan, "The Role of Central Banks and the Financial System in Emerging Market Economies," *Federal Reserve Bank of New York Quarterly Review* (Summer 1990), pp. 1–7; Lawrence Brainard, "Reform in Eastern Europe: Creating a Capital Market," *Federal Reserve Bank of Kansas City Economic Review* (January–February 1991), pp. 49–58; Thomas H. Hanley and others, *Banking in Eastern Europe: A New Market Opens Up* (New York: Salomon Brothers, June 1991); Alan H. Gelb and Cheryl W. Gray, "The Transformation of Economies in Central and Eastern Europe: Issues, Progress and Prospects," Policy and Research Series, no. 17 (Washington: World Bank, June 1991); and "Gelingen der Reformen im Osten setzt leistungsfähiges Bankensystem voraus," *Handelsblatt*, September 30, 1991.

69. In Hungary and Poland, for example, the savings rate in 1986 was 25 percent and 30 percent of GDP, respectively. Similarly, the investment rate was 26 percent of GDP for Hungary and 29 percent of GDP for Poland. See Institute for International Finance, *Building Free Market Economies in Central and Eastern Europe: Challenges and Realities* (Washington, April 1990).

70. For an overview of financial systems in Central and Eastern Europe, see Anne Hendrick, *Banking in COMECON* (London: Financial Times Business Information, 1989); George Garvy, *Money, Banking, and Credit in Eastern Europe* (New York: Federal Reserve Bank of New York, 1966); and OECD, *OECD, Services in Central and Eastern Europe* (Paris, 1991).

71. See, for example, "Privatbanken werden öffentlichen Kapital-gebern den Vortritt lassen," *Handelsblatt*, December 31, 1990. However, this has created problems. Since many countries now allow their citizens to buy foreign exchange, depositors have been paid interest rates in line with inflation to encourage them to hold some of their savings in local currency. Given the high inflation in some countries—especially in what used to be Yugoslavia, Poland, and Hungary—emerging businesses have refused to borrow at such high rates, with the result that the transformation process has been stifled.

72. The lack of an indigenous system of financial sources has been one of the principal factors for Latin America's dependence and debt accumulation.

73. The ability to control the money supply is still limited. For the most part, credit ceilings and the refinancing of bank credits to enterprises have remained the principal tool of monetary control. In Hungary since December 1988, the central bank has guided short-term interest rates through regular treasury bill auctions. Poland started to sell so-called national bank bills early in 1991.

74. See, for example, IMF, "Financial Market Constraints and Private Investment in a Developing Country," Working Paper 90/121 (Washington, December 1990).

75. Norbert Kloten, "Beseitigung des Geldüberhangs und Inflationsbekämpfung," *Auszüge aus Presseartikeln* (Deutsche Bundesbank), no. 79 (October 1990), pp. 11–12. See also A. Khandruev, "Monetary Aspects of the Stabilization," *Nomisma*, vol. 1 (1990), pp. 43–51.

76. Obviously, such a strategy only works if there are attractive investments that can pay higher interest rates. In a much less popular measure, the Soviet Union

attempted to reduce this overhang by withdrawing large-denomination notes from circulation. For additional ways to reduce the overhang, see Guillermo A. Calvo and Jacob A. Frenkel, "Obstacles to Transforming Centrally-Planned Economies: The Role of Capital Markets," Working Paper 3776 (Cambridge, Mass.: National Bureau of Economic Research, July 1991).

77. On the importance of capital markets in the Polish privatization, see "Erste Aktien im April notiert," *Handelsblatt*, March 14, 1991. For more on the status of the Polish stock exchange, see PlanEcon, *PlanEcon, Review and Outlook* (Washington, July 1991), pp. 125–26.

78. See, for example, the contributions by the participants from Central and Eastern Europe in *Central Banking Issues in Emerging Market-Oriented Economies*, a symposium sponsored by the Federal Reserve of Kansas City, Jackson Hole, Wyoming, August 23–25, 1990. For an excellent overview see V. Sundararajan, "Financial Sector Reform and Central Banking in Centrally Planned Economies," in Patrick Downes and Reza Vaez-Zadeh, *The Evolving Role of Central Banks* (Washington: IMF, 1991); Herbert Poenisch, "The New Central Banks of Eastern Europe," *Central Banking*, vol. 1, no. 4 (1991). While Hungary started with basic economic reforms in 1968, it did not introduce a two-tier banking system until 1988. See T. Erdös, "Monetary Regulation and Its Perplexities in Hungary," *Acta Oeconomica*, vol. 40 (1989), pp. 1–16. See also Ted Gardener, "Big Bang in Budapest," *Banking World*, August 1990; "Für das neue Bankensystem ist der Grundstein gelegt," *Süddeutsche Zeitung*, June 6, 1991.

79. For some background information on these systems see Istvan Szekely, "The Reform of the Hungarian Financial System," *European Economy*, no. 43 (March 1990), pp. 107–23.

80. Richard A. Debs, Harvey Shapiro, and Charles Taylor, *Financing Eastern Europe*, A Study Group Report (Washington: Group of Thirty, 1991); Institute for International Finance, Inc., *Financial Sector Reform in Central and Eastern Europe* (Washington, January 1991). In Bulgaria commercial banks still have not gained full independence from the former state bank. See *PlanEcon, Review and Outlook.*

81. Donald Franklin and Michael Harnett, "Central and Eastern Europe in Transition," *Journal of International Securities Markets* (Autumn 1991), pp. 247–60; "Heisse Eisen werden nicht angepackt," *Handelsblatt*, November 20, 1991; and Poenisch, "The New Central Banks of Eastern Europe."

82. Bank for International Settlements, *61st Annual Report* (Basle, June 10, 1991).

83. "Slovak Companies' Debt Reach 20 Billion Korunas," *FBIS-EEU*, July 11, 1991.

84. Data provided by the deputy governor of the National Bank of Yugoslavia, as cited in Brainard, "Reform in Eastern Europe."

85. "Reconstruction Is a Priority," *Financial Times*, April 28, 1992.

86. Thomas H. Hanley and others, *Banking in Eastern Europe* (New York: Salomon Brothers, June 1991), pp. 9–10.

87. "Wohin mit dem Geld in Polen?" *Süddeutsche Zeitung*, April 11, 1991; "Bank Scandal May Help Belgrade Reform," *Financial Times*, January 18, 1991; "Plot Thickens in Polish Bank Scandal," *RFE/RL Daily Report*, no. 151 (August 9, 1991);

"Poland's Central Bank Is Rattled by Scandal," *New York Times*, August 12, 1991; "Poles Charged in Financial Scandal," *Financial Times*, November 14, 1991; "Former Polish Bank Chief Charged," *Financial Times*, September 24, 1991; "Poles Seek $330m Proceeds from Country's Biggest Fraud," *Financial Times*, November 8, 1991; and "Further Arrests in Polish Scandal," *RFE/RL Daily Report*, August 16, 1991.

88. Poland had agreed not to undertake such transactions. See "Former Head of Polish Debt Fund Arrested," *Financial Times*, August 23, 1991; "Polens Schulden-Unterhändler Sawicki entlassen," *Süddeutsche Zeitung*, August 26, 1991; and "Polish Report Links US Bank to Debt Buy-Backs," *Financial Times*, October 11, 1991. In early September a new chief negotiator, Wladyslaw Golebiewski, deputy president for International Affairs of the National Bank of Poland was appointed. See "New Debt Negotiating Chief Appointed in Poland," *RFE/RL Daily Report*, September 6, 1991.

89. "Polish Parliament Rejects Bank Chief," *Financial Times*, September 14–15, 1991; "Walesa Proposes New National Bank President," *FBIS-EEU*, December 9, 1991; "Sejm Rejects Walesa's National Bank Nominee," *FBIS-EEU*, December 18, 1991; "Walesa Reopens Bank Chief Row," *Financial Times*, February 26, 1992; "Walesa Urges Support for Bank President Candidate," *FBIS-EEU*, February 26, 1992; ". . . And [Walesa] Endorses National Bank Chairman," *RFE/RL Daily Report*, March 6, 1992.

90. "Comment on Dismissal of Bank Chairman Suranyi," *FBIS-EEU*, December 5, 1991.

91. On the links between proper banking supervision and the failure of financial reforms see Jacques Gautier, "Financial Reform, Financial Policy, and Bank Regulation," in Patrick Downes and Reza Vaez-Zadeh, *The Evolving Role of Central Banks* (Washington: IMF, 1991).

92. "Polish MPs Approve Bank Reform," *Financial Times*, September 23, 1991.

93. Interview with the president of the Polish National Bank, Grzegorz Wojtowicz, *FBIS-EEU*, May 16, 1991.

94. Grzegorz Wojtowicz, "Dynamische Zunahme neuer Institute, aber Mängel bei der Infrastruktur," *Handelsblatt*, May 28, 1991.

95. "Schon 100,000 Aktionäre in Polen," *Süddeutsche Zeitung*, March 12, 1991; "Erste Aktien im April notiert," *Handelsblatt*, March 14, 1991; and "Capitalism of a Sort," *Economist*, December 1, 1990.

96. "Hungary Lays Ground for Sell-off of Banks," *Financial Times*, November 15, 1991; and "Assembly Passes Law on Financial Institutions," *FBIS-EEU*, November 15, 1991. See also "Hungarian Banks Prepare for Rough Transition," *Journal of Commerce*, June 17, 1991.

97. The rather conservative legislation ensures that the state will retain a 40–50 percent equity stake in the country's six leading commercial banks. Foreign investors will be allowed to buy up to 25 percent of any bank's equity, but no one investor will be allowed to hold more than a 10 percent share. These provisions are designed to allay fears that foreign capital will dominate the banking sector. See "Prague Approves Banking Reform Act," *Financial Times*, November 22, 1991; "Umgestaltung des Bankensystems der CSFR," *Neue Zürcher Zeitung*, December 14, 1991; and "Assembly Chamber Approves Law on Banks," *FBIS-EEU*, December 27, 1991.

98. "Council of Ministers Endorses Banking Bill," *FBIS-EEU*, July 9, 1991; "Government Approves Banking, Credit Bill," *FBIS-EEU*, November 19, 1991; and "Bulgarian Parliament Adopts Law on Banks," *RFE/RL Daily Report*, February 28, 1992. See also "National Bank Asked to Monitor Commercial Banks," *FBIS-EEU*, March 18, 1992.

99. "Die Tschechoslowakei muss aus eigener Kraft Banken und Betriebe sanieren," *Handelsblatt*, April 4, 1991; and "Bereinigung der Bilanzen bleibt weiter umstritten," *Handelsblatt*, July 1, 1991.

100. "Signs That All Is Not Well," *Financial Times*, April 28, 1992.

101. Banks were following instructions by the various ministries to lend to state enterprises, irrespective of their ability to service or repay the loan. For the Polish case, see "The Players Lack Experience," *Financial Times*, November 20, 1991; for the CSFR, see "Umgestaltung des Bankensystems der CSFR," *Neue Zürcher Zeitung*, December 14, 1992.

102. Customers had no choice of a bank, and the low and often arbitrary interest rates were not considered an instrument to encourage people to deposit money with financial institutions, nor did they reflect risk in the return on an asset. Still, given the shortage of goods, savings ratios were often high.

103. "Run on Poland's First Private Bank," *RFE/RL Daily Report*, January 22, 1992; "Banker Held as U.S. Requests Extradition," *Financial Times*, February 3, 1992; see also "Poland Jails Banker after Request For Extradition," *Journal of Commerce*, April 2, 1992; and "Poland Agrees to Extradite US Tax Evader," *RFE/RL Daily Report*, March 20, 1992.

104. With the help of the World Bank, Yugoslavia, for example, founded the Federal Agency for Deposit Insurance and Bank Rehabilitation to help restructure the financial system. But such a move is likely to be unpopular and carry a heavy political cost. Given that roughly 20,000 enterprises are now either illiquid or insolvent, many of them would have to close as well. See "Enterprise Culture," *Financial Times*, June 27, 1991. Similar plans exist in Czechoslovakia. See, for example, "Die Tschechoslowakei muss aus eigener Kraft Banken und Betriebe sanieren," *Handelsblatt*, April 4, 1991; and "Bereinigung der Bilanzen bleibt weiter umstritten," *Handelsblatt*, July 1, 1991. See also "End of a Communist Banking System," *Financial Times*, July 5, 1991; and "Gaddum: Abwicklung des Zahlungsverkehrs erschwert," *Handelsblatt*, December 29, 1990.

105. Convertible bonds worth about $0.58 billion will be issued to the commercial banks by three national property funds, which were set up for the privatization process. See "Prague to Ease Path to Private Sector," *Financial Times*, October 18, 1991.

106. "Czechoslovak Banks Get Government Credit," *RFE/RL Daily Report*, October 9, 1991.

107. For a similar proposition to recapitalize the banking system see Donald Franklin and Michael Harnett, "Central and Eastern Europe in Transition," *Journal of International Securities Markets*, (Autumn 1991), pp. 247–60.

108. Thomas H. Hanley and others, *Banking in Eastern Europe*; and "Ausländische Banken beschränken sich zumeist noch auf eine Beobachterrolle," *Handelsblatt*, May 14, 1991.

109. Recently, the Lazard Bank of France and the Polish Bank Handlowy formed

a joint venture. See *RFE/RL Daily Report*, April 12, 1991. Similarly, the Austrian bank Kreditanstalt-Bankverein, which is already active in Hungary, recently opened branches in Poland and the CSFR. On telecommunications see "Reconstruction Is a Priority," *Financial Times*, April 28, 1992.

110. "Polish Banks in 'Twinning' Deal with West," *Financial Times*, July 12, 1991. The scheme is partly financed through a World Bank loan. Numerous other joint operations are being planned or have already been established. See, for example "European Arm of CSFB Opens Office in Budapest," *Financial Times*, December 4, 1990; "Neue Banken in Ungarn gegründet," *Handelsblatt*, December 12, 1990; "Eine Bank Troika für Ungarn," *Süddeutsche Zeitung*, December 23, 1990; "Securities Firm to Join Hungary SE," *Financial Times*, February 20, 1991; "Ein Dutzend Gemeinschaftsinstitute und 37 Banken haben Repräsentanzen," *Handelsblatt*, May 27, 1991; and "12 buhlen um die Gunst der Gewerbebanken," *Süddeutsche Zeitung*, May 6, 1991.

111. "Treasury Awards Contract for Central and Eastern European Financial Training," *Treasury News*, May 1, 1992.

112. "Bank of England Training E Europe Central Bankers," *Financial Times*, September 26, 1991. The central banking department of the IMF has also offered technical assistance to the National Bank of Poland. See "IMF Central Banking Department Organizes Aid to National Bank of Poland," *IMF Survey*, August 13, 1991. On the EBRD's project see "Developing Eastern Europe's Capital Markets," *Financial Times*, February 6, 1992.

113. "New York, Budapest Exchanges to Cooperate," *RFE/RL Daily Report*, February 25, 1992; and "Hungarian Exchange in Deal with Nymex," *Journal of Commerce*, February 25, 1992.

114. On the decision to use convertible currencies, see, for example, "Death of the Surreal Transferable Ruble," *Financial Times*, December 31, 1990; and "Noch viele ungelöste Rechtsfragen beim Umtausch von Transferrubeln," *Handelsblatt*, January 2, 1991. On the end of the CMEA see "Members Agree to Bury Comecon," *Financial Times*, January 7, 1991; and "Die Wirtschaftsgemeinschaft des Ostens löst sich auf," *Süddeutsche Zeitung*, January 7, 1991. For an excellent discussion of the trade relationships among the former CMEA members, see UN Economic Commission for Europe, "Reforms in Foreign Economic Relations of Eastern Europe and the Soviet Union," Economic Studies, no. 2 (New York: United Nations, 1991).

115. On the collapse, see "Export Ban on Russian Goods," *RFE/RL Daily Report*, January 10, 1992; and "Das Verbot des Tauschgeschäfts hat den Handel mit RGW-Staaten hart getroffen," *Handelsblatt*, June 11, 1991. See also *FBIS-EEU*, July 30, 1991; and "Significant Decline in Soviet Trade Reported," *FBIS-EEU*, August 29, 1991. Michael S. Lelyveld, "Plan to Aid Soviets Expected to Boost E. European Trade," *Journal of Commerce*, June 4, 1991, p. 5; "Balcerowics Seeks Western Aid for Exports," *FBIS-EEU*, June 5, 1991; and "Den Reformen fehlt oft die letzte Konsequenz," *Handelsblatt*, December 31, 1991.

116. "Deputy Minister Pancir on Foreign Trade Problems," *FBIS-EEU*, July 30, 1991.

117. "Kadar Reports Foreign Trade Statistics," *FBIS-EEU*, July 9, 1991.

118. "Der Kollaps im Osten wird dynamisch überspielt," *Handelsblatt*, December 27–28, 1991. See also *FBIS-EEU*, July 31, 1991; "Hungary Goes West with a New Urgency," *Financial Times*, May 2, 1991; and "Auf dunkle Zeiten vorbereitet," *Süddeutsche Zeitung*, August 21, 1991.

119. The companies had signed their contracts before January 1991. In Poland, the government had to pay 15 trillion zlotys to compensate private Polish companies. See "Losses in Trade with the Soviet Union Outlined," *FBIS-EEU*, July 26, 1991.

120. On the collapse of trade among the member countries, see UN Economic Commission for Europe, *Economic Survey of Europe in 1990–1991* (New York: United Nations, 1991), esp. pp. 74–82; and "High Hopes Give Way to Empty Shelves," *Financial Times*, April 2, 1991. On the problems of East Germany's exit from the CMEA, see András Inotai, "Economic Impact of German Reunification on Central and Eastern Europe," mimeo, July 1991. The Czech figures are from "Economic Repercussions for CEMA Felt," *FBIS-EEU*, May 30, 1991. Figures for Hungary are from "Economic Effects of CEMA's Collapse Assessed," *FBIS-EEU*, August 7, 1991.

121. "Budapest zeigt dem Kreml die kalte Schulter," *Handelsblatt*, March 15–16, 1991. On the subsidy, see Organization for Economic Cooperation and Development, *Economic Outlook* (Paris, 1990), here p. 49. For the Baltics, this subsidy is estimated at about $2 billion to $3 billion a year. On the Baltic energy dependence and the higher costs, see "Skandinavier werben um die Baltenstaaten," *Neue Zürcher Zeitung*, November 12, 1991; and "Baltic States Consider Costs of Breaking Free," *Financial Times*, November 7, 1991.

122. Juri Dienstbier, "Die Aussenpolitik der Tschechoslowakei in einer neuen Zeit, Vorschläge zur Wirtschaftlichen Gesundung Osteuropas," *Europa-Archiv*, vol. 45, no. 13–14 (1990), pp. 397–407, here p. 398.

123. "Charta für neue Organization," *Handelsblatt*, January 7, 1991; "Teure Marktwirtschaft," *Handelsblatt*, January 8, 1991; and "Endloser Schlussakt," *Die Zeit*, March 1, 1991. Countries such as Austria, Finland, Yugoslavia, and Germany (as the legal representative of the former German Democratic Republic) were invited to join, and there was speculation about whether the European Community would be invited to have an observer status. "Valuation Row Could Mar COMECON Talks," *Financial Times*, January 2, 1991; "Die Wirtschaftsgemeinschaft des Ostens löst sich auf," *Süddeutsche Zeitung*, January 7, 1991; "Charta für eine Organisation," *Handelsblatt*, January 7, 1991; and "Editorial Analyzes Relations with CMEA," *FBIS-EEU*, May 24, 1991.

124. "High Hopes Give Way to Empty Shelves," *Financial Times*, April 2, 1991; "RGW Konferenz in Moskau," *Handelsblatt*, March 14, 1991; and "COMECON: desaccord sur une nouvelle organization," *Agence Europe*, March 16, 1991. See also "East Europe Cool on Soviet Trade Proposal," *Financial Times*, September 5, 1991. The three opposed any follow-up organization that would include Mongolia, Vietnam, and Cuba. See "Comecon Put Out of Misery after 42 Years," *Financial Times*, June 29–30, 1991; and "Die Reformländer fegen ihre Scherben zusammen," *Handelsblatt*, June 28–29, 1991.

125. "Rat für Gegenseitige Wirtschaftshilfe aufgelöst," *Süddeutsche Zeitung*, June

29–30, 1991. The dissolution was delayed for several months because of a domestic disagreement in the Soviet Union over the need to dissolve the trading bloc.

126. "Budapest zeigt dem Kreml die kalte Schulter," *Handelsblatt,* March 15–16, 1991; "CSFR Tariffs Would Prove 'Surprising'" *FBIS-EEU,* June 20, 1991; and "New Customs Tariffs Become Effective Early 1992," *FBIS-EEU,* December 17, 1991.

127. "Hungary, Poland, CSFR to Coordinate on EC," *FBIS-EEU,* October 29, 1991; and "Biliecki Interviewed on Regional Cooperation," *FBIS-EEU,* June 28, 1991. The Soviet Union traded principally oil (also coal, wood products, construction materials, tractors, and artificial fertilizers) for buses and pharmaceutical, agricultural, and light industry products; in June and July 1991 Poland, Hungary, and Czechoslovakia each signed major barter agreements with the Russian Republic of the Soviet Union worth $360 million, $670 million, and $130 million, respectively. See *FBIS-EEU,* July 24, 1991; "Agricultural Agreement with Russian Republic," *FBIS-EEU,* June 3, 1991; "Hungarian-RSFSR Trade Agreement Signed," *RFE/RL Daily Report,* June 17, 1991; and "Problems in Trade with Soviet Union Discussed," *FBIS-EEU,* May 29, 1991. On the lifting of the barter agreement, see "Official on Trade Problems With USSR," *FBIS-EEU,* May 22, 1991; and "Horn Discusses Economic Ties with USSR," *FBIS-EEU,* July 16, 1991.

128. The problem with such exchanges at present is that Soviet oil and gas production has declined considerably over the past year, and exports to Central and Eastern Europe have suffered most from that decline. See General Accounting Office, *Soviet Energy, U.S. Attempts to Aid Oil Production Are Hindered by Many Obstacles* (Washington, May 1991).

129. See, for example, "Russia to Restrict Natural Gas Supplies," *FBIS-EEU,* January 13, 1992; "Poland Concerned about Russian Fuel Deliveries," *RFE/RL Daily Report,* January 24, 1992; "Soviet Oil Deliveries Resume; Gas Shortage," *FBIS-EEU,* January 28, 1992; "Russia Breaks Polish Barter Deal," *RFE/RL Daily Report,* January 29, 1992; and "Russia to Increase Gas, Resume Oil Supplies," *FBIS-EEU,* January 30, 1992. See also "Dienstbier on Treaties with Commonwealth Nations," *FBIS-EEU,* December 27, 1991; "Trade Talks with USSR Begin," *FBIS-EEU,* June 17, 1991; and "Minister Views Economic Ties with USSR," *FBIS-EEU,* August 27, 1991.

130. "Comecon Successor in the Works?" *RFE/RL Daily Report,* July 12, 1991; and "Bulgarien für gemeinsame Regierungs-konsultationen," *Süddeutsche Zeitung,* July 15, 1991.

131. "Warschau, Budapest und Prag wollen sich gemeinsam um die Zukunft bemühen," *Handelsblatt,* February 18, 1991; "Kadar on Trade and Hungary's Foreign Debt," *RFE/RL Daily Report,* March 19, 1991; "Europe De L'Est: Vers Une Zone De Libre Echange Hongrie-Tchecoslovaquie-Pologne," *Europe,* Lundi–Mardi, April 8–9, 1991; "Hungary Proposes Trade Zone Talks," *RFE/RL Daily Report,* April 11, 1991. In general Poland and the CSFR reacted positively to such a proposal. See, for example, "Bilecki on EC Integration Forecast," *FBIS-EEU,* June 18, 1991; and "Rychetsky: Central European Cooperation Suitable," *FBIS-EEU,* June 25, 1991. Still some resistance to cooperation remains for domestic and foreign policy reasons. See "Klaus Views Economic Progress, Transformation," *FBIS-EEU,* August 12, 1991, here p. 11. See also "Free Trade Talks with Poland, CSFR Open," *FBIS-EEU,*

July 30, 1991; "Die Idee des Dreierbundes," *Handelsblatt*, September 19, 1991; "Customs Union, EC Ties Viewed," *FBIS-EEU*, October 8, 1991; "Declaration Issued," *FBIS-EEU*, October 8, 1991; "Poland, CSFR, Hungary Meet on Trade Issues," and "Agreement Signed," *FBIS-EEU*, December 3, 1991; and "Article Views Trilateral Free Trade Agreement," *FBIS-EEU*, December 10, 1991.

132. Given the prospect of trade liberalization between each of these countries and the European Community some common framework had to be found for trade among themselves to avoid distorting trade through differential tariff rates. See also "Dienstbier Has High Hopes for Free Trade Zones," *FBIS-EEU*, May 15, 1992.

133. "Toward a Baltic Customs Union," *RFE/RL Daily Report*, February 5, 1992; "Balts for Commercial Council," *RFE/RL Daily Report*, November 21, 1991; and "Eine Freihandelszone als Scharnier zwischen den Sowjetrepubliken und Europa," *Handelsblatt*, August 26, 1991.

134. The European Energy Charter signed on December 17, 1991, by forty-five states, including the twelve Russian republics, is an important step in that direction. On East-West cooperation in energy and environment, see Helmut Schreiber and Ulrich Weissenburger, *Europäischer Umweltplan*, Europäischer Plan für die Zusammenarbeit beim ökologischen Aufbau in Mittel- und Osteuropa (Bonn: Institut für Europäische Umweltpolitik e.V, Berlin: Deutsches Institut für Wirtschaftsforschung, 1991); and Peter Palinkas, "Ost-West Kooperation im Energie- und Umweltbereich: Probleme und Aussichten," *Zeitschrift für Energiewirtschaft*, vol. 3 (1991), pp. 154–66.

135. The triangle countries had agreed in December to coordinate their policy on recognizing Slovenian and Croatian independence in accordance with the resolutions of the European Community Council of Foreign Ministers. See "CSFR-Hungary-Poland Agree on SFRY Policy," *FBIS-EEU*, December 19, 1991; and "SFRY Republic Recognition Discussed," *FBIS-EEU*, December 17, 1991.

136. It is often forgotten that the European Economic Community was founded primarily for political not economic purposes. See Wilhelm Hankel, "Die Idee einer Ost-EG ist realistisch," *Handelsblatt*, September, 20–21, 1991, p. S1.

137. The controversy broke out and Romania asked to be invited to the summit after Poland suggested that Transylvania should be included in the cooperative scheme. See "Jeszensky Examines Regional Economic Cooperation," *FBIS-EEU*, October 17, 1991; and Viktor Maier, "Europas Osten sucht nach einer neuen Ordnung," *Frankfurter Allgemeine*, February 27, 1991.

138. PHARE stands for Pologne/Hongrie-assistance à la réconstruction économique. Currently, only 15 percent of the resources allocated within the framework of PHARE can go to regional projects.

139. During a recent visit by Lech Walesa, the president of the commission indicated that the Community may be willing to consider such a policy move. See "Importance of 'Stable' Poland," *FBIS-EEU*, July 8, 1991.

140. Revival of regional trade is undoubtedly important. However, it cannot substitute for access to Western markets, particularly in such products as agriculture, textiles, and coal and steel.

141. This scheme was originally proposed by the CSFR Foreign Minister Jiri

Dienstbier, see "CSFR Proposes EC Aid to Boost Exports," *FBIS-WEU*, June 6, 1991. More recently, Japan has also indicated it may promote triangular trade. See "Japan Plans Soviet Food Loans," *Financial Times*, January 25–26, 1992.

142. This triangular trade had already been proposed by the commissioner for external affairs, Frans Andriesen. Recounting his experience during the council meeting, when he realized that his proposal would not pass, Andriessen intervened, "'Mr. Chairman, I would like to withdraw my proposal.' Because I preferred that it not be rejected, so I may get another chance to bring it back," as quoted in "Commissioner Andriessen Discusses EC Expansion," *FBIS-WEU*, August 15, 1991.

143. "EC Food Credit Signed for Russia," *Financial Times*, March 5, 1992. For more background, see "Pirek Views Western Aid for Exports to USSR," *FBIS-EEU*, November 14, 1991. The Central and East Europeans wrote to the Community expressing their "astonishment that until now it [the aid scheme] has been so very modest." See "Agreement Signed," *FBIS-EEU*, December 3, 1991. The whole debate about triangular trade started when Central and East Europeans correctly argued that Western aid to the Soviet Union would undermine their trade with the USSR. See, for example, "Kritik an Hilfe für die Sowjetunion," *Süddeutsche Zeitung*, June 12, 1991. The first actual deal in September broke down, however, when much of the 100,000 tons of Hungarian grain that the Commission had announced it would buy to ship to Albania was discovered to have gone bad because of difficulties in shipping it there.

144. "Hungary Wants EC Help to Export Pharmaceutical to USSR," *RFE/RL Daily Report*, October 15, 1991.

145. "Pharmaceutical Industry to Send Supplies to CIS," *FBIS-EEU*, January 27, 1992.

146. "Triangular Plan Accepted," *FBIS-EEU*, January 27, 1992; and "Comments on Supplying Medicine," *FBIS-EEU*, January 27, 1992.

147. "Jeszenszky Appraises Conference on CIS Aid," *FBIS-EEU*, January 27, 1992; "Visegrad Triangle Considers Aid Program to CIS," *FBIS-EEU*, January 23, 1992; "EE Plan for Aid to Ex-USSR," *RFE/RL Daily Report*, January 23, 1992; and "Participation in Commonwealth Aid Program Pending," *FBIS-EEU*, February 14, 1992.

148. Originally composed of only five states, the Pentagonale was expanded on July 27, 1990, to include Poland. More recently, the group decided to drop Yugoslavia from the arrangement, which is likely to be succeeded by several newly independent republics. "Regional Cooperation," *RFE/RL Daily Report*, January 24, 1992; and "Hexagonal Group Meets in Venice Nov. 30, to Recognize Slovenia, Croatia," *FBIS-EEU*, December 2, 1991.

149. See, respectively, "Pushkarov Supports Black Sea 'Common Market,'" *FBIS-EEU*, November 27, 1991; "Balkan-Staaten wollen enger zusammenarbeiten," *Frankfurter Allgemeine*, October 26, 1991; "Italien plant in Triest eine Freihandelszone," *Handelsblatt*, January 7, 1991; "Nordic Council to Increase Cooperation with Baltic States," *RFE/RL Daily Report*, November 14, 1991; "Skandinavier werben um die Baltenstaaten," *Neue Zürcher Zeitung*, November 12, 1991; "Dicke Fragen vor der Idee einer Hanseregion," *Handelsblatt*, September 11, 1991; "Baltic States Aim for EFTA Membership," *RFE/RL Daily Report*, October 14, 1991; "Die Europäische Freihandelszone kann ihre Funktion als Drehscheibe ausbauen," *Handelsblatt*, No-

vember 14, 1991; and Marion Gräfin von Dönhoff, "Ein Bogen bis zum Baltikum: Auf den Spuren der Hanse," *Die Zeit*, October 26, 1990.

150. "Baltic Neighbors Seek to Bridge East-West Divide," *Financial Times*, March 6, 1992; and "Baltic Regional Conference Starts in Copenhagen," *RFE/RL Daily Report*, March 5, 1992.

151. For a detailed discussion, see, for example, Jozef M. van Brabant, *A Central European Payments Union: Technical Aspects*, Public Policy Paper, no. 3 (New York: Institute for East-West Security Studies, June 1991); Economic Commission for Europe, "Reforms in Foreign Economic Relations of Eastern Europe and the Soviet Union," Economic Studies, no. 2 (New York: United Nations, 1991), esp. chapters, 3.8–3.10; Wojeiech Kostrzewa and others, "A Marshall Plan for Middle and Eastern Europe," *World Economy*, vol. 1 (1990), pp. 27–49; Norman S. Fieleke, "The Liberalization of International Trade and Payments in Eastern Europe," *New England Economic Review* (March–April 1991), pp. 41–51; Renzo Daviddi and Efisio Espa, "Foreign Aid and Monetary Integration in Central and Eastern Europe," CIDEI Working Paper 4 (Rome, June 1991); and John Williamson, *The Economic Opening of Eastern Europe* (Washington: Institute for International Economics, May 1991). For a more critical perspective, see Perter B. Kenen, "Transitional Arrangements for Trade and Payments among the CMEA Countries," *International Monetary Fund Staff Papers*, vol. 38 (June 1991), pp. 235–67.

152. The three Western banks supporting the scheme were Deutsche Bank, Credit Lyonnais, and San Paolo Bank. See "Clearing für Osteuropa," *Handelsblatt*, December 7, 1990; "Eastern Banks Back Ecu Trade System," *Financial Times*, April 24, 1991; and "Moscow to Discuss Ecu Payments System," *Financial Times*, April 23, 1991. The EBRD is also currently developing a proposal to establish a European payments union.

153. "Association for the Monetary Union of Europe, A Proposal to Create an Ecu Zone to Assist Eastern Europe's Transition to a Market Economy," mimeo, Paris, November 13, 1991.

154. Ronald Freemen, the EBRD's vice-president proposed that a separate bank be created to finance trade from Central and Eastern Europe to the Soviet Union. See "Bank to Finance Europe-Soviet Trade Is Mooted," *Financial Times*, October 30, 1991. On the role of export credit agencies, see Daniel L. Bond, *Trade or Aid?* Public Policy Paper, no. 4 (New York: Institute for East West Security Studies, June 1991).

155. Some of that increase reflects the impact of the depreciation of the dollar in the second half of 1990.

156. "Bulgaria Rules Out Debt Forgiveness," *Financial Times*, April 17, 1991; "Full Bulgarian Debt Rescheduling in View," *Financial Times*, April 22, 1991; and "Bulgaria's Foreign Debt," *RFE/RL Daily Report*, March 16, 1992.

157. Creditor governments can choose among three forms of debt relief: they can write off part of Poland's debt; they can accept lower interest payments, while leaving the debt's face value unchanged; and they can allow interest payments to be reduced and some of the interest to be rolled up into capital.

158. "Yugoslavia Seeks to Reschedule $1.3bn Debt Payments," *Financial Times*, July 30, 1991.

159. "Net Foreign Debt Decreases by $2 Billion," *FBIS-EEU*, March 31, 1992. See

also "Hungary's Foreign Debt Drops," *RFE/RL Daily Report*, April 9, 1991; and "Sinkende Exporterlöse," *Handelsblatt*, April 4, 1991.

160. "Ungarn will keine Schuldenreduzierung," *Handelsblatt*, March 21, 1991; and "Foreign Trade Minister Discusses Trade, Debt," *FBIS-EEU*, July 8, 1991. Strong pressure has also been exercised by the IMF. It advised Hungary against seeking debt relief since that would be a sign of weakness and would undermine the credibility of the reform effort, and thus the confidence of international creditors. See "IMF Tells Hungary to Avoid Debt Relief," *RFE/RL Daily Report*, April 22, 1991.

161. This ratio declined to 30 percent in 1991 owing to the strong export performance of Hungary's economy. See "Der Kollaps im Osten wird dynamisch überspielt," *Handelsblatt*, December 27–28, 1991.

162. "Hungarian Government Divided over Whether to Seek Debt Deal," *Financial Times*, March 18, 1991; and "Kadar on Trade and Hungary's Foreign Debt," *RFE/RL Daily Report*, March 19, 1991. According to the Hungarian finance minister, Mihaly Kupa, the West's decision to reduce Poland's foreign debt is aggravating social tensions in Hungary and increasing pressures for rescheduling. "The Polish government does whatever it wishes on repayment, someone who behaves well is penalized and someone who behaves badly gets special rewards and benefits." See "Hungarians Angered by Polish Debt Deal," *Financial Times*, March 6, 1991.

163. Presenting the 1991 budget to the Czechoslovak parliament, Finance Minister Vaclav Klaus stated that he expects the country's debt to increase by about $3 billion from the current level. See "CSFR rechnet mit starkem Anstieg der Schulden," *Süddeutsche Zeitung*, December 28, 1990.

164. "Romania to Borrow $2bn," *Financial Times*, May 14, 1991.

165. "Germany Reschedules Bulgarian Debt," *Journal of Commerce*, May 15, 1992.

166. Bank for International Settlements, *The Maturity and Sectoral Distribution of International Bank Lending*, Second Half of 1989 (Basle, July 1990).

167. Bank for International Settlements, *The Maturity and Sectoral Distribution of International Bank Lending*, First Half of 1990 (Basle, January 1991).

168. Bank for International Settlements, *The Maturity and Sectoral Distribution of International Bank Lending*, Second Half of 1990 (Basle, July 1991); and Bank for International Settlements, *61st Annual Report* (Basle, June 1991). See also "Die Internationale Schuldenkrise verlagert sich immer mehr in die östlichen Länder," *Handelsblatt*, June 13, 1991. During the first six months of 1991, Western banks' exposure to Central and Eastern Europe dropped by an additional $5.9 billion (16 percent in current dollars), from $92.5 billion to $77.3 billion. The Soviet Union accounted for $3.6 billion. The reduction in claims was the greatest in relation to Hungary and Czechoslovakia—about -10 percent each. See *The Maturity and Sectoral Distribution of International Bank Lending*, First Half of 1991 (Basle, January 1992).

169. These estimates include the Polish debt reduction, which so far has only been cleared by the governments of the United States and Austria. Excluding Polish debt reduction, these figures would be $90.5 billion and $129.1 billion, respectively.

170. PlanEcon, *Review and Outlook*, Analysis and Forecasts to 1995 (Washington,

July 1991). According to the OECD, "a further weakening [of the debt exposure] seems inevitable before changes in the economic structure can produce any tangible improvement." See "OECD Caution on East Europe Reforms," *Financial Times*, February 28, 1990. These figures do not include DM 23 billion that the former CMEA members owe to the Federal Republic of Germany as a result of claims from trade between the former German Democratic Republic and its Eastern partners. See "Former CMEA Members Reluctant to Pay Debts," *FBIS-EEU*, August 15, 1991.

171. "Zehn Millarden Dollar Zinsen," *Handelsblatt*, July 9, 1991.

172. To a certain degree, this will depend on the West's willingness and ability to open its markets to products from Central and Eastern Europe. This point is elaborated in the following paragraphs.

173. "Die Reformländer Mittel- und Osteuropas benötigen neue Mittel zur Finanzierung ihrer Importe," *Handelsblatt*, December 19, 1991.

174. On the status of the implementation of the agreements that have to be ratified at the national level, see "Debt Reduction Accords with Paris Club Planned," *FBIS-EEU*, April 9, 1992.

175. One element that was not helpful was the feud among various Western governments attempting to take credit for the agreement. See, for example, "USA über alles," *Handelsblatt*, March 22–23, 1991.

176. The United States reduced its share by 70 percent. See, for example, "Balcerowics: U.S. Debt Agreement 'Good Example,'" *FBIS-EEU*, July 18, 1991. Though initially irritated by the U.S. decision, France quickly moved to cut its debt with Poland by another 10 percent as well. See "France Irritated by 70% US Write-off," *Financial Times*, March 22, 1991; "Walesa Signs Friendship Treaty with France," *RFE/RL Daily Report*, April 10, 1991; and "Walesa schliesst Freundschaftsvertrag mit Paris," *Süddeutsche Zeitung*, April 10, 1991. Germany officially announced its debt reduction early in 1992. See "Germany Forgives Half of Poland's Government Debt," *RFE/RL Daily Report*, February 20, 1992.

177. "Die Schuldenhalbierung hält Warschau den Rücken frei," *Süddeutsche Zeitung*, March 20, 1991. This idea dates back to Germany's so-called jumbo credit of 1989 under Chancellor Helmut Schmidt, whereby part of the credit was transformed into a zloty fund for joint projects.

178. "Schulden gegen Umweltschutz," *Süddeutsche Zeitung*, June 12, 1991.

179. "Poles Offer Debt-For-Nature Swap ," *Financial Times*, June 12, 1991; and "Der Umwelttrick," *Handelsblatt*, June 27, 1991. Though much smaller in size, this proposal is similar to a recent plan for the Inter-American Development Bank to buy $100 million of Mexico's debt in the secondary market and use the funds to plant trees around Mexico City.

180. Poland's different creditor profile dates back to Polish martial law, when the authorities stopped repaying governments and continued to service their debt with commercial banks. The resulting unpaid interest accumulated and eventually dwarfed the bank debt burden.

181. Poland stopped paying interest to commercial banks at the end of 1989. Until recently, private banks, led by Barclays, have demanded that Poland pay 30 percent of its $1.03 billion in overdue interest arrears before they make a proposal on a plan.

See "Poland Secures Deal to Cancel Half Its Debt," *Financial Times*, March 16–17, 1991.

182. "Polish Offer to Banks on Debt Arrears," *Financial Times*, February 27, 1991.

183. "Westliche Gläubigerbanken signalisieren Einlenken," *Handelsblatt*, June 14–15, 1991. There have been reports that Poland plans to use a quarter of the $1.6bn IMF loan secured as a result of the Paris Club agreement to cover part of the outstanding interest. See "Poland Committed to Tight Controls on Money Supply," *Financial Times*, April 24, 1991.

184. Until recently, the relations between the London Club and the Polish government were strained. According to Janusz Sawicki, deputy finance minister and Poland's chief negotiator, Polish authorities "have never had any reasonable word from the banks. We have not had an opportunity to negotiate with the banks." See "Relief at Last from a Poisonous Legacy," *Financial Times*, May 3, 1991; and "Poles to Restart Debt Reduction Talks," *Financial Times*, March 10, 1992. For further details on the delay, see "Government Unable to Pay Interest on Debt," *FBIS-EEU*, April 17, 1992. According to Stefan Kawalec, deputy finance minister, Poland envisages an agreement similar to that reached with the Paris Club. See "Official Notes 'General Agreement' with IMF," *FBIS-EEU*, May 13, 1992. See also "Creditor Banks Press for Polish Debt Talks," *Financial Times*, May 13, 1992; and "Banking on a Reduction Agreement," *Financial Times*, April 28, 1992.

185. "Polish Offer to Banks on Debt Arrears," *Financial Times*, February 27, 1991.

186. As a result of the Paris Club agreement, the market value of outstanding debt to private creditors rose by 12 percent, from 18 percent to 30 percent. "Relief at Last from a Poisonous Legacy," *Financial Times*, May 3, 1991.

187. This presupposes the existence of functioning capital markets, as discussed earlier.

188. The Support for the East European Democracy Act of 1989 already envisions such swaps on behalf of the United States. The problem with such a conversion program is that countries like Czechoslovakia or Bulgaria would be penalized for having avoided excessive debt accumulation. Some compensatory scheme would have to be found.

189. For some background information on debt-equity swaps, see UN Commission on Transnational Corporations, *Debt Equity Conversion: A Guide for Decision Makers* (New York, 1990). This form of debt relief has become quite important in recent years. According to recent World Bank estimates, debt-equity swaps retired some $45 billion of developing country debt from 1985 to 1990. See World Bank, *World Debt Tables 1990–91*, vol. 1 (Washington, 1991), p. 64; and United Nations, ECLAC, *Preliminary Overview of the Economy of Latin America and the Caribbean 1990*, no. 500–501 (New York, December 1990).

190. For some background on debt-for-nature swaps, see, for example, Jens Rosebrock and Harald Sondhof, "Debt-for-Nature Swaps: A Review of the First Experiences," *Intereconomics*, vol. 26, no. 2 (1991), pp. 82–87; and M. Potier, "Swapping Debt for Nature," *OECD Observer* (August–September 1990), pp. 17–20.

191. Note that swaps have a potentially adverse impact on inflation. Policymakers in the East and the West may oppose them because the domestic money supply may

grow above the target agreed on in a stabilization program that allows the countries to gain access to loans from international organizations.

192. At the opening meeting of the EBRD, EC Commissioner Henning Christophersen called for debt forgiveness for Bulgaria along similar lines as Poland: "There must be a debt relief agreement for Bulgaria. Without this, it will be impossible for that country to get out of its difficulties." See "Bulgaria Rules Out Debt Forgiveness," *Financial Times*, April 17, 1991. More recently, the Council of Europe also agreed to consider debt relief for Central and Eastern European countries when it can be established that the debt burden hinders the transformation process. See "Schuldenlast für Reformländer prüfen," *Woche im Bundestag*, vol. 17–91, October 16, 1991, p. 62.

193. During the initial months after the revolutions in Central and Eastern Europe, there was doubt whether further unity could be achieved because the line that divided Europe was disappearing. See, for example, "Remixing Europe," *Economist*, November 11, 1990. Commission President Jacques Delors initially opposed any serious debate about any widening of the European Community at least until the completion of the internal market project in January 1993. As events in Central and Eastern Europe and the Soviet Union unfolded, however, he changed his position, for he recognized that Europe cannot avoid taking on this challenge. See "The EC's Own Visionary," *Financial Times*, August 5, 1991. Margaret Thatcher, echoing the tenor of her 1988 Brugge speech, seized on the events and argued that the prospect for democracy in Central and Eastern Europe meant that the Community should be broadened not deepened. Many continental members concluded, however, that the events in the East strengthened the case for closer integration of Western Europe and made it more urgent to broaden the Community at the same time. See Edward Mortimer, "The New Europe, Building a Peacetime Order around Germany," *World Press Review*, (September 1990), p. 12.

194. Gianni De Michelis, "Reaching Out to the East," *Foreign Policy*, no. 79 (Summer 1990), pp. 44–55, here p. 44. See also "In Stufen auch zur Politischen Union," Deutsche Bundesbank, *Auszüge aus Presseartikeln*, no. 43 (June 11, 1991), pp. 7–8.

195. As quoted in *Liberation*, September 6, 1991, pp. 21–23.

196. The current wave of emigration from Yugoslavia to Western Europe, particularly to Germany, indicates the potential magnitude of the problem.

197. To some degree this can already be observed as a result of the war in Yugoslavia.

198. For a more detailed history of EC-CMEA relations, see Avi Shlaim and G. N. Yannopolous, *The EEC and Eastern Europe* (London: Cambridge University Press, 1978); John Maslen, "The European Community's Relations with the State-Trading Countries of Europe 1984–1986," in F. J. Jacobs, ed., *Yearbook of International Law* (Oxford University Press, 1987); and Marc Maresceau, ed., *The Political and Legal Framework of Trade Relations between the European Community and Eastern Europe* (Dordrecht: Martinus Nijhoff, 1989).

199. Once it became clear that COCOM restrictions forced the Community to reject any discussion of industrial, technological, and scientific cooperation, cooperation

was of lesser interest. See Hans-Jörg Seeler, *Report on the Relations between the European Community and the Council of Mutual Economic Assistance (CMEA) and the Eastern European Member States of the CMEA*, European Parliament Working Documents, A 2–187/86 (December 19, 1986). For a discussion of EC-Soviet relations, see Klaus Hänsch, *Report on Political Relations between the European Community and the Soviet Union*, European Parliament Session Document, A 2–0155/ 88 (July 18, 1988). An exception to this was the establishment of a relationship with Romania in 1980, but the agreement proved to be relatively modest in economic terms. See Commission of the European Communities, *EC-Eastern Europe Relations*, ICC Background Brief (Brussels, May 29, 1990).

200. One of the central points in the treaty was the acceptance of West Berlin by the CMEA under the jurisdiction of the EC treaties. See, for example, Horst G. Krenzler, "Die Europäische Gemeinschaft und der Wandel in Mittel- und Osteuropa," *Europa-Archiv*, no. 3 (1990), pp. 89–96.

201. The Commission was especially quick in developing a comprehensive response to the developments in Central and Eastern Europe. See, for example, Kommission der Europäischen Gemeinschaften, Mitteilung der Kommission an den Rat, *Auswirkungen der jüngsten Veränderungen in Mittel- und Osteuropa auf die Beziehungen der Gemeinschaft zu den dortigen Ländern*, SEK (90)111 endg. (Brussels, January 23, 1990); and Commission of the European Communities, Communication from the Commission to the Council, *The Development of the Community's Relations with the Countries from Central and Eastern Europe*, SEC(90)196 final (Brussels, February 1, 1990).

202. PHARE was started at the Paris G-7 summit in July 1989, the program was originally designed for Poland and Hungary. At the G-24 meeting in December 1989, the decision was taken to extend, in principle, the aid to other countries of Central and Eastern Europe, provided they carried out the requisite political reforms. See "Declaration of Ministers of the Group of 24 for Economic Assistance to Poland and Hungary," *European Community News*, December 14, 1989. In July 1990 in Brussels, the program was officially extended to Czechoslovakia, Bulgaria, Yugoslavia, and Romania. See "Declaration of Ministers of the 'Group of 24' Countries Engaged in Economic Assistance to Central and East European Countries," *Information Memo*, Brussels, July 4, 1990. Though not often acknowledged, it was Chancellor Helmut Kohl who first proposed to President George Bush at the G-7 summit that the commission be given the mandate to coordinate the aid program to Central and Eastern Europe. Bush subsequently endorsed Kohl's proposal and announced it at the press conference.

203. For more on the PHARE program and a more detailed description of the projects, see, for example, Commission des Communeautés Européennes, *Perspective de l'assistance du G-24 aux pays d'Europe Centrale et d'Europe l'Est*, Le Groupe des 24, Reunion ministrielle (Bruxelles, le 4 juillet 1990) Sommet economique occidentale, Houston, les 9 et 10 juillet 1990; Commission of the European Communities, *Action Plan, Coordinated Assistance from the Group of 24 to Bulgaria, Czechoslovakia, the German Democratic Republic, Romania, and Yugoslavia*, SEC

(90) 843 final (Brussels, May 2, 1990); Commission of the European Communities, *PHARE, Coordinated Support for the Restructuring of the Economies of Certain Central and Eastern European Countries* (Brussels, January 30, 1991); and Commission of the European Communities, *PHARE*, Assistance for Economic Restructuring in the Countries of Central and Eastern Europe (Brussels, 1992).

204. If the EFTA contributions are included, the share rises to 70 percent, Commission of the European Communities, *Scoreboard of G-24 Assistance* (Brussels, April 8, 1992). See also "Brüssel kann bereits auf massive Hilfen verweisen," *Handelsblatt*, July 15, 1991.

205. The European Investment Bank (EIB) and the Community subscribe to 6 percent of the capital. The twelve member states subscribe to another 45 percent, making a total Community representation of 51 percent. The United States, with 10 percent, is the second largest shareholder. For more on the EBRD, see Ibrahim Shihata, *The European Bank for Reconstruction and Development: A Comparative Analysis of the Constituent Agreement* (London: Graham and Trotman, 1990); and Karen Donfried, *The European Bank for Reconstruction and Development: An Institution of and for the New Europe*, 91-611F (Washington: Congressional Research Service, August 15, 1991).

206. To link Germany's recent tight monetary policy and the resultant high interest rates to a new "assertiveness" thus overlooks the fact that the Bundesbank has had almost complete monopoly over European monetary policy for the past decade.

207. These difficulties allowed France and Britain to gain limited independence from German macroeconomic policy and lower their interest rates in May 1992 without any serious repercussions on the value of their currencies. At the same time, the sharp appreciation of the deutsche mark in response to the Danish referendum reconfirmed the mark's continued strength.

208. Whatever the eventual merit of Germany's position on Yugoslavia is, it was particularly unfortunate that Germany's insistence on the early recognition of Slovenia and Croatia came on the heels of the Maastricht decisions on a common foreign and security policy.

209. On the SPD, see "SPD Says Constitution Will Have to Be Changed," *Financial Times*, May 8, 1992; on the CSU, "Die CSU knüpft Zustimmungen zu Maastricht an Bedingungen," *Frankfurter Allgemeine*, March 30, 1992; and on the FDP, "Lambsdorff Critical of Maastricht Outcome," *FBIS-WEU*, January 10, 1992. For excerpts of the Parliamentary debate on Maastricht, see *Das Parlament*, December, 20–27, 1991; and "Kohl Struggles to Land His Catch," *Financial Times*, March 17, 1992.

210. "EC Commission President Delors Grants Interview," *FBIS-WEU*, January 6, 1992.

211. The most obvious example of such a change in the distribution of power is Europe's move toward a monetary union and the establishment of the European System of Central Banks (ECSB). For all practical purposes, European monetary policy is currently made by the Bundesbank. The establishment of the ECSB will return some of the decisionmaking power to individual countries and their central

banks, albeit in a multilateral context. In other words, rather than losing sovereignty, most EC members, with the exception of Germany, are regaining some of the sovereignty they lost to Germany during the 1970s and 1980s.

212. "Club List Closed for Rule Changes," *Financial Times*, December 8–9, 1990.

213. See, for example, Luis Planas Puchades, *Report on Community Enlargement and Relations with other European Countries*, European Parliament Session Documents, A3–0077/91 (March 26, 1991).

214. "Streit um Erweiterung der EG," *Süddeutsche Zeitung*, February 16, 1991; "Wer wen nicht will im Zwölfer Club," *Auszüge aus Presseartikeln* (Deutsche Bundesbank), no. 39 (May 28, 1991); "EG-Erweiterung spaltet die Mitgliedstaaten," *Süddeutsche Zeitung*, July 26, 1991; and "The EC's Moment of Truth," *Financial Times*, August 7, 1991.

215. This position was confirmed by François Mitterrand's surprise meeting with Mikhail Gorbachev in Kiev and the French position during the initial rounds of the Two-plus-Four negotiations. During the meeting in Kiev, Mitterrand warned West Germany not to push for unification with East Germany because it would upset the delicate balance in Europe and the process of European integration. See "Mitterrand, in Kiev, Warns Bonn Not to Press Reunification Issue," *New York Times*, December 7, 1989; and "Paris and Moscow Agree on Germany," *Financial Times*, December 12, 1991. The first shift in the French position, at least with respect to Germany, was indicated when Mitterrand and the German president, Richard von Weizäcker, traveled together through East Germany in September 1991, even before political unification had occurred.

216. "Wer wen nicht will im Zwölfer Club," *Auszüge aus Presseartikeln* (Deutsche Bundesbank), no. 39 (May 28, 1991). Conversely, there has always been a fear that the new Community would be tilted toward the Mediterranean. In a recent speech to the Nordic Council, Chancellor Helmut Kohl indicated that this attitude has changed: "There were many fears, even in my country, that this EC-Europe would drift away in the direction of the Mediterranean, that it would become a Latin Europe. The danger of drifting away to a Latin Europe should not be feared by anyone in Northern Europe anymore." "FRG's Kohl Addresses Council," *FBIS-WEU*, March 6, 1992.

217. This has been reflected in radically different interpretations by the press of a major policy speech by President Mitterrand during a visit to East Germany in September of 1991. See "Mitterrand springt auf den Zug nach Osten auf," *Süddeutsche Zeitung*, September 17, 1991; "Mitterrand für Erweiterung der EG," *Süddeutsche Zeitung*, September 20, 1991; "Mitterrand warnt vor zu raschem Beitritt Osteuropas," *Handelsblatt*, September 20–21, 1991; and "Mitterrand mauert weiter," *Süddeutsche Zeitung*, September 21–22, 1991. Similarly, under the French-CSFR friendship and cooperation treaty signed in October 1991, France has pledged to support Czechoslovakia's associate membership in the Community, even though French resistance to open EC markets for agricultural products from Central and Eastern Europe had led to the breakdown of negotiations between the Community and the three Central and East European countries. For the treaty declaration, see "Support for CSFR in EC," *FBIS-WEU*, October 2, 1991.

218. For an early statement of that, see "Die Fakten des Monsieur Delors," *Die Zeit*,

August 19, 1988; and "Dumas Interviewed on Relations with Poland," *FBIS-WEU*, January 22, 1992.

219. "Mitterrand Clarifies Scheme for Grand European Cooperation," *Financial Times*, June 13, 1991; and "Views Steps toward Integration," *FBIS-WEU*, June 10, 1991.

220. "French Dream, Czech Nightmare," *Economist*, June 1, 1991; and "Ambiguity Clouds Idea of Pan-Europe Confederation," *Financial Times*, June 12, 1991.

221. See, for example, the joint ten-point declaration by the foreign ministers of Poland, France, and Germany, which among other things states that France and Germany support all efforts by Poland to pave the way for the country's entry into the Community. "Neue Demokratien an EG heranführen," *Frankfurter Allgemeine*, August 28, 1991.

222. "Bérégovoy Insists France Must Lead over Maastricht," *Financial Times*, May 11, 1992.

223. "Dumas Reaffirms Value of European Confederation," *FBIS-WEU*, February 19, 1992; and "Mitterrand Pleads for European Confederation," *FBIS-WEU*, March 2, 1992.

224. "Kohl Urges Bar on ex-Soviet States from EC Membership," *Financial Times*, April 4–5, 1992; and "FRG's Kohl Opposes CIS Association in EC," *FBIS-WEU*, April 3, 1992.

225. "Noch zahlreiche Probleme und Fallstricke," *Handelsblatt*, November 30, 1990; and "The Balance of Power Changes in Europe," *Financial Times*, December 6, 1990. For a different perspective, see "Neue Ost-Märkte sind keine Konkurrenz für den Süden," *Handelsblatt*, December 17, 1990.

226. "Wer wen nicht will im Zwölfer Club," *Auszüge aus Presseartikeln* (Deutsche Bundesbank), no. 39 (May 28, 1991); "EG-Erweiterung spaltet die Mitgliedstaaten," *Süddeutsche Zeitung*, July 26, 1991; "Streit um Erweiterung der EG," *Süddeutsche Zeitung*, February 16, 1991; and "Southern Discomfort," *Financial Times*, June 18, 1991.

227. As quoted in "Aid to Eastern Europe, USSR Raise Concern," Lisbon RDP Commercial Radio Network, December 11, 1991, in *FBIS-WEU*, December 17, 1991, p. 34; see also "Portugal Seeks Greater Unity within the EC," *Financial Times*, October 10, 1991, p. 1.

228. See, for example, "Mittelmeeraum befrieden," *Europa Forum*, May 1991; and "EC Free Trade with Maghreb Sought," *Financial Times*, March 3, 1992. The fear that the transformation process in Central and Eastern Europe will divert resources away from the Middle East was confirmed during a visit to Egypt by Jacques Delors in late 1991. See "EC Tells Arab Leaders E. Europe to Get Priorities," *Journal of Commerce*, November 12, 1991.

229. "Commissioner Interviewed on EC Presidency," *FBIS-WEU*, January 23, 1992.

230. "Bonn will Warschau der EG näher bringen," *Handelsblatt*, March 7, 1991; "Bereitschaft zur weiteren Öffnung der EG bekräftigen," *Handelsblatt*, April 4, 1991; "Kohl Calls on EC to Support Reform States," *FBIS-WEU*, June 4, 1991; and "Sofia: Unterzeichnung im Spätherbst," *Süddeutsche Zeitung*, August 1, 1991.

231. This does not include assistance from international financial institutions such as the IBRD, IMF, and EBRD. Commission of the European Communities, *Scoreboard of G-24 Assistance* (Brussels, April 8, 1992).

232. Note, however, that measured as a percentage of GDP, Germany ranks second after Austria, whose assistance amounts to 1.2 percent of GDP, and is closely followed by Turkey and Sweden. See table A-12.

233. Immigrants from Central and Eastern Europe brought the number of asylum seekers in 1991 to a new record in the history of the Federal Republic of Germany: 256,112 refugees requested political asylum, which represents an increase of 32.7 percent over the previous year, with 78,854 (or 31 percent) of refugees from the republics of the former Yugoslavia constituting the largest percentage of the asylum seekers. See "Interior Ministry Announces Asylum Figures," *FBIS-WEU*, January 8, 1992. For January 1992 alone, this number jumped to 31,000, a new record high, with 12,573 or 41 percent from the former Yugoslavia. *The Week in Germany*, February 7, 1992.

234. For a recent statement to that effect, see "Genscher Proposes States to Join EC," *Financial Times*, February 1992. The German government was particularly grateful to Hungary. At a meeting on August 25, 1989, Hungary's premier Miklos Nemeth revealed to Chancellor Kohl that the country had decided to reopen its border with Austria. The leaders then reportedly discussed aid for Hungary and associate membership in the EC. A similar exchange took place between Czechoslovak and German officials after the Czechoslovak embassy was filled with East Germans. See Jim Hoagland, "Europe's Destiny," *Foreign Affairs*, vol. 69, no. 1 (1990), pp. 33–50. See also "Goncz Discusses Future Organization of Europe," *FBIS-EEU*, February 14, 1992; and "Kohl Backs Prague's EC Drive," *Financial Times*, February 28, 1992. As for Poland, the Polish-German treaty explicitly mentions German support for Poland's membership in the European Community. See also "Budapest hofft auf Hilfe bei Annäherung zur EG," *Handelsblatt*, May 7, 1991; Géza Jeszenszky, "Eckpfeiler ungarischer Europolitik: EG-Mitgliedschaft und gesamteuropäische Zusammenarbeit," in Gerhard Eickhorn, ed., *Ungarn und Deutschland im künftigen Europa* (Bonn: Europa Union Verlag, 1991), pp. 30–34; and "Bonn soll Warschau die Wege ebnen," *Handelsblatt*, June 17, 1991.

235. For the British position, see, for example, "EC 'Should Expand Trade with E. Europe,'" *Financial Times*, July 5, 1991, p. 16. According to the Danish foreign minister Uffe Ellemann-Jensen, "We [Denmark] want to enlarge it [the EC] with new member states: the EFTA [European Free Trade Association] countries and the countries in central and eastern Europe," as quoted in "New World Order Requires Wider and Deeper EC," *Financial Times*, April 25, 1991, p. 2.

236. "Grosszügige Erweiterung erwünscht," *Das Parlament*, November 1, 1991; and "Schlüter: EG soll verhandeln," *Handelsblatt*, September 24, 1991.

237. "Major Urges EC to Admit East European States," *Financial Times*, September 13, 1991, p. 1; and "Major: EG nach Osten öffnen," *Süddeutsche Zeitung*, September 13, 1991. See also "Hurd Wants to Bind E. Europe Closer to West," *Financial Times*, January 15, 1992; and "Hurd Sees 20-member Community by 2000," *Financial Times*, February 8–9, 1992.

238. See, for example, "Club List Closed for Rule Changes," *Financial Times*, December 8–9, 1990; and "Der Elfenbeinturm gerät ins Wanken," *Frankfurter Allgemeine*, May 3, 1991.

239. The experience of the former East German economy is a good example of the social, political, and economic repercussions that occur when a former centrally planned economy is integrated rapidly into the Community and exposed to the competition of the international economy and the resources required to mitigate some of those consequences.

240. Centrally planned economies, especially Hungary, have been exposed to some form of limited international competition for the past twenty years. Unlike the German Democratic Republic, which experienced a sharp revaluation of its currency as a result of monetary union, these countries can use the exchange rate, and to a limited degree wage policies, to enhance the international competitiveness of their products. However, both the experience and the availability of additional policy instruments are unlikely to sufficiently cushion the expected adjustment shock in the short run.

241. Commission des Communeautés Européennes, Communication de la Commission au Conseil et au Parliament, *Accords d'association avec les pays d'Europe centrale et orientale: Cadre general*, COM(90) 398 final (Brussels, August 27, 1990). For the European Parliament's position, see Christa Randzio-Plath, *Report of the Committee on External Economic Relations on a General Outline for Association Agreements with the Countries of Central and Eastern Europe*, European Parliament Session Documents, A3–0055/91 (Luxembourg, March 1991). It is interesting to note that the possibility of association for some Eastern bloc countries was raised as early as May 1989. See Valéry Giscard d'Estaing, Yasuhiro Nakasone, and Henry A. Kissinger, *Ost-West Beziehungen, Ein Bericht an die Trilaterale Kommission* (Trilateral Commission, 1989). At a more official level, the Community first decided at its Council of Ministers meeting in December 1989 to examine appropriate forms of associations for those countries that would successfully and purposefully follow the path of political and economic reform. In February of 1990 the Commission presented a proposal that offered Czechoslovakia, Hungary, and Poland the closest possible relations, short of membership, which was approved by the foreign ministers. Such an offer has never been made to countries such as Austria, Norway, Sweden, and Switzerland. This indicates the political importance and urgency of embracing these Central European countries.

242. It is true that the Community has already concluded association agreements, some of which are still in effect. The only definite aspect of an association agreement is that it must contain more than just a trade and cooperation agreement. This is why early agreements with the participants of the Lomé Convention and the Maghreb countries (1967) were later renamed cooperation agreements. For Greece, the association agreement of 1962 was the first step toward membership. For Turkey, which concluded an agreement in 1964, the agreement includes a clause of prospective membership. One could interpret these precedents as a partial explanation for the European Community's reluctance to include the membership clause in the current negotiations with Central and Eastern Europe. Malta (1971) and Cyprus (1973) also

concluded association agreements. None of these agreements, however, is as elaborate and far-reaching as those with Central and Eastern Europe, as is clear from their alternative name, European agreements.

243. See "EC Paves Way for Free Trade with E Europe," *Financial Times*, November 23–24, 1991; and "Balcerowicz: Accord 'Turning Point,'" *FBIS-EEU*, December 17, 1991. For the Czechoslovak and Hungarian reactions, see "Calfa Views Agreement's Importance," *FBIS-EEU*, December 17, 1991, and "Official Views EC Membership Prospects," *FBIS-EEU*, December 18, 1991, respectively.

244. "Europe's Reluctant Empire-Builders," *Financial Times*, December 2, 1991, p. 15; "Economic Official Views Effect of EC Association," *FBIS-EEU*, December 4, 1991; and "Calfa Views Agreement's Importance," *FBIS-EEU*, December 17, 1991.

245. After joining the European Community as a full member, Portugal has had its foreign investment increase twenty-two-fold.

246. See, for example, "News Conference Details Agreement," *FBIS-EEU*, March 4, 1992; "Temporary Trade Agreement Signed with EC," *FBIS-EEU*, March 2, 1992; and "Temporary Trade Agreement with EC Outlined," *FBIS-EEU*, March 11, 1992.

247. "Delors: Slow East European Integraton into EC," *FBIS-WEU*, September 6, 1991, p. 3; and "Zheleve Says EC Association Government Priority, " *FBIS-EEU*, November 20, 1991. EC Commission president Delors has indicated his interest in concluding an association agreement similar to those already concluded. "Eastern Europe and the EC," *RFE/RL Daily Report*, October 30, 1991; "Dimitrov Meets EC Official on Membership," *FBIS-EEU*, December 20, 1991; "President Zhelev Views EC's Role in E. Europe," *FBIS-EEU*, December 11, 1991; "EC Talks with Bulgaria Considered 'Positive,'" *FBIS-EEU*, January 22, 1992; "Ganev Says Conditions Met for EC Association," *FBIS-EEU*, May 12, 1992; "Meeting on Cooperation with EFTA Countries Held," *FBIS-EEU*, January 14, 1992; "EC Plans Agreements with Bulgaria, Romania," *Journal of Commerce*, April 29, 1992; "EC Postpones Association Talks with Romania," *FBIS-EEU*, September 30, 1991; "Nastase Comments on G-24 Meeting in Brussels," *FBIS-EEU*, November 13, 1991; and "Spokeswoman on EC, Military Pay, Economic Issues," *FBIS-EEU*, December 20, 1991.

248. After some initial resistance, the European Parliament has approved the agreements. During its first reading of the 1992 budget plan, the Parliament made clear that it will not accept any budgetary cuts in other fields to provide for any financial commitments that arise from Community programs to assist Central and Eastern Europe and has requested that the Community's budgetary limits be raised. This indicates that the future of such agreements may be in doubt, as the allocation of funds is likely to depend on increases in the EC budget, which involves complicated negotiations and requires the approval of the Council, the Commission, and the Parliament. "Erste Lesung des Haushalts 1992," *Europa Forum*, no. 9 (1991), p. 2; and "Parlament und Ministerrat streiten um Osteuropahilfe," *Handelsblatt*, September 23, 1991.

249. This position is also taken by the German government despite the overall favorable position on Polish-EC relations. See, for example, "Opening EC Market Viewed," *FBIS-EEU*, July 15, 1991; and "Breitere Öffnung der Märkte," *Handelsblatt*,

July 15, 1991. Britain, which has long favored a reduction in agricultural import prices, supports the Central and East European countries' position. See "EC 'Should Expand Trade with Europe,'" *Financial Times*, July 5, 1991.

250. "Polish-EC Talks Hit Deadlock," *RFE/RL Daily Report*, no. 132, July 13, 1991. According to chief negotiator Jaroslaw Mulewicz, "We will ask ourselves whether it will be worth appearing at a further round of negotiations." As quoted in "Poland May Stay Out of EC Talks," *RFE/RL Daily Report*, July 16, 1991. See also "Der EG Markt als Heilsbringer," *Handelsblatt*, July 23, 1991; and "Polens Bauern mit Regierung unzufrieden," *Süddeutsche Zeitung*, February 28, 1991.

251. "EG will Verhandlugen mit östlichen Nachbarn beschleunigen," *Süddeutsche Zeitung*, August 20, 1991; "Der Westen fordert Gorbatschows Rückkehr," *Süddeutsche Zeitung*, August 21, 1991; "Schneller Konsens," *Handelsblatt*, August 21, 1991; and "EC Seen Easing Restrictions on E. European Farm Imports," *Journal of Commerce*, September 6, 1991.

252. As quoted in "Europeans Hope Soviets Will Quicken Shift to Market System," *New York Times*, August 22, 1991; and "Der Spielball liegt bei den Mitgliedstaaten," *Handelsblatt*, September 2, 1991.

253. "Brussels Aims to Open Door Wider to EC's Eastern Neighbours," *Financial Times*, August 22, 1991; and "Europeans Hope Soviets Will Quicken Shift to Market System," *New York Times*, August 22, 1991.

254. "With Soviet Trouble, Former Satellites Look West for Help," *New York Times*, August 25, 1991; and "Walesa drängt auf einen zügigen Anschluss an die Europäische Gemeinschaft," *Handelsblatt*, August 22, 1991.

255. Among other things, the proposal included a 60 percent cut in the level of tariffs over three years on imports of agricultural products. This was combined with a preferential treatment that would allow an increase in volume by 50 percent over the next five years. The Commission also asked Spain and Germany to end their national restrictions on Polish coal imports within five years. In the area of textiles, the Commission proposed that curbs on imports of textiles be phased out within six years. "Brussels Seeks Import Concessions," *Financial Times*, September 5, 1991; "A New Wave of Eastern Approaches," *Financial Times*, September 6, 1991; "Brussels Opens Its Arms to the East," *Financial Times*, September 4, 1991; "EC Proposes Stronger Links with Eastern Europe," *FBIS-EEU*, September 5, 1991; and "Flexibilität gegenüber Osteuropa gefordert," *Handelsblatt*, September 9, 1991.

256. In the end the talks foundered more than 550 tons of beef, which amounts to 0.008 percent of annual beef consumption in the European Community. It is unlikely that Belgium and Ireland would have maintained their opposition without France as the main opposition. France even rejected a compromise solution of 5 percent of meat imports. "No Accord with East Europe," *FBIS-EEU*, September 9, 1991; "Frankreich verhindert Marktöffnung nach Osten," *Süddeutsche Zeitung*, September 9, 1991; and "EC, E. Europe Fail to Reach Farm Deal," *Journal of Commerce*, September 9, 1991.

257. "Osteuropäer setzen Verhandlungen mit EG aus," *Süddeutsche Zeitung*, September 11, 1991; and "East European Disappointment with the EC Trade Talks," *RFE/RL Daily Report*, September 10, 1991. There were some different interpretations

of this, but in essence it amounted to a break of talks. See "Olechowski Denies Talks with EC Cancelled," *FBIS-EEU*, September 10, 1991; and "Poland Threatens to Call Off EC Trade Talks," *Financial Times*, September 10, 1991.

258. "EG Assoziierung in Osteuropa rückt näher," *Frankfurter Allgemeine*, September 30, 1991; and "EC Finesses French Complaints, Offers Trade Benefits to East," *Washington Post*, October 1, 1991. The Polish side accepted this as a workable compromise. See "Government Satisfied with EC Compromise," *FBIS-EEU*, October 2, 1991. The Commission had already offered such a triangular deal in September for 5 percent of the additional meat imports. See also "EC to Boost Quotas for East Europe Meats," *Journal of Commerce*, October 1, 1991; and "EC's Decision to Buy More Meat Salvages Talks with Eastern Europe," *Journal of Commerce*, October 2, 1991.

259. Portugal and Greece asked for additional guarantees for their domestic textile industry. Spain raised doubts about its willingness to continue to honor the original agreements on steel. "CSFR Resumes Talks on Association with EC," *FBIS-EEU*, November 6, 1991; "Disputed Matters Delay Signing of EC Agreement," *FBIS-EEU*, November 15, 1991; "EC to Delay Signing East European Protocols," *FBIS-EEU*, November 15, 1991; "Initialling of Poland's EC Association Agreement Delayed," *RFE/RL Daily Report*, November 18, 1991; "Concessions Obstacle to EC, Hungary Association," *FBIS-EEU*, November 18, 1991; "Kadar on EC Treaty of Association Talks," *FBIS-EEU*, November 18, 1991; "Hungarian-EC Agreement Delayed," *RFE/ RL Daily Report*, November 21, 1991; and EC Imports of Iron, Steel from East Opposed," *FBIS-EEU*, November 26, 1991.

260. "Negotiators Say 'EC Bureaucracy' Undermined Talks," *FBIS-EEU*, October 24, 1991.

261. "Spain Delays Signing," *FBIS-EEU*, December 17, 1991; and "EC Signs Treaties with Poland, Hungary, CSFR," *FBIS-EEU*, December 27, 1991.

262. Unemployment figures were expected to reach 9.1 percent in 1992, which amounts to an increase of 0.5 percent. See "Annual Economic Report, 1991–92," *European Economy*, vol. 50 (December 1991), statistical annex, table 3, p. 216.

263. "OH Claims Slovakia Could Jeopardize the Accord," *FBIS-EEU*, October 28, 1991; "Carnogursky Unhappy with EC Accord Preparations," *FBIS-EEU*, October 29, 1991; and "Scotland on the Danube River," *Financial Times*, November 6, 1991.

264. "Calfa Expects EC Agreement Mid-December," *FBIS-EEU*, November 14, 1991; and "Czech Prime Minister Views Association Plan," *FBIS-EEU*, December 16, 1991.

265. As quoted in "EC Commission Pleased with Phare Program," *FBIS-EEU*, December 3, 1991. See also "Says EC No Threat to Agriculture," *FBIS-EEU*, December 4, 1991.

266. "Balcerowicz: Accord 'Turning Point,'" *FBIS-EEU*, December 17, 1991.

267. As quoted in "East Europeans Fear Delays in Timetable for EC Entry," *Financial Times*, December 9, 1991.

268. "EC's New Associate States Fear Deficits," *Financial Times*, February 28, 1992. See also "Walesa: Stop Flooding Poland with Imports," *RFE/RL Daily Report*, March 20, 1992.

269. Commission des Communeautés Européennes, Communication de la Com-

mission au conseil et au Parliament, *Accords d'association avec les pays d'Europe centrale et orientale: Cadre general,* COM(90) 398 final (Brussels, August 27, 1990), p. 2.

270. Czechoslovakia, for example, hopes to join the European Community by the year 2000. See "Havel Wants EC membership by 2000," *RFE/RL Daily Report,* June 14, 1991. The chairman of the Foreign Affairs Committee of the Hungarian Parliament recently stated that he thought Hungary required another four years before it meets the requirement of full membership. See "Hungarian Government Divided over Whether to Seek Debt Deal," *Financial Times,* March 18, 1991.

271. "East Europe Given New Hope for EC Links," *Financial Times,* April 16, 1991; and "Die Gemeinschaft will ihr Angebot an die östlichen Reformstaaten noch verbessern," *Handelsblatt,* July 31, 1991. It is important to note that the Commission has pressed the Council of Ministers for a wider negotiating mandate. Such a mandate would include a firm commitment to membership, possibly even indicating a time frame. This position is also supported by the Parliament's Committee on External Relations. See Committee on External Economic Relations, "Association Agreements with the Countries of Central and Eastern Europe," *Resolution,* PE 150.654 (April 18, 1991); and Christa Randzio-Plath, *Report on a General Outline for Association Agreements with the Countries of Central and Eastern Europe,* European Parliament, PE 146.342 fin. (March 13, 1991). The Soviet coup initially led some to conclude that the membership question now would be slave to the satisfaction of the Central and East Europeans. However, just as in the case of market liberalization the effect of the coup was short-lived. See "Brüssels Hilfe an Osteuropa stösst an ihre Grenzen," *Handelsblatt,* September 19, 1991.

272. ". . . and Walesa Warns of Explosion," *RFE/RL Daily Report,* July 15, 1991. See also "Havel Warns of Potential 'Chaos,'" *Financial Times,* March 21, 1991; and "Europe's Reluctant Empire-Builders," *Financial Times,* December 2, 1991.

273. See "EC, Hungary, Poland, CSFR Initial Treaties," *FBIS-EEU,* November 25, 1991.

274. As quoted in "EC Paves Way for Free Trade with E Europe," *Financial Times,* November 23–24, 1991.

275. "EC Signs Treaties with Poland, Hungary, CSFR," *FBIS-EEU,* December 27, 1991, p. 1.

276. Douglas Nelson, "The Domestic Political Preconditions of U.S. Trade Policy: Liberal Structure and Protectionist Dynamics," paper presented at the Conference on Political Economy of Trade: Theory and Policy, World Bank, Washington, D.C., 1987, as quoted in Jagdish Bhagwati, *Protectionism* (MIT Press, 1988), p. 39. For a more general discussion of the relevance of the Marshall Plan, see Donald C. Stone, "Assistance to Central and Eastern Europe," *The Bureaucrat* (Winter 1990–91), pp. 7–12.

277. Harry Bayard Price, *The Marshall Plan and Its Meaning* (Cornell University Press, 1955); Gerd Hardach, "Transnationale Wirtschaftspolitik: Der Marshall-Plan in Deutschland, 1947–1952," in Diter Petzina, ed., *Ordnungspolitische Weichenstellung nach dem Zweiten Weltkrieg* (Berlin: Duncker and Humblot, 1991); and Alan S. Milward, *The Reconstruction of Europe 1945–51* (London: Methuen, 1984).

278. For an early analysis of export possibilities of agricultural goods, see Center for Economic Policy Research, *Monitoring European Integration: The Impact of Eastern Europe* (London: CEPR, 1990).

279. "Handelspolitik der EG im Zuge der Öffnung nach Osten," *Wochenbericht*, DIW 35/90 (August 30, 1990). See also Leah Haus, "The East European Countries and GATT: The Role of Realism, Mercantilism, and Regime Theory in Explaining East-West Trade Negotiations," *International Organization*, vol. 45, no. 2 (1991), pp. 163–82; Leah Haus, *Globalizing the GATT* (Brookings, 1992); and "Die versprochene Öffnung der Märkte stösst oft an Quoten und Kontingente," *Handelsblatt*, July 29, 1991.

280. "Czech Prime Minister Views EC Association Plan," Prague Federal Television Network, December 13, 1991, in *FBIS-EEU*, December 16, 1991, pp. 10–11.

281. "EEC Negotiator on Association Talks," *FBIS-EEU*, June 28, 1991. After six rounds the negotiations were deadlocked, and Poland threatened to break off the negotiations. "Polish-EC Talks Hit Deadlock," *RFE/RL Daily Report*, July 13, 1991.

282. "Hungary at Impasse on Brussels Farm Trade," *Financial Times*, April 9, 1991; "Round of Talks between Hungary, EC Opens," *FBIS-EEU*, July 25, 1991; "Die Tschechoslowakei braucht schnell Zugang zu den Märkten der Gemeinschaft," *Handelsblatt*, June 16, 1991; and "CSFR über Verhandlungen mit EG enttäuscht," *Süddeutsche Zeitung*, August 5, 1991.

283. "Europe's Reluctant Empire-Builders," *Financial Times*, December 2, 1991, p. 15.

284. As quoted in "Die versprochene Öffnung der Märkte stösst oft an Quoten und Kontingente," *Handelsblatt*, July 29, 1991. See also "EC Producers May Act to Block Polish Steel," *Journal of Commerce*, January 14, 1992.

285. "Europe's Reluctant Empire-Builders," *Financial Times*, December 2, 1991, p. 15.

286. "Framers' Roadblock in Poland," *RFE/RL Daily Report*, March 29, 1991; and "Der EG-Market als Heilsbringer," *Handelsblatt*, July 23, 1991. The reinstatement of tariffs will be even more complicated for countries like Czechoslovakia, which will need the permission of GATT to raise its current tariffs (on average about 4–5 percent).

287. For the Hungarian case, see "Jerenszky Interviewed on Foreign Policy," *FBIS-EEU*, June 5, 1991. For Czechoslovakia, see "Slovak Farmers Stage Big Protest," *RFE/RL Daily Report*, July 12, 1991. For the Czechoslovak case, see "Ministry Notes Agricultural Marketing Crisis," *FBIS-EEU*, July 5, 1991; and "Controversy over Agriculture Minister Continues," *FBIS-EEU*, July 22, 1991. In Czechoslovakia the EC's attitude even supports the secessionist forces in the Slovak Republic. In mid-June the Slovak agriculture minister announced the Republic would defend itself "against heedless food imports" by setting up a customs policy department. See "Klaus Announces Measures to Protect Farmers," *FBIS-EEU*, June 19, 1991.

288. "EC-Poland Free Trade Pact Hits Car Import Snag," *Financial Times*, February 26, 1992; and "Car Dispute Delays Poland's EC Association Accord," *RFE/RL Daily Report*, March 24, 1992.

289. "Hungary to Put Up Steel Barriers Next Week," *Financial Times*, March 5, 1992.

290. For an interesting discussion of some of these issues, see "West Hides behind Polish Tariffs," *Financial Times*, March 9, 1992.

291. "Poland, Hungary, and Czechoslovakia Initial EC Agreements," *RFE/RL Daily Report*, November 25, 1991.

292. "Official Cited on Warsaw Treaty," *FBIS-EEU*, June 6, 1991; "No Agreement Reached on Controversial EC Issues," *FBIS-EEU*, July 15, 1991; and "Freihandelszone mit östlichen Nachbarn," *Süddeutsche Zeitung*, November 25, 1991.

293. Up to now, resources for external activities have been lumped together with other mostly internal policies. As a result, the Commission has often had to trade off money for external aid with demands for more money by the European Parliament for other categories.

294. Commission of the European Communities, *Scoreboard of G-24 Assistance: Summary of ECU Tables and Graphics* (Brussels, April 1992).

295. Commission des Communeautés Européennes, Communication de la Commission au Conseil et au Parliament, *Accords d'association avec les pays d'Europe centrale et orientale: Cadre général*, COM(90) 398 final (Bruxelles, le 27 aout 1990), pp. 6–10.

296. In the end, it was a legal issue that postponed the signing of the EEA agreement for another two months, not an economic one.

297. This figure is likely to rise if regional programs are included, since most of them are allocated in Poland, Hungary, and the CSFR.

298. "Europe's Lost Cousins," *Financial Times*, December 5, 1990. As of September 5, 1991, Albania and the three Baltic states have been included in the PHARE program. With the recognition of several former Yugoslav republics as independent states, a similar move by the EC is only a matter of time.

299. "EC Partial Membership Suggested," *Financial Times*, April 20, 1991; "Andriessen: EG sollte Teilmitgliedschaft anbieten," *Süddeutsche Zeitung*, April 20–21, 1991; "Beitrittswünsche erfordern eine klare Antwort," *Handelsblatt*, April 26, 1991; "Der Druck wird stärker," *Handelsblatt*, August 6, 1991; and "Geschlossene Gesellschaft," *Der Spiegel*, May 6, 1991.

300. To some degree this cooperation has already started. The European Energy Charter is an example for cooperation in the field of energy and environment; for cooperation in the field of Science and Technology, see Wolfgang H. Reinicke, "Current European Efforts in Eastern Europe," paper presented at a conference on Science, Technology, and Economic Growth: The Case of Eastern Europe, National Academy of Sciences, Washington, D.C., November 13–14, 1991.

301. Czechoslovakia, Hungary, and Poland have officially requested that they be allowed to participate in the European Political Cooperation. See "Brussels Opens Its Arms to the East," *Financial Times*, September 4, 1991; and "A New Wave of Eastern Approaches," *Financial Times*, September 6, 1991.

302. "Commissioner Andriessen Discusses EC Expansion," *FBIS-WEU*, August 15, 1991.

303. Following the example of the former East Germany's integration into the European Community, Central and East Europeans would be observers in the Parliament.

304. On Central and Eastern Europe and the EMS, see "Tietmayer: Monetäre

Anker für Osteuropa," *Frankfurter Allgemeine*, June 22, 1991. Initially such a linkup would probably require an exchange rate stabilization fund. In addition, it could prevent what some have referred to as a "currency divide." See "Pöhl Warns of Europe's 'Currency Divide,'" *Financial Times*, October 25, 1991.

305. The Council and the Parliament rejected Andriessen's trial balloon because it involved participation by the affiliates in the Council as well as the Parliament. Despite the criticism and the internal conflicts it caused, Andriessen has renewed his proposal on several occasions. See, for example, "Kritik an Hilfe für Sowjetunion," *Süddeutsche Zeitung*, June 12, 1991.

306. "Commissioner Andriessen Discusses EC Expansion," *FBIS-WEU*, August 15, 1991.

307. The republics of Latvia, Lithuania, and Estonia have already expressed their interest in closer cooperation with the Community, and it is only a matter of time until they will have aspirations similar to those of other Central and East European countries.

308. During 1991 the EC's unemployment rate rose more sharply than in any other year since the Community started compiling comparative figures in 1983. The seasonally adjusted unemployment rate, excluding the new five German *Länder*, rose to 9.3 percent in 1991 from 8.4 percent in 1990. See "EC Unemployment Up Sharply," *Financial Times*, January 25–26, 1992.

309. In this context it should be remembered that Britain, Denmark, and Portugal all belonged to EFTA before joining the European Community. For some background on EC-EFTA relations and the impact of the creation of an EES, see Andrea de Guttry, "EFTA and Its Member States," *International Spectator*, vol. 25 (October-December 1990), pp. 251–60; and "The Impact of the EC's Internal Market on Non-member Countries: The Case of EFTA," IMF Working Paper, WP/90/68 (August 1990).

310. EFTA has already proposed to cooperate closely with the EC in its support for the Baltics. See "Neue Rettungspläne für Europas Wirtschaftsraum," *Handelsblatt*, September 11, 1991.

311. "Die Europäische Freihandelszone kann ihre Funktion als Drehscheibe ausbauen," *Handelsblatt*, November 14, 1991.

312. "EC-EFTA/EEA: Agreement Will Be Mixed Because It Includes a 'Political Dialogue' Section Which Does Not Come Under Community Competence," *Agence Europe*, November 1, 1991.

313. "EFTA Sidetracked by the Lure of EC Membership," *Financial Times*, May 2, 1991. The only EFTA country that has publicly stated that it will not become an EC member is Liechtenstein. On the difficulties that a Norwegian application may pose, see "Norway, EC Differ on Free Trade Agreement," *FBIS-WEU*, February 10, 1992.

314. The statement, however, did not mention Cyprus, Malta, and Turkey. See "Austria and Sweden Top EC Entry Waiting List," *Financial Times*, December 11, 1991.

315. "Wette und Zeit verloren," *Handelsblatt*, June 20, 1991; "Paraphierug des EWR-Vertrags muss verschoben werden," *Süddeutsche Zeitung*, June 20, 1991; "EC Goes Fishing in Norwegian Waters," *Financial Times*, July 30, 1991; "The EC's Moment of Truth," *Financial Times*, August 7, 1991; and "EFTA Wants Norway Concessions in Fishing Talks," *FBIS-WEU*, September 12, 1991.

316. "EC, EFTA Face Their Last Chance Today," *Financial Times*, October 21, 1991; "Streit über Alpentransit offenbar beigelegt," *Süddeutsche Zeitung*, October 22, 1991; and "Talks on Free Trade Zone Close to Success," *Financial Times*, October 22, 1991.

317. For more on the agreement, see, for example, "Nahezu integral freier Warenhandel," *Neue Zürcher Zeitung*, November 6, 1991.

318. "EC-EFTA/EEA: The Court of Justice Calls for Information on the Impact of the Creation of and 'EEA' Court on Its Competencies and Autonomy," *Agence Europe*, November 20, 1991; and "Der EWR auf dem rechtlichen Prüfstand," *Neue Zürcher Zeitung*, November 28, 1992. On the rejection, see, "EWR-Gerichtshof auf dem Schafott," *Neue Zürcher Zeitung*, December 17, 1991; "Neue Hausaufgaben für die EWR-Alchimisten," *Neue Zürcher Zeitung*, December 18, 1991; and "Die Pannen und Pleiten halten an," *Neue Zürcher Zeitung*, December 17, 1992. On the court's increasingly powerful position, see Articles 171–84 in the Maastricht Treaty; see also "Judges Sent into Battle to Hold Maastricht Line," *Financial Times*, February 20, 1992.

319. This arises because much of EEA law is made up of EC law and directives, and the court has always insisted that it has the sole right to interpret law. The EEA court consists of four judges from the European Court of Justice and three from EFTA. In addition, Spain and Belgium raised questions about the treaty and caused the EFTA countries to be concerned about the legal difficulties, suggesting they could be an opportunity to reopen other negotiating points. See "EC/EEA/Court of Justice," *Agence Europe*, November 29, 1991.

320. "Der Institutionelle Bereich als Achillesferse," *Neue Zürcher Zeitung*, December 25–26, 1991; "EC Tackles Legal Hurdle to 19-Nation Trade Zone," *Financial Times*, February 4, 1992; and "EC-EFTA Near Deal on Single Market," *Financial Times*, February 15–16, 1992.

321. "Court Gives Go-ahead to EC-EFTA Accord," *Financial Times*, April 13, 1992; and "Grünes Licht vom EuGH," *Handelsblatt*, April 13, 1992. However, the European Court made it a condition for its approval that the joint committee appointed to resolve disagreements in the EEA must not be allowed to interfere in the judgments of the Court. This is binding for all parties to the agreement.

322. "EEA Signing Set to Intensify Talks over Bigger EC," *Financial Times*, May 2–3, 1992. The EEA market has 380 million consumers and in 1990 handled 47.2 percent of global exports and 46.4 percent of global imports; and 68 percent of this trade is intra-EEA trade.

323. Under the agreement, the EFTA countries have to be consulted by the Commission on new proposals, but they cannot vote on EC legislation.

324. An agreement is mixed if it contains sections that do not come under EC competence. See "EC-EFTA/EEA: Agreement Will Be Mixed Because It Includes a 'Political Dialogue' Section Which Does Not Come under Community Competence," *Agence Europe*, November 1, 1991.

325. Calling the agreement the "European Free Ride Association," many members of the European Parliament have expressed their concern that EFTA countries got an unfair advantage. See "Irony of EEA Sop that Spurred Flood to Join EC," *Financial Times*, October 23, 1991; and "Europäischer Wirtschaftsraum: EG und EFTA einigen

sich," *Das Parlament*, October 25, 1991. Since the beginning of the negotiations, the Parliament has complained that the agreement could not threaten the decision making autonomy of the EC institutions. "EG-Parlament will mitreden," *Handelsblatt*, March 15–16, 1991.

326. "EC Parliament Committee Cites EEA Objections," *FBIS-WEU*, March 30, 1992; and "Fears Delay in EEA Implementation," *FBIS-WEU*, March 27, 1992.

327. "Westeuropäer bilden Freihandelszone vom Nordkap bis zum Mittelmeer," *Süddeutsche Zeitung*, October 23, 1991.

328. Proposals to reform the Community go further back than the signing of the Single European Act. However, their success was limited, and it was not possible to get any sweeping reform. For an overview, see Werner Weidenfeld, ed., *Nur verpasste Chancen? Die Reformberichte der Europäischen Gemeinschaft*, Mainzer Beiträge zur Europäischen Einigung, Band 2 (Bonn: Europa Union Verlag, 1983). See also the discussion in Roy Price, ed., *The Dynamics of European Union* (New York: Croon Helm, 1987).

329. On the deficit provisions, see Article 104c, pp. 27–28, and "Protocol on the Excessive Deficit Procedure," pp. 183–84, in particular Article 1; on the criterion of price stability, see Article 109j, section 1, and "Protocol on the Convergence Criteria Referred to in Article 109j of the Treaty Establishing the European Community," pp. 185–86, all in *Treaty on European Union* (Luxembourg: Office for Official Publications of the European Communities, 1992). For a critique of the independence of the central bank and the plans for economic convergence, see "EC Council Seen Controlling Central Bank," and "EMU Economic Harmonization Policy Criticized," both in *FBIS-WEU*, January 27, 1992; and "EC Treaty Permits EMU without Convergence," *FBIS-WEU*, February 11, 1992.

330. That the treaty actually set a fixed date was criticized by the Bundesbank, which pointed out that "the fulfillment of the entry criteria or the convergence conditions must not be impaired by any dates set." See "The Maastricht Decisions on the European Economic and Monetary Union," *Monthly Report of the Deutsche Bundesbank*, vol. 44 (February 1992), pp. 43–52; quotation from p. 52.

331. On the exception rules for both the deficit ratio and the government debt ratio, see Article 104c, section 2 (a) and (b), in *Treaty on European Union*, p. 27.

332. However, in a recent survey in Germany based on almost 1,500 company directors, 18 percent believed Germany would *not* meet the conditions. See "Maastricht Pact Loses Appeal in Germany," *Financial Times*, April 29, 1992.

333. On the Spanish plans for a convergence program, see "Madrid plant ehrgeiziges Konvergenzprogramm," *Handelsblatt*, April 4, 1992.

334. See "Protests Grow as Portugal Faces up to Euro-Integration," *Financial Times*, March 5, 1992.

335. For a different perspective, see Martin Feldstein, "Wirtschaftliche und politische Aspekte der Europäischen Währungsunion," *Auszüge Aus Presseartikeln* (Deutsche Bundesbank), January 23, 1992.

336. The acceptance of the escape clause may also have set a precedent for other countries in other issue areas, perhaps severely undermining the cohesion and credibility of the EC policymaking and its decisions.

337. Even in the United Kingdom, the Confederation of British Industry (CBI) has strongly supported the formation of the Single Market and the Economic and Monetary Union. In addition, the CBI supports the enforcement of Community legislation and directives and considers them vital to the success of the European Community. See "(EU) Maastricht Summit: Single Market and Monetary Union Are Priorities for British Industry," *Europe* (Agence Europe), November 22, 1991. See also "Business Urged to Act on EMU Opt-out Clause," *Financial Times*, May 15, 1992.

338. "The Maastricht Decisions on the European Economic and Monetary Union," *Monthly Report of the Deutsche Bundesbank*, vol. 44 (February 1992), pp. 43–52, quotation on p. 51. See also "Kohl Faces Tough Line on EMU from Bundesbank," *Financial Times*, January 29, 1992, p. 1; and "Family Quarrel at the Bundesbank," *Financial Times*, January 29, 1992.

339. Commission of the European Communities, *From Single Act to Maastricht and beyond: The Means to Match our Ambitions*, Communication from the Commission, COM(92) 2000 (Brussels, February 1992). See also "The Bill for Maastricht," *Financial Times*, February 13, 1992. On an inflation-adjusted basis, this represents an annual increase of 5.6 percent. See "EG soll sparen statt neue Ausgaben schaffen," *Die Woche Im Bundestag*, March 18, 1992, p. 31.

340. "Brussels Targets Poorest States," *Financial Times*, January 20, 1992.

341. "FRG's Waigel Rejects EC Budget Increase," *FBIS-WEU*, March 19, 1992; and "Bonn Rejects Delors II Package Increase," *FBIS-WEU*, February 19, 1992. In particular, Germany fears that the two notions of cohesion and convergence will get mixed up and has insisted that the cohesion funds should only become available once the convergence program has been fulfilled. See "Gnadenloser Zielkonflikt," *Die Woche im Bundestag*, March 25, 1992. Germany is also insisting on a renegotiation of the annual budget rebate (worth ECU 3.3 billion in 1991) that had been conceded to Britain in 1984 because of its relatively small share in the agricultural subsidies handed out by the Community.

342. "Brussels Faces United German Opposition on Budget Increase," *Financial Times*, February 22–23, 1992; "EC Faces Battle over Budget," *Financial Times*, March 3, 1992; "Germany and Italy Express Concern about Delors Budget," *Financial Times*, March 17, 1992; and "EC Accord Unlikely on Plans for Spending," *Financial Times*, March 18, 1992.

343. See, for example, "Portugal Warns on EC Spending," *Financial Times*, March 19, 1992; "Der Geist von Maastricht muss Konsolidiert werden," *Handelsblatt*, March 25, 1992; "Cavaco Silva Doubts Approval of EC Budget," *FBIS-WEU*, May 11, 1992; "EC Braces for Fight over Major Hike in Budget," *Journal of Commerce*, May 12, 1992; and "North-South Split over Plan to Raise Revenue by 35%," *Financial Times*, May 12, 1992.

344. Article 117 of the Treaty of Rome was supplemented by an agreement that was signed by eleven of the twelve member states. See *Treaty on European Union* (Luxembourg: Office for Official Publications of the European Communities, 1992), pp. 197–201. However, the eleven members will be able to use the institutions of the Community to formulate and implement policy. In other words, the European

Commission will develop directives that will be agreed on with a majority of forty-four (instead of the usual fifty-four) votes.

345. "Employers Cast Doubt on Value of Maastricht 'Opt-Out,'" *Financial Times*, February 24, 1992; and "Opting Out and Cashing In," *Financial Times*, February 28, 1992. See also "EC Ministers Put Social Policy on Hold until after UK Poll," *Financial Times*, March 14, 1992; "(EU) Maastricht Summit: Single Market and Monetary Union Are Priorities for British Industry," *Europe* (Agence Europe), November 22, 1991.

346. Citizenship of the Union will come into effect on or before December 31, 1994. The same principle will be applied for elections to the European Parliament. See *Treaty on European Union*, Article 8a–e, pp. 15–16.

347. The only real change occurred in the Parliament's ability to partake in the election of the Commission president and its members.

348. For the procedure see, *Treaty on European Union*, Article 189a–c, pp. 75–79.

349. *Treaty on European Union*, Article 158, pp. 66–67.

350. A vote that would have called for a new summit to renegotiate the treaty failed by one vote. "Das EG-Parlament billigt Maastrichter Vertragsreformen," *Frankfurter Allgemeine Zeitung*, April 8, 1992; and "Ein klares Ja zu Maastricht," *Das Parlament*, April 10, 1992.

351. European Parliament, *Report of the Committee on Institutional Affairs on the Results of the Intergovernmental Conferences*, A3–0123/92/Part I–III (Luxembourg, March 26, 1992). In fact, given that some decisions in the Council are now made on a majority basis, which reduces the control of individual national parliaments even further, one could argue that the democratic deficit has increased.

352. For a summary of the list, see "Ja zu Maastricht," *Europa Forum*, April 6–10, 1992.

353. "Europaparlament fordert Verbesserungen," *Das Parlament*, December 20–27, 1991; and "Ja zu Maastricht," *Europa Forum*, April 6–10, 1992.

354. "Leaders Address Bundestag on Maastricht Summit, Kohl Speech," *FBIS-WEU*, December 13, 1991; and "Mitterrand Discusses Maastricht, USSR, Issues," *FBIS-WEU*, December 16, 1991.

355. "Ein Wechsel auf Europas Zukunft," *Die ZEIT*, December 13, 1991; "Beschränkt belastbar," *Der Spiegel*, February 10, 1992, pp. 20–22; and "Opposition to Maastricht Accord Stiffens," *FBIS-WEU*, February 26, 1992, pp. 6–7. In this context, it is interesting to note that the final decision to replace the deutsche mark with the ECU is due in late 1997, shortly before the next general election in Germany. The strong performance of the deutsche mark in the aftermath of the Danish referendum confirmed that point.

356. Between September 1990 and January 1992 Germany pledged ECU 35.9 billion, or 57.4 percent of all public Western aid to the successor states of the Soviet Union. Commission of the European Communities, "Assistance to the Independent States (ex-USSR)," Brussels, January 20, 1992.

357. In the long run, however, it may well be the German states' critical position toward further integration that presents the greatest challenge to the federal government. In essence, the *Länder* demanded that they be given an effective veto on future

transfers of sovereignty to Brussels. See "Laender Not Ready to Agree to Maastricht Accords," *FBIS-WEU*, March 16, 1992; "German States Seek Veto on EC Deals," *Financial Times*, March 13, 1992; "Kohl Struggles to Land his Catch," *Financial Times*, March 17, 1992; "Land Minister Critiques Maastricht Treaty," *FBIS-WEU*, March 25, 1992; and "Kohl Agrees More Power for Länder," *Financial Times*, May 16–17, 1992.

358. "Further on Mitterrand's Comments on Maastricht," *Le Monde*, January 12–13, 1992, in *FBIS-WEU*, January 14, 1992, p. 23; "French Prepare for Debate on Maastricht," *Financial Times*, April 23, 1992, p. 3; "Verfassungskorrektur für Maastricht in Paris," *Neue Zürcher Zeitung*, April 24, 1992; "Divisions Ease Path in France for EC Treaty," *Financial Times*, May 13, 1992, p. 3; "Assembly Approves Constitutional Amendments," *FBIS-WEU*, May 13, 1992; and "France Clears Its First Maastricht Hurdle," *Financial Times*, May 14, 1992. On Mitterrand's decision to hold a referendum, see "Mitterrand Raises the Stakes," *Financial Times*, June 4, 1992.

359. Although he has been the target of most criticism, Jacques Delors, the president of the European Commission, has publicly emphasized the need to engage the public in the debate over European Union. But except for those in Great Britain, politicians have avoided the issue for the most part. On Delors, see "Final Uphill Push for the Treaty," *Financial Times*, April 23, 1992, p. 16.

360. The idea that Europe should return to the traditional concept of balance of power is not new, but it has recently been reiterated by Margaret Thatcher.

361. In the aftermath of the Danish referendum, various legal responses have been considered on how to deal with the situation.

362. For the procedure, see *Treaty on European Union*, Title V, Article J.3.

363. Gunther Nonnenmacher, "Nach Maastricht wird es ernst," *Frankfurter Allgemeine*, December 12, 1992. The decisionmaking procedure has also been criticized by the Commission's president. According to Delors, "We will need to get back to the drawing board and devise simple, effective evaluation and decisionmaking procedures." See "1992: A Pivotal Year," address by Jacques Delors, President of the Commission to the European Parliament, *Bulletin of the European Communities*, Supplement 1/92 (Luxembourg, 1992), quotation on p. 9.

364. "Delors enttäuscht über den fehlenden Willen zu Mehrheitsentscheidungen," *Handelsblatt*, December 13–14, 1992.

365. *Treaty on European Union*, Title V, Article J.4, p. 126; and "Declaration On Western European Union," Final Act, pp. 242–46, 243, 242, and 246.

366. Britain, Ireland, and Portugal also resisted this move.

367. "Danish Referendum Frays Brussels' Nerves," *Financial Times*, March 31, 1992, p. 2; "Lone Dane in Maastricht Campaign," *Financial Times*, May 18, 1992, p. 3; and "WEU Row Fuels Danish Debate on EC Treaties," *Financial Times*, February 21, 1992, p. 3.

368. *Treaty on European Union*, pp. 13–14.

369. Ibid., p.14.

370. A case in point is the conflict that erupted over the inclusion of the word "federal" in the preamble of the treaty and its subsequent rephrasing to "resolved to continue the process of creating an ever closer union among the peoples of Europe, in

which decisions are taken as closely as possible to the citizens in accordance with the principle of subsidiarity."

371. The European Commission even has the right to withdraw a proposal during a Council of Ministers meeting if it becomes clear that it will fail the unanimity test. The most recent case of such a withdrawal took place when Andriessen proposed the affiliate membership option.

372. According to Article 100 of the Treaty of Rome, the Council shall act unanimously on a proposal from the Commission. This article was amended with the implementation of the Single European Act in 1986. With a few, though important, exceptions, the countries agreed to adopt the measures designed to approximate the legal, regulatory, and administrative aspects of the single market by a qualified majority vote. Decisions that would be exempted from qualified majority voting for example would be new memberships or matters related to national or European military security.

373. Karlheinz Neunreither, "The Constitutional Debate in the European Community: Towards Which Europe? How to Govern It?" paper presented at the Conference on the New European Architecture, International Political Science Association, Research Committee on European Unification, Luxembourg, May 6–7, 1991.

374. It is not certain, however, whether Denmark will be able to take on the presidency in January 1993, pending its future status in the Community. Belgium, which would follow Denmark in July 1993, may thus take over as early as January 1993.

375. The divisibility of sovereignty is one of the initial principles on which the Community is built. See Europe Federalists' Union, *European Federation Now* (Paris: Union Européenne des Federalists; distributed by the American Committee on a United Europe, New York, 1951).

376. The Committee of the Regions is composed of 189 members representing the "regional and local bodies" in Europe and has an advisory status, being consulted by the Council and the Commission. See *Treaty on European Union*, Article 4, section 2, p. 14, and Article 198 a–c. In the long run, such a Committee could well develop into a second legislative chamber representing the sub-national interests.

377. "Hurd Attacks Opposition Proposals for Scotland," *Financial Times*, February 29–March 1, 1992, p. 1.

378. *Webster's Third New International Dictionary* (Springfield, Mass.: Merriam Company, 1961), p. 2179.

379. Ralf Dahrendorf, *Betrachtungen über die Revolution in Europa* (Stuttgart: Deutsche Verlags-Anstalt, 1990).

380. For an account indicating that the costs of unification were deliberately played down, see Wolfgang Schäuble, *Der Vertrag—Wie ich über die Deutsche Einheit verhandelte* (Stuttgart: Deutsche Verlags-Anstalt, 1991), esp. pp. 184–87.